TOP 10 BOOK TWO

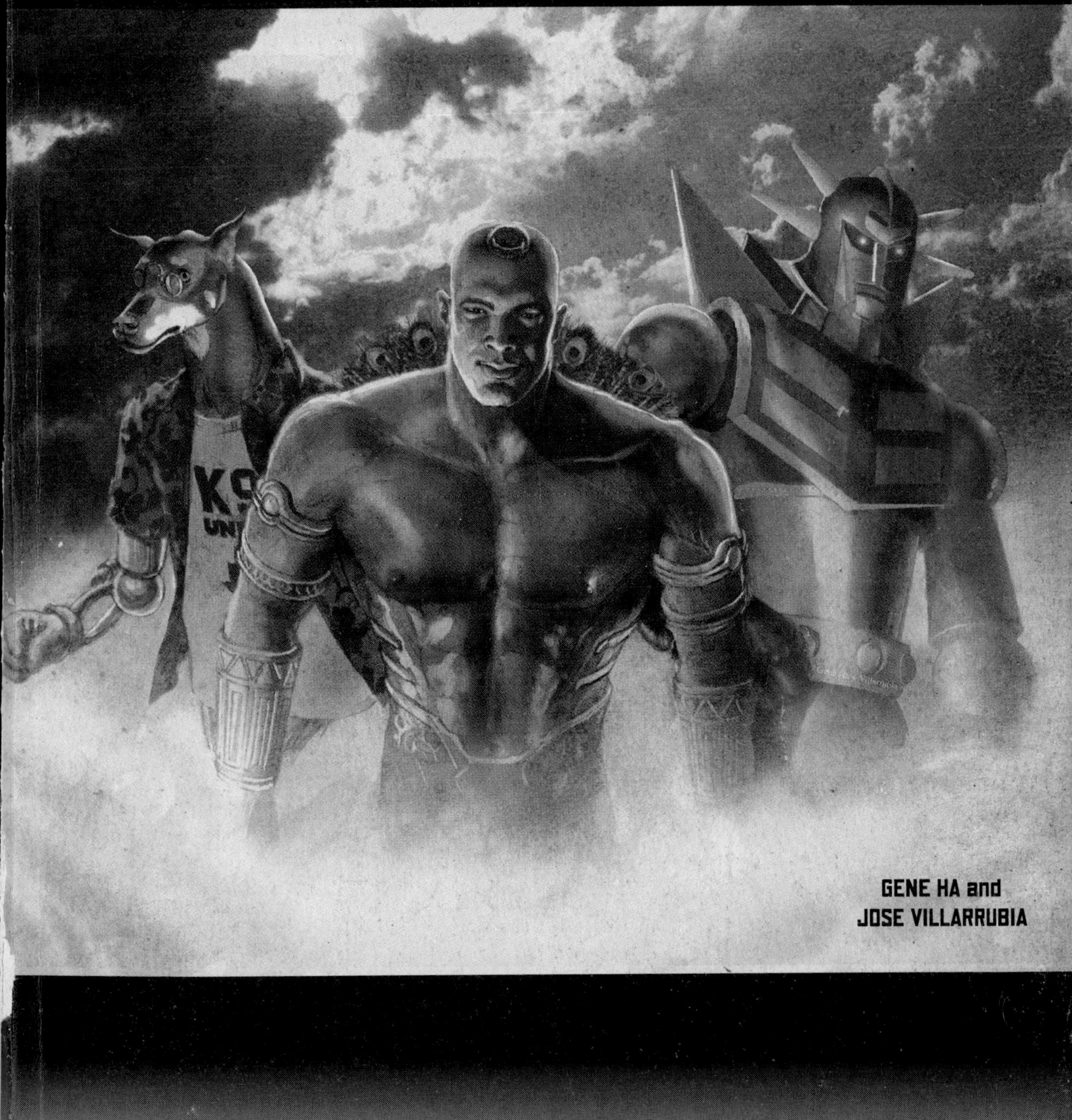

GENE HA and
JOSE VILLARRUBIA

JIM LEE
Editorial Director

JOHN NEE
VP and General Manager

SCOTT DUNBIER
Group Editor

ERIC DeSANTIS
JEFF MARIOTTE
NEAL POZNER
KRISTY QUINN
Assistant Editors

TOP 10: BOOK 2. Published by America's Best Comics, LLC. Cover, design pages and compilation © 2002 America's Best Comics, LLC. Top 10 and all related characters and elements are trademarks of America's Best Comics. All Rights Reserved. Originally published in single magazine form as TOP 10, #8-12. Copyright © 2000, 2001 America's Best Comics. Editorial Offices: 888 Prospect St., Suite 240, La Jolla, CA 92037. Any similarities to persons living or dead is purely coincidental. America's Best Comics does not read or accept unsolicited submissions of ideas, stories or artwork. PRINTED IN CANADA. FIRST PRINTING.
ISBN 1-56389-876-4

TOP 10

COLLECTED EDITION BOOK 2

ALAN MOORE
writer

GENE HA
finishing artist

ZANDER CANNON
layout artist

ALEX SINCLAIR
WILDSTORM FX
coloring

TODD KLEIN
lettering,
logos and
design

AMERICA'S
BEST COMICS

TOP 10
created by
Alan Moore
& Gene Ha

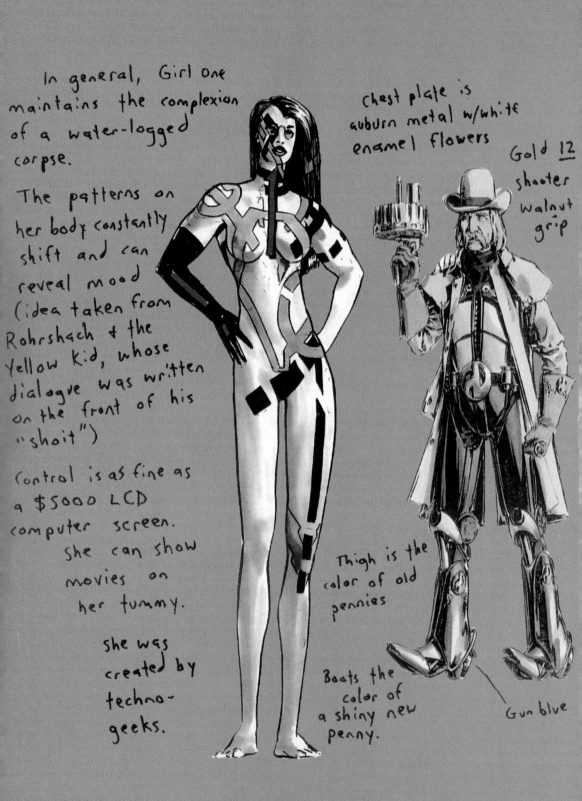

In general, Girl One maintains the complexion of a water-logged corpse.

The patterns on her body constantly shift and can reveal mood (idea taken from Rohrshach + the Yellow Kid, whose dialogue was written on the front of his "shoit")

Control is as fine as a $5000 LCD computer screen. She can show movies on her tummy.

She was created by techno-geeks.

chest plate is auburn metal w/white enamel flowers

Gold 12 shooter walnut grip

Thigh is the color of old pennies

Boots the color of a shiny new penny.

Gun blue

Girl One and Dust Devil character sketches by Gene Ha

CHAPTER ONE

ON THE DOCKET:
Peregrine handles traffic detail,
Captain Traynor defends an arrest,
and Girl One puts on her best game.

Cover art:
Gene Ha and
Zander Cannon

AMERICA'S BEST COMICS
TOP 10
VERSION 8.0
ON DUTY
HEALTH: 92%
POWER: 86%
GIRL 1
ARRESTS: 05
HEALTH: 95%
POWER: 88%
PARTNER
JUST SAY NO TO THE UN
IRMA 6
BACKUPS
SMAX
JACK PHANTOM
PETER
LEVEL: 04
TIME LEFT: 0:25
P
Jump
A
W
HI-REZ GAME
by ScoDee!
+
Switch
View
-
wildstorm.com
ALAN MOORE • GENE HA
ZANDER CANNON • TODD KLEIN

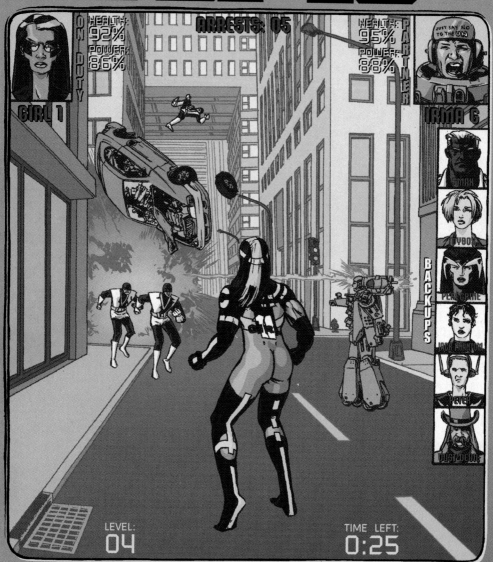

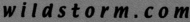

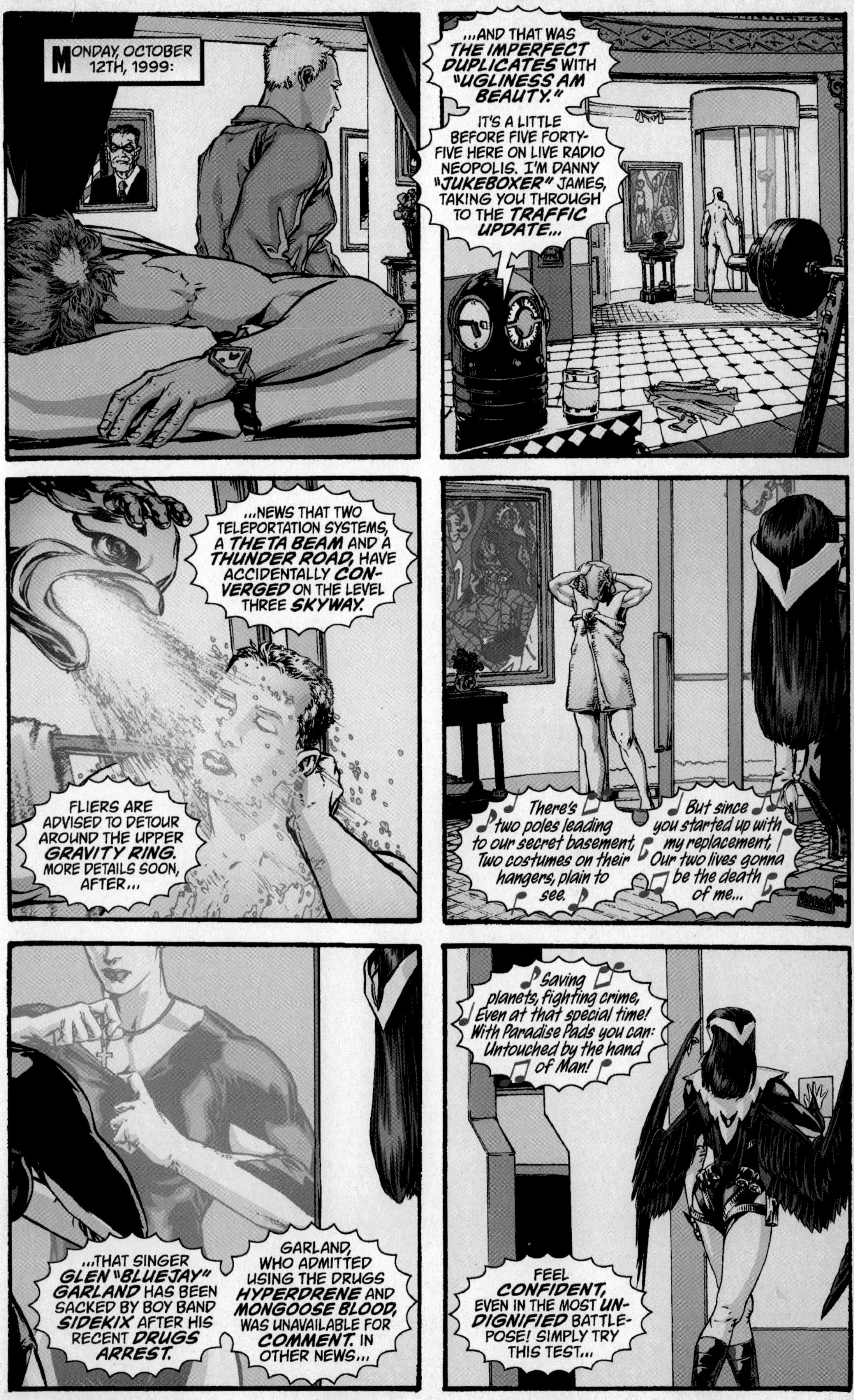
MONDAY, OCTOBER 12TH, 1999:
...AND THAT WAS THE IMPERFECT DUPLICATES WITH "UGLINESS AM BEAUTY."
IT'S A LITTLE BEFORE FIVE FORTY-FIVE HERE ON LIVE RADIO NEOPOLIS. I'M DANNY "JUKEBOXER" JAMES, TAKING YOU THROUGH TO THE TRAFFIC UPDATE...
...NEWS THAT TWO TELEPORTATION SYSTEMS, A THETA BEAM AND A THUNDER ROAD, HAVE ACCIDENTALLY CON-VERGED ON THE LEVEL THREE SKYWAY.
FLIERS ARE ADVISED TO DETOUR AROUND THE UPPER GRAVITY RING. MORE DETAILS SOON, AFTER...
There's two poles leading to our secret basement, Two costumes on their hangers, plain to see.
But since you started up with my replacement, Our two lives gonna be the death of me...
...THAT SINGER GLEN "BLUEJAY" GARLAND HAS BEEN SACKED BY BOY BAND SIDEKIX AFTER HIS RECENT DRUGS ARREST.
GARLAND, WHO ADMITTED USING THE DRUGS HYPERDRENE AND MONGOOSE BLOOD, WAS UNAVAILABLE FOR COMMENT. IN OTHER NEWS...
Saving planets, fighting crime, Even at that special time! With Paradise Pads you can: Untouched by the hand of Man!
FEEL CONFIDENT, EVEN IN THE MOST UN-DIGNIFIED BATTLE-POSE! SIMPLY TRY THIS TEST...

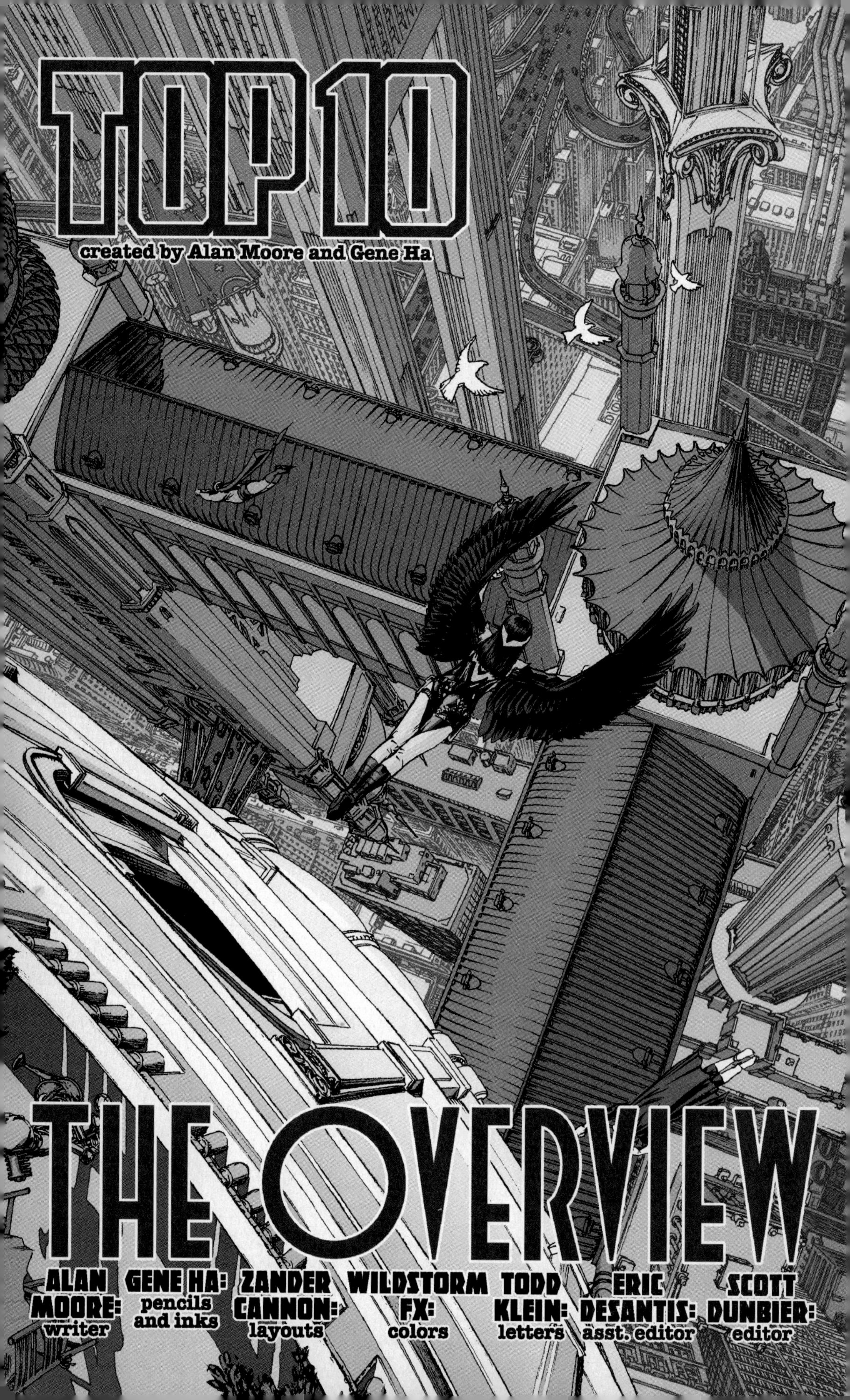
TOP 10
created by Alan Moore and Gene Ha
THE OVERVIEW
ALAN MOORE: writer
GENE HA: pencils and inks
ZANDER CANNON: layouts
WILDSTORM FX: colors
TODD KLEIN: letters
ERIC DESANTIS: asst. editor
SCOTT DUNBIER: editor

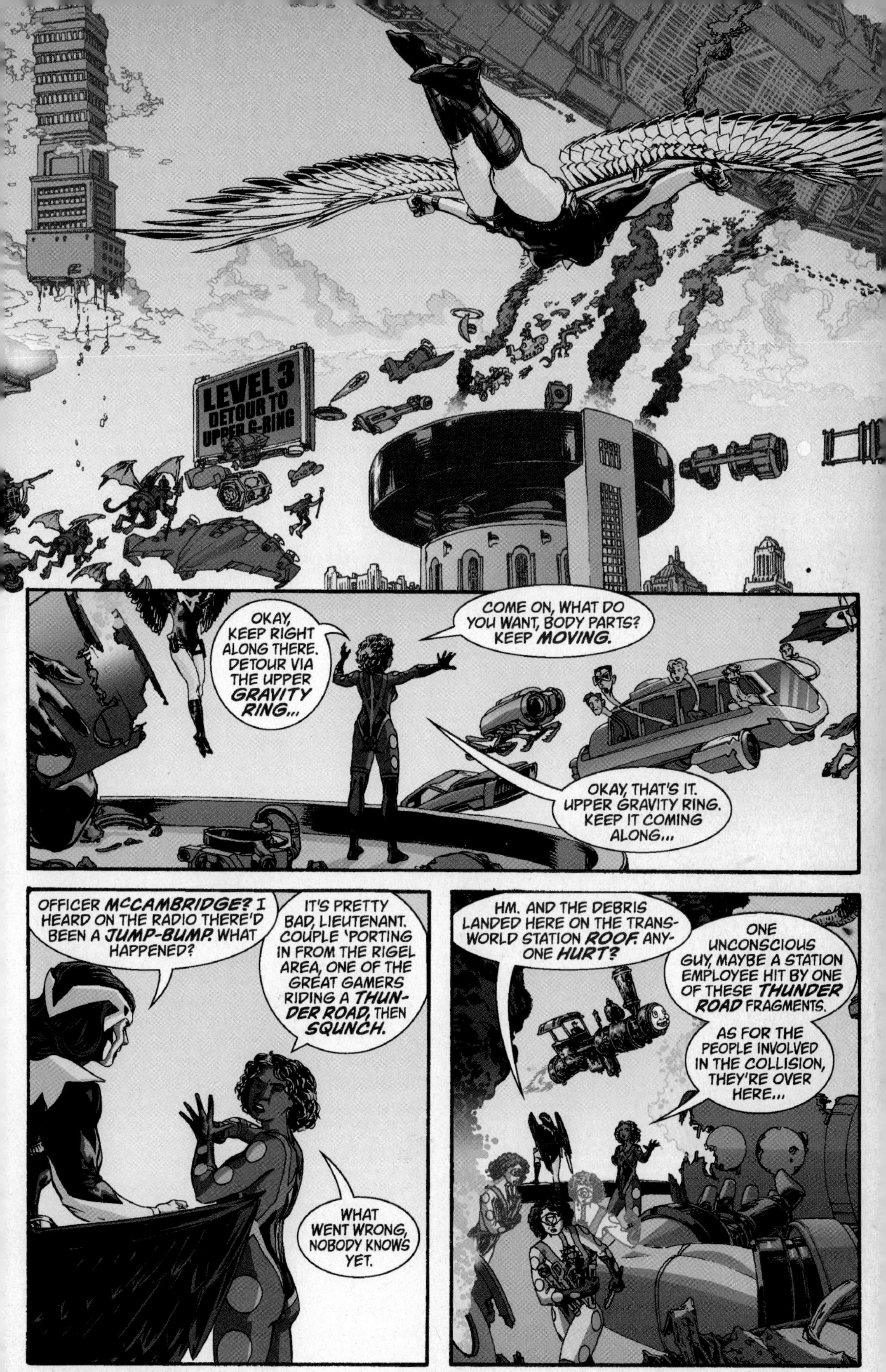
LEVEL 3 DETOUR TO UPPER G-RING
OKAY, KEEP RIGHT ALONG THERE. DETOUR VIA THE UPPER GRAVITY RING...
COME ON, WHAT DO YOU WANT, BODY PARTS? KEEP MOVING.
OKAY, THAT'S IT. UPPER GRAVITY RING. KEEP IT COMING ALONG...
OFFICER McCAMBRIDGE? I HEARD ON THE RADIO THERE'D BEEN A JUMP-BUMP. WHAT HAPPENED?
IT'S PRETTY BAD, LIEUTENANT. COUPLE 'PORTING IN FROM THE RIGEL AREA, ONE OF THE GREAT GAMERS RIDING A THUNDER-ROAD, THEN SQUNCH.
WHAT WENT WRONG, NOBODY KNOWS YET.
HM. AND THE DEBRIS LANDED HERE ON THE TRANS-WORLD STATION ROOF. ANY-ONE HURT?
ONE UNCONSCIOUS GUY, MAYBE A STATION EMPLOYEE HIT BY ONE OF THESE THUNDER ROAD FRAGMENTS.
AS FOR THE PEOPLE INVOLVED IN THE COLLISION, THEY'RE OVER HERE...

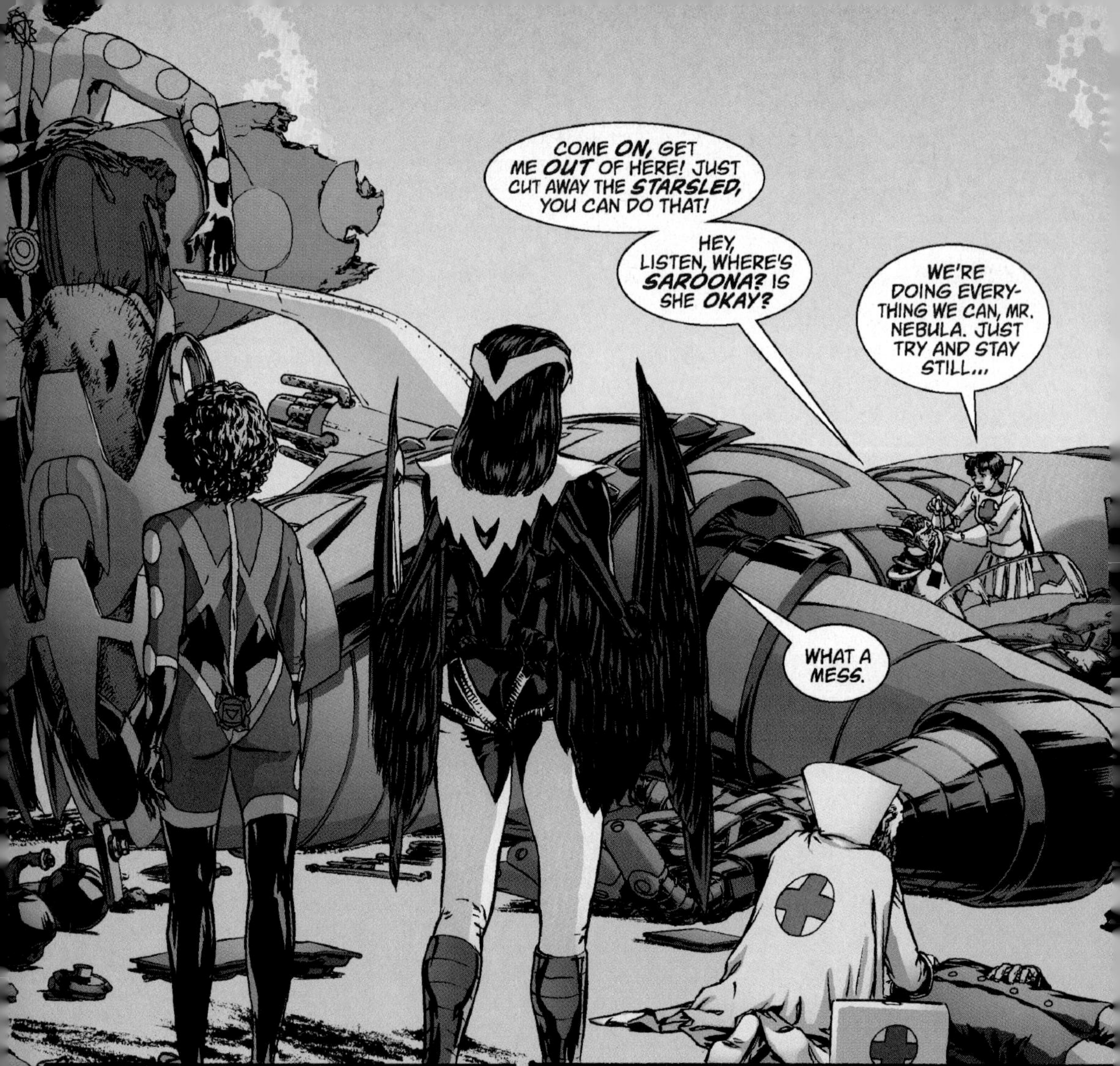
COME ON, GET ME OUT OF HERE! JUST CUT AWAY THE STARSLED, YOU CAN DO THAT!
HEY, LISTEN, WHERE'S SAROONA? IS SHE OKAY?
WE'RE DOING EVERY-THING WE CAN, MR. NEBULA. JUST TRY AND STAY STILL...
WHAT A MESS.
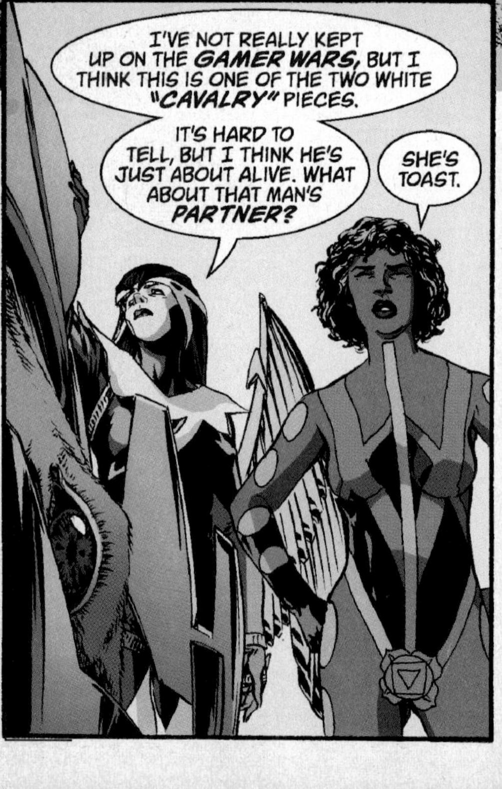
I'VE NOT REALLY KEPT UP ON THE GAMER WARS, BUT I THINK THIS IS ONE OF THE TWO WHITE "CAVALRY" PIECES.
IT'S HARD TO TELL, BUT I THINK HE'S JUST ABOUT ALIVE. WHAT ABOUT THAT MAN'S PARTNER?
SHE'S TOAST.
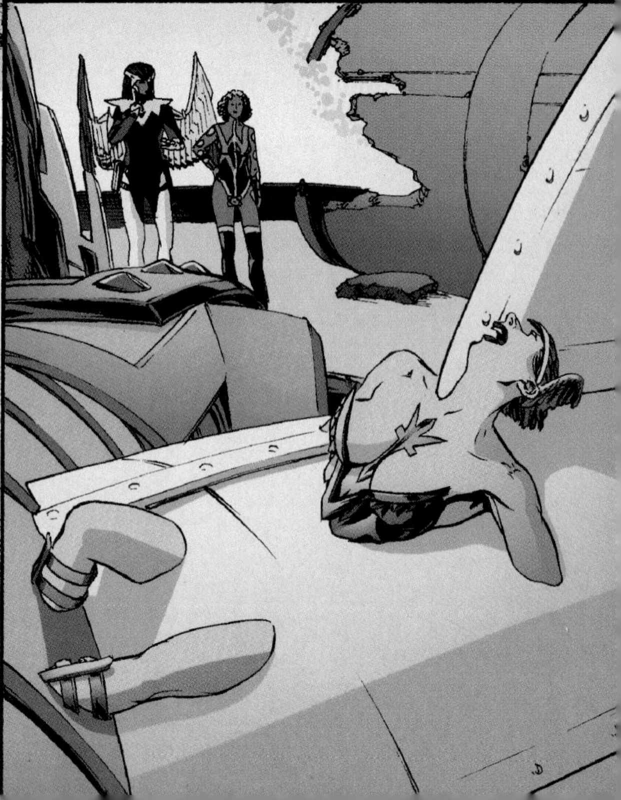

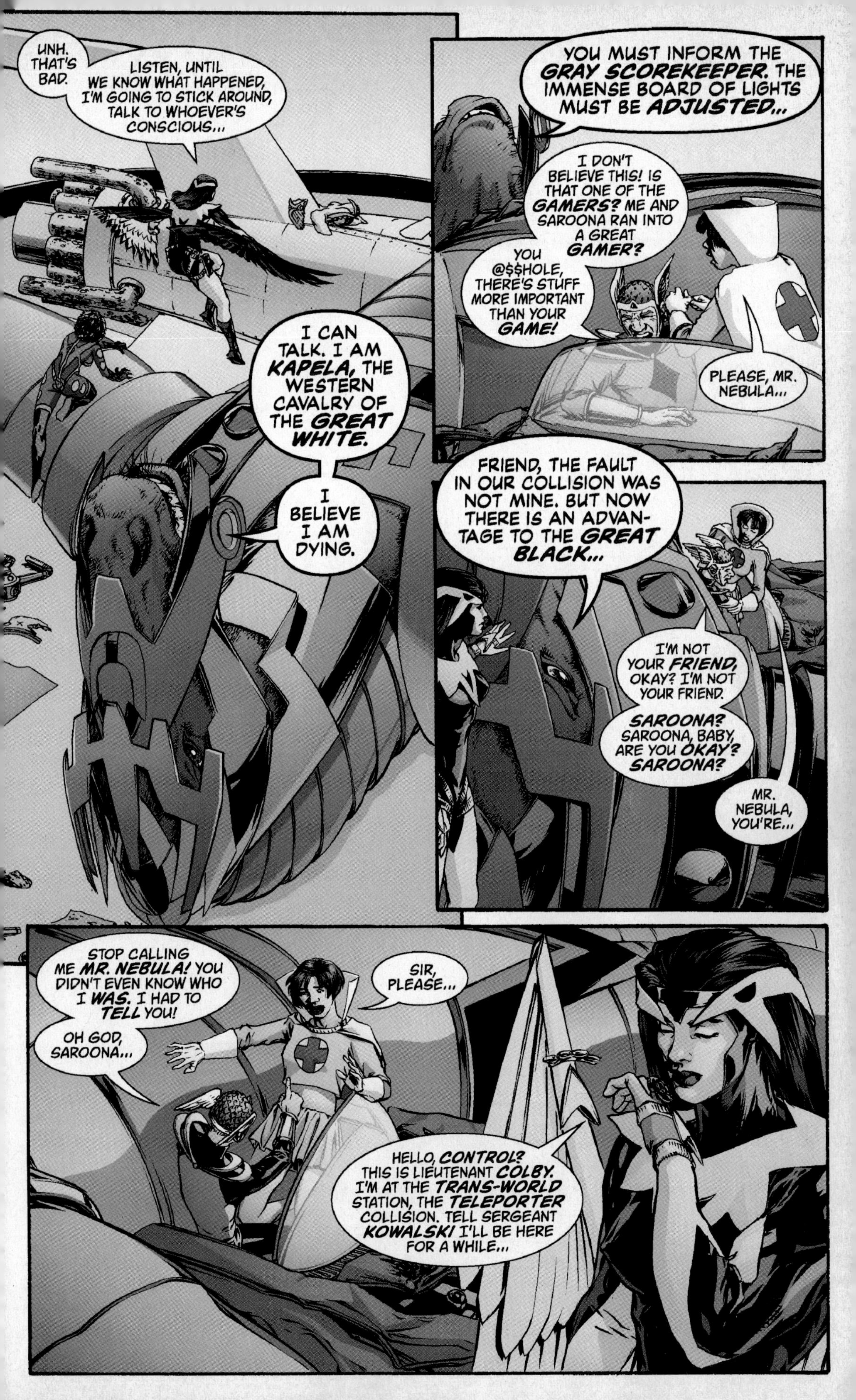

UNH. THAT'S BAD.
LISTEN, UNTIL WE KNOW WHAT HAPPENED, I'M GOING TO STICK AROUND, TALK TO WHOEVER'S CONSCIOUS...
I CAN TALK. I AM KAPELA, THE WESTERN CAVALRY OF THE GREAT WHITE.
I BELIEVE I AM DYING.
YOU MUST INFORM THE GRAY SCOREKEEPER. THE IMMENSE BOARD OF LIGHTS MUST BE ADJUSTED...
I DON'T BELIEVE THIS! IS THAT ONE OF THE GAMERS? ME AND SAROONA RAN INTO A GREAT GAMER?
YOU @$$HOLE, THERE'S STUFF MORE IMPORTANT THAN YOUR GAME!
PLEASE, MR. NEBULA...
FRIEND, THE FAULT IN OUR COLLISION WAS NOT MINE. BUT NOW THERE IS AN ADVANTAGE TO THE GREAT BLACK...
I'M NOT YOUR FRIEND, OKAY? I'M NOT YOUR FRIEND.
SAROONA? SAROONA, BABY, ARE YOU OKAY? SAROONA?
MR. NEBULA, YOU'RE...
STOP CALLING ME MR. NEBULA! YOU DIDN'T EVEN KNOW WHO I WAS. I HAD TO TELL YOU!
OH GOD, SAROONA...
SIR, PLEASE...
HELLO, CONTROL? THIS IS LIEUTENANT COLBY. I'M AT THE TRANS-WORLD STATION, THE TELEPORTER COLLISION. TELL SERGEANT KOWALSKI I'LL BE HERE FOR A WHILE...

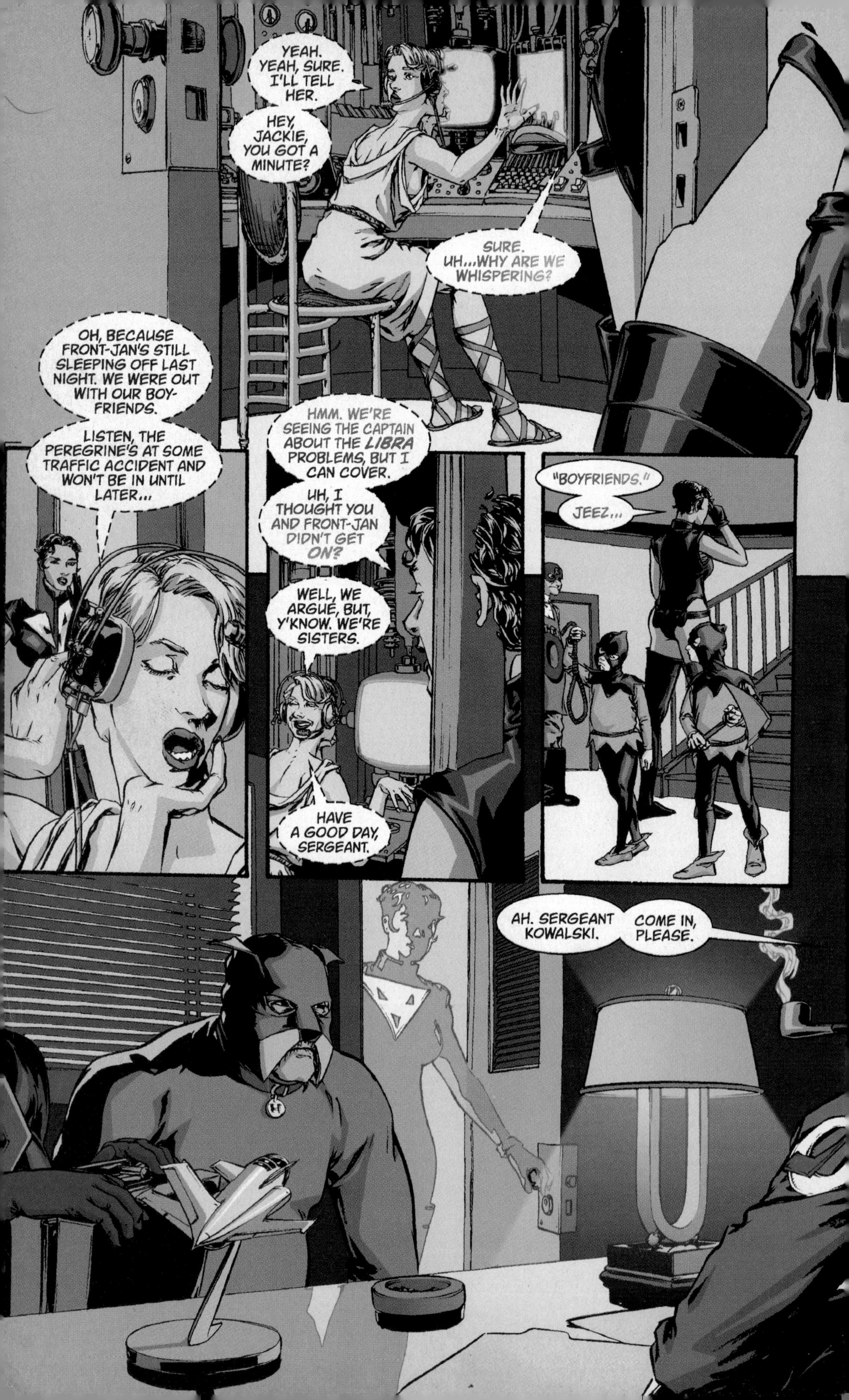
YEAH. YEAH, SURE. I'LL TELL HER.
HEY, JACKIE, YOU GOT A MINUTE?
SURE. UH...WHY ARE WE WHISPERING?
OH, BECAUSE FRONT-JAN'S STILL SLEEPING OFF LAST NIGHT. WE WERE OUT WITH OUR BOY-FRIENDS.
LISTEN, THE PEREGRINE'S AT SOME TRAFFIC ACCIDENT AND WON'T BE IN UNTIL LATER...
HMM. WE'RE SEEING THE CAPTAIN ABOUT THE *LIBRA* PROBLEMS, BUT I CAN COVER.
UH, I THOUGHT YOU AND FRONT-JAN DIDN'T GET *ON*?
WELL, WE ARGUE, BUT, Y'KNOW. WE'RE SISTERS.
HAVE A GOOD DAY, SERGEANT.
"BOYFRIENDS."
JEEZ...
AH. SERGEANT KOWALSKI.
COME IN, PLEASE.

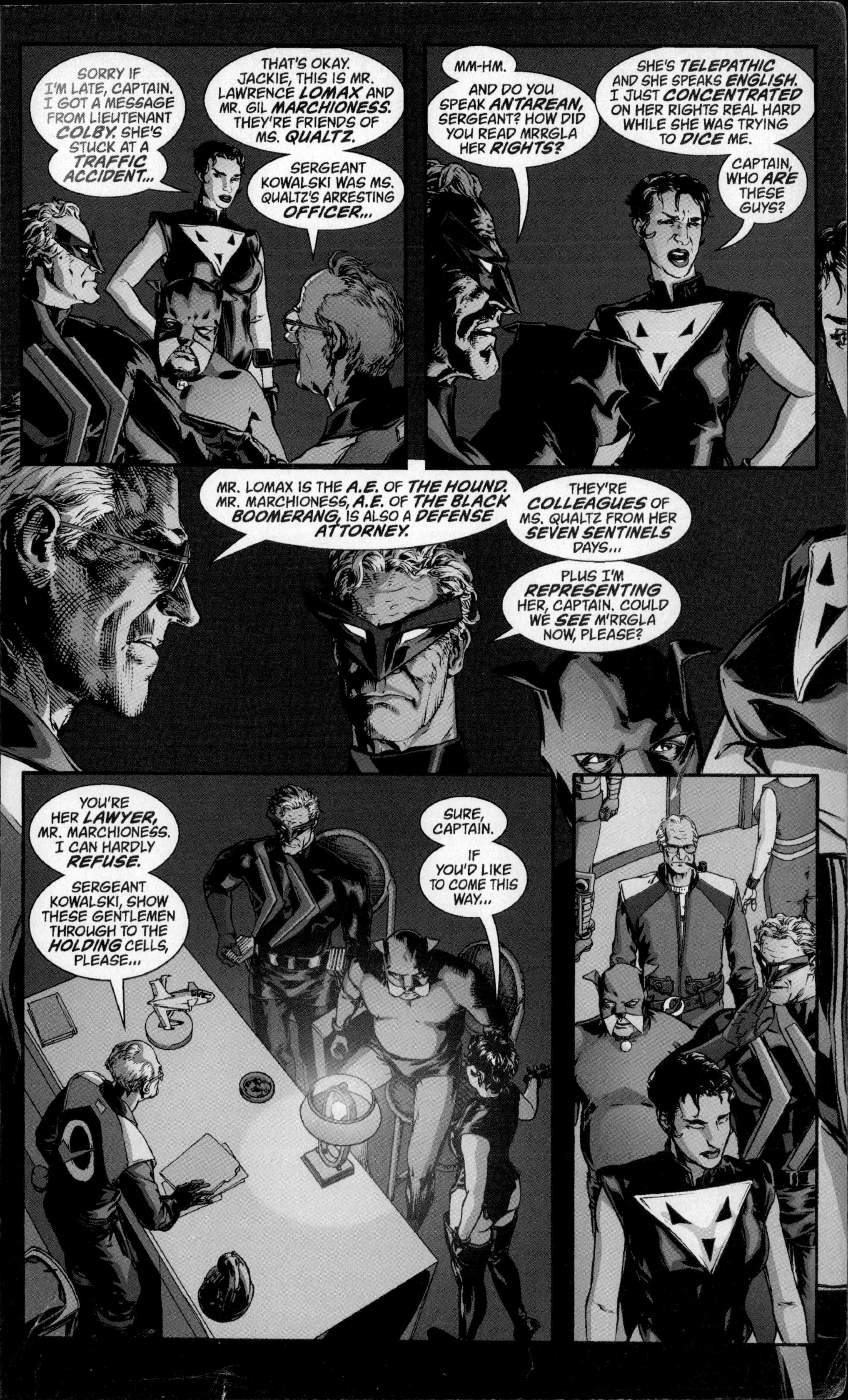
SORRY IF I'M LATE, CAPTAIN. I GOT A MESSAGE FROM LIEUTENANT COLBY. SHE'S STUCK AT A TRAFFIC ACCIDENT...
THAT'S OKAY. JACKIE, THIS IS MR. LAWRENCE LOMAX AND MR. GIL MARCHIONESS. THEY'RE FRIENDS OF MS. QUALTZ.
SERGEANT KOWALSKI WAS MS. QUALTZ'S ARRESTING OFFICER...
MM-HM.
AND DO YOU SPEAK ANTAREAN, SERGEANT? HOW DID YOU READ MRRGLA HER RIGHTS?
SHE'S TELEPATHIC AND SHE SPEAKS ENGLISH. I JUST CONCENTRATED ON HER RIGHTS REAL HARD WHILE SHE WAS TRYING TO DICE ME.
CAPTAIN, WHO ARE THESE GUYS?
MR. LOMAX IS THE A.E. OF THE HOUND. MR. MARCHIONESS, A.E. OF THE BLACK BOOMERANG, IS ALSO A DEFENSE ATTORNEY.
THEY'RE COLLEAGUES OF MS. QUALTZ FROM HER SEVEN SENTINELS DAYS...
PLUS I'M REPRESENTING HER, CAPTAIN. COULD WE SEE M'RRGLA NOW, PLEASE?
YOU'RE HER LAWYER, MR. MARCHIONESS. I CAN HARDLY REFUSE.
SERGEANT KOWALSKI, SHOW THESE GENTLEMEN THROUGH TO THE HOLDING CELLS, PLEASE...
SURE, CAPTAIN.
IF YOU'D LIKE TO COME THIS WAY...

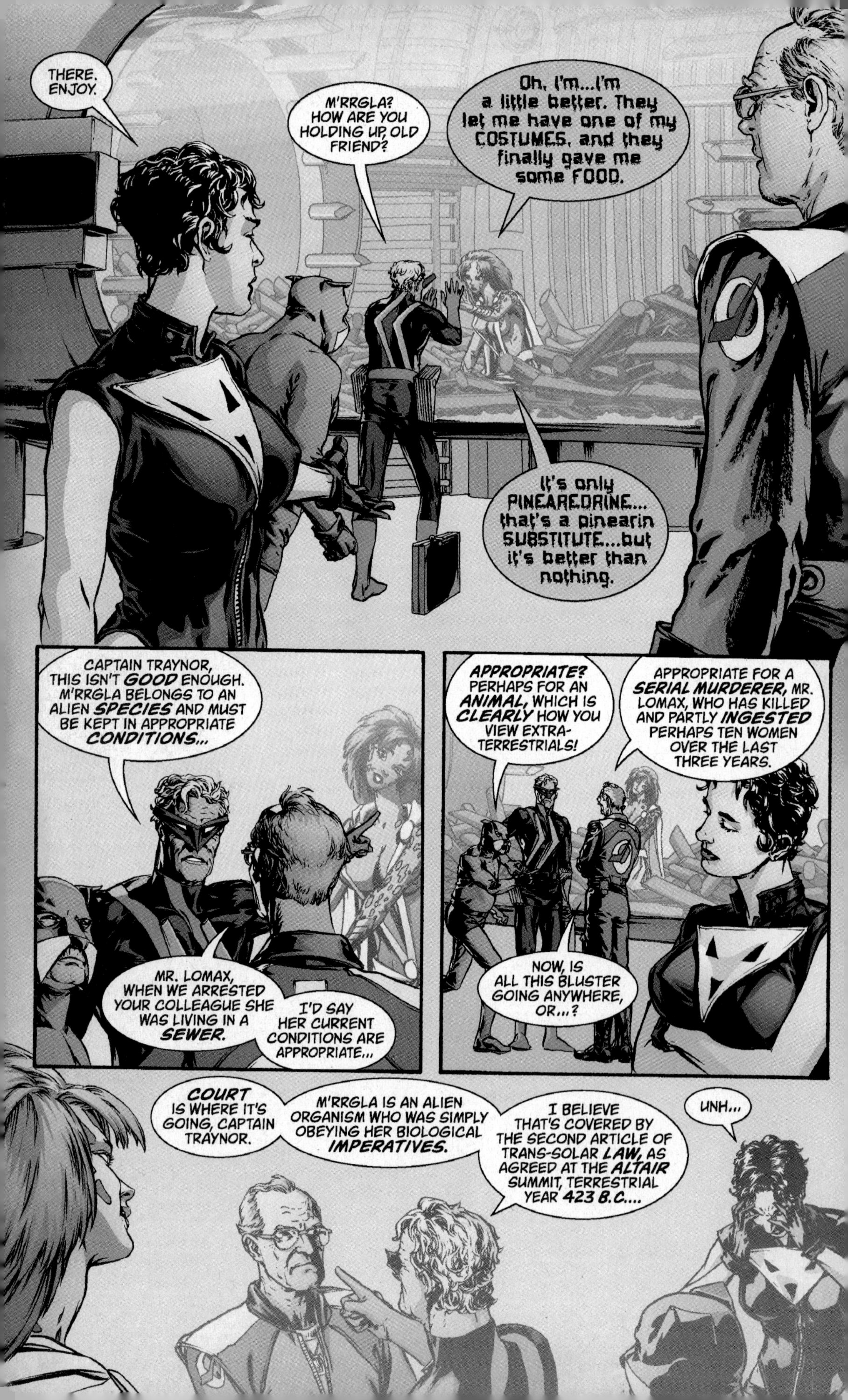

THERE. ENJOY.
M'RRGLA? HOW ARE YOU HOLDING UP, OLD FRIEND?
Oh, I'm...I'm a little better. They let me have one of my COSTUMES, and they finally gave me some FOOD.
It's only PINEAREDRINE... that's a pinearin SUBSTITUTE...but it's better than nothing.
CAPTAIN TRAYNOR, THIS ISN'T GOOD ENOUGH. M'RRGLA BELONGS TO AN ALIEN SPECIES AND MUST BE KEPT IN APPROPRIATE CONDITIONS...
MR. LOMAX, WHEN WE ARRESTED YOUR COLLEAGUE SHE WAS LIVING IN A SEWER.
I'D SAY HER CURRENT CONDITIONS ARE APPROPRIATE...
APPROPRIATE? PERHAPS FOR AN ANIMAL, WHICH IS CLEARLY HOW YOU VIEW EXTRA-TERRESTRIALS!
APPROPRIATE FOR A SERIAL MURDERER, MR. LOMAX, WHO HAS KILLED AND PARTLY INGESTED PERHAPS TEN WOMEN OVER THE LAST THREE YEARS.
NOW, IS ALL THIS BLUSTER GOING ANYWHERE, OR...?
COURT IS WHERE IT'S GOING, CAPTAIN TRAYNOR.
M'RRGLA IS AN ALIEN ORGANISM WHO WAS SIMPLY OBEYING HER BIOLOGICAL IMPERATIVES.
I BELIEVE THAT'S COVERED BY THE SECOND ARTICLE OF TRANS-SOLAR LAW, AS AGREED AT THE ALTAIR SUMMIT, TERRESTRIAL YEAR 423 B.C....
UNH...

WELL, YOU CLEARLY KNOW MORE ABOUT ALIEN LAW THAN I DO, MR. MARCHIONESS.

HOWEVER, HAVING LIVED HERE SINCE 1949, I *AM* FAIRLY FAMILIAR WITH *NEOPOLIS* LAW...

...AND A MAJOR *TENET* OF THAT LEGISLATION IS THE POSSIBLY PROVINCIAL IDEA THAT KILLING AND EATING PEOPLE IS *WRONG.* IN FACT...

JACKIE? ARE YOU OKAY?

GEHHHH... GOD *DAMN*...

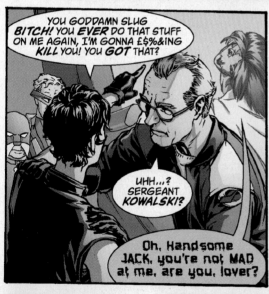

YOU GODDAMN SLUG *BITCH!* YOU *EVER* DO THAT STUFF ON ME AGAIN, I'M GONNA £$%&ING *KILL* YOU! YOU *GOT* THAT?

UHH...? SERGEANT *KOWALSKI!?*

Oh, Handsome JACK, you're not MAD at me, are you, lover?

CAPTAIN TRAYNOR, "SLUG" IS WHAT I WOULD CONSIDER A TERM OF TRANS-SPECIES *ABUSE.* AS FOR THE *DEATH-THREAT*...

THAT WAS NOT A THREAT, THAT WAS A *PROMISE,* YOU...OH, YOU £$%&ING *BITCH!*

JACKIE, COME *ON.* OUTSIDE AND COOL *OFF.*

NOW, SERGEANT...

MORNIN', JACKS. HOW'S...

BOY. YOU LOOK LIKE YOUR GRANMA DIED AND LEFT YOU CONTROLLIN' SHARES IN *BETAMAX*. WHAT'S UP?

IT'S THAT £$%&ING *QUALTZ* THING! SHE...OH, FORGET IT.

SHE'S JUST GOT ALL THESE BIG-SHOT PLAYBOY *SCIENCE GUYS* ROOTING FOR HER AND I'M SCARED SHE'S GOING TO *WALK*.

ANYWAY, WHY'RE *YOU* IN SO EARLY?

LONG STORY. C'MON, LET'S GET *COFFEE*...

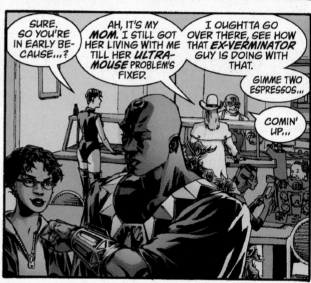

SURE. SO YOU'RE IN EARLY BE-CAUSE...?

AH, IT'S MY *MOM*. I STILL GOT HER LIVING WITH ME TILL HER *ULTRA-MOUSE* PROBLEM'S FIXED.

I OUGHTTA GO OVER THERE, SEE HOW THAT *EX-VERMINATOR* GUY IS DOING WITH THAT.

GIMME TWO ESPRESSOS...

COMIN' UP...

YOU AND YOUR MOM DON'T GET ON?

HELL, JACK, I HAD TO TAKE DOWN ALL MY...UH, ALL MY *ART PRINTS* AN' STUFF.

ALSO, SHE'S GOT THIS *POWER*, RIGHT? EARLY SIXTIES, SHE WAS *"RUTH O'DARE."*

SHE'S, LIKE, THIS HUMAN *LIE DETECTOR*.

I THOUGHT *ALL* MOMS DID THAT?

YEAH, BUT *MY* MOM *SPECIALIZED*.

TELLYA, SOON AS *PETE* GETS IN, I'M GOING TO SEE ABOUT THOSE *MICE*. STOMP THE LITTLE BASTARDS MYSELF IF I HAVE TO...

SO, JOHN, YOU AT ALL READY FOR YOUR *TRIP*?

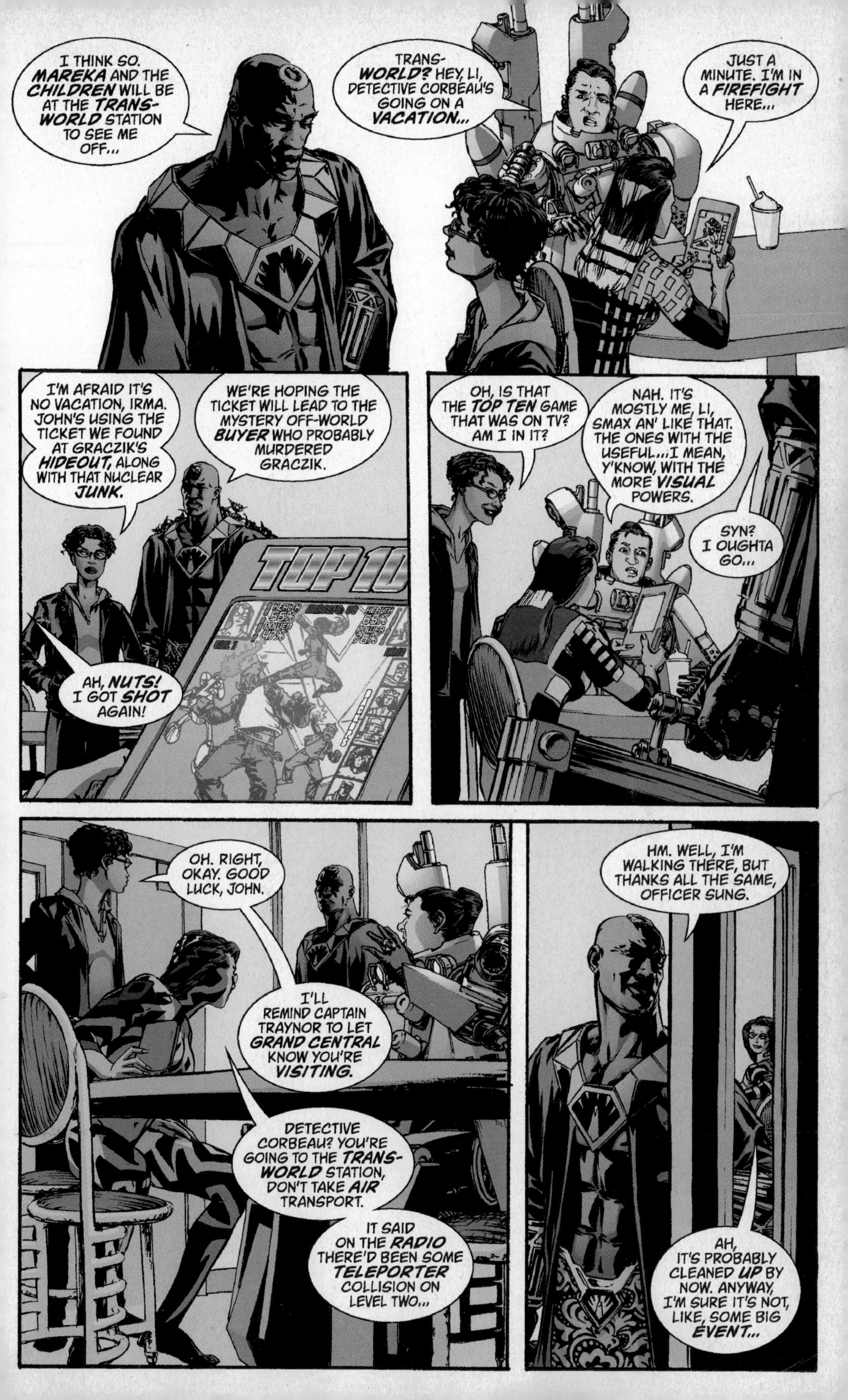
I THINK SO. MAREKA AND THE CHILDREN WILL BE AT THE TRANS-WORLD STATION TO SEE ME OFF...
TRANS-WORLD? HEY, LI, DETECTIVE CORBEAU'S GOING ON A VACATION...
JUST A MINUTE. I'M IN A FIREFIGHT HERE...
I'M AFRAID IT'S NO VACATION, IRMA. JOHN'S USING THE TICKET WE FOUND AT GRACZIK'S HIDEOUT, ALONG WITH THAT NUCLEAR JUNK.
WE'RE HOPING THE TICKET WILL LEAD TO THE MYSTERY OFF-WORLD BUYER WHO PROBABLY MURDERED GRACZIK.
TOP 10
AH, NUTS! I GOT SHOT AGAIN!
OH, IS THAT THE TOP TEN GAME THAT WAS ON TV? AM I IN IT?
NAH. IT'S MOSTLY ME, LI, SMAX AN' LIKE THAT. THE ONES WITH THE USEFUL...I MEAN, Y'KNOW, WITH THE MORE VISUAL POWERS.
SYN? I OUGHTA GO...
OH. RIGHT, OKAY. GOOD LUCK, JOHN.
I'LL REMIND CAPTAIN TRAYNOR TO LET GRAND CENTRAL KNOW YOU'RE VISITING.
DETECTIVE CORBEAU? YOU'RE GOING TO THE TRANS-WORLD STATION, DON'T TAKE AIR TRANSPORT.
IT SAID ON THE RADIO THERE'D BEEN SOME TELEPORTER COLLISION ON LEVEL TWO...
HM. WELL, I'M WALKING THERE, BUT THANKS ALL THE SAME, OFFICER SUNG.
AH, IT'S PROBABLY CLEANED UP BY NOW. ANYWAY, I'M SURE IT'S NOT, LIKE, SOME BIG EVENT...

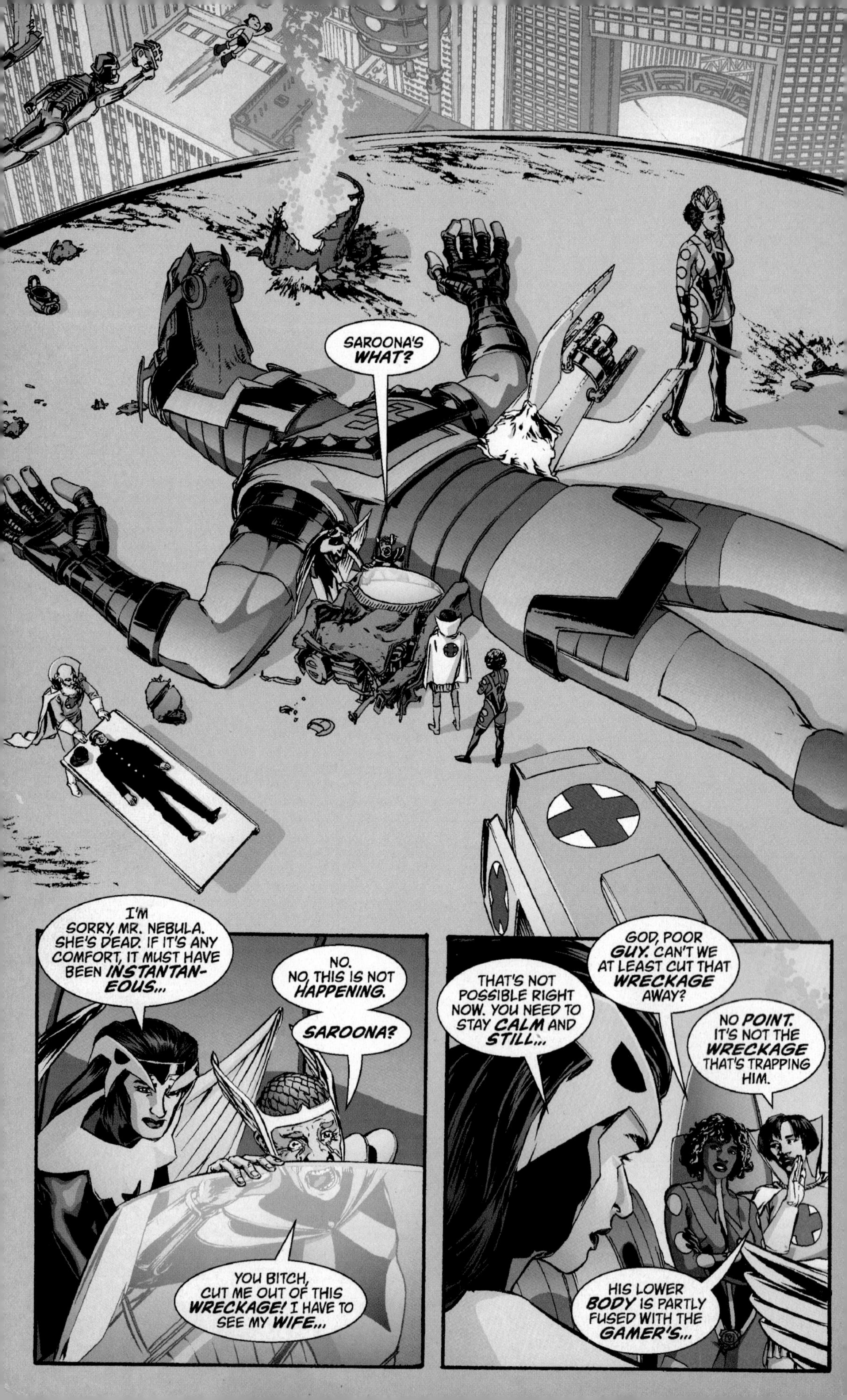
SAROONA'S WHAT?
I'M SORRY, MR. NEBULA. SHE'S DEAD. IF IT'S ANY COMFORT, IT MUST HAVE BEEN INSTANTANEOUS...
NO. NO, THIS IS NOT HAPPENING.
SAROONA?
YOU BITCH, CUT ME OUT OF THIS WRECKAGE! I HAVE TO SEE MY WIFE...
THAT'S NOT POSSIBLE RIGHT NOW. YOU NEED TO STAY CALM AND STILL...
GOD, POOR GUY. CAN'T WE AT LEAST CUT THAT WRECKAGE AWAY?
NO POINT. IT'S NOT THE WRECKAGE THAT'S TRAPPING HIM.
HIS LOWER BODY IS PARTLY FUSED WITH THE GAMER'S...

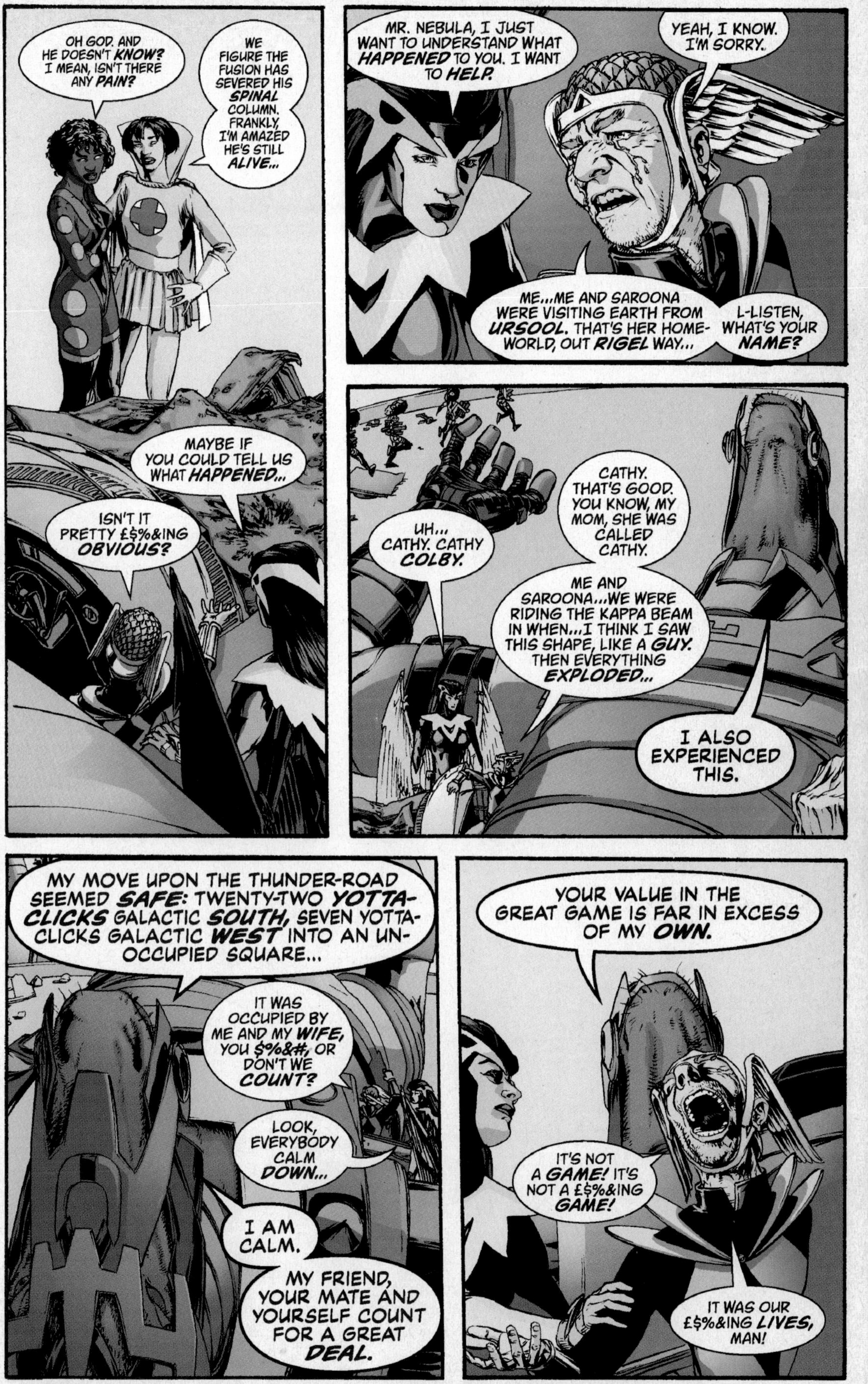
OH GOD. AND HE DOESN'T KNOW? I MEAN, ISN'T THERE ANY PAIN?
WE FIGURE THE FUSION HAS SEVERED HIS SPINAL COLUMN. FRANKLY, I'M AMAZED HE'S STILL ALIVE...
MAYBE IF YOU COULD TELL US WHAT HAPPENED...
ISN'T IT PRETTY £$%&ING OBVIOUS?
MR. NEBULA, I JUST WANT TO UNDERSTAND WHAT HAPPENED TO YOU. I WANT TO HELP.
YEAH, I KNOW. I'M SORRY.
ME...ME AND SAROONA WERE VISITING EARTH FROM URSOOL. THAT'S HER HOME-WORLD, OUT RIGEL WAY...
L-LISTEN, WHAT'S YOUR NAME?
UH... CATHY. CATHY COLBY.
CATHY. THAT'S GOOD. YOU KNOW, MY MOM, SHE WAS CALLED CATHY.
ME AND SAROONA...WE WERE RIDING THE KAPPA BEAM IN WHEN...I THINK I SAW THIS SHAPE, LIKE A GUY. THEN EVERYTHING EXPLODED...
I ALSO EXPERIENCED THIS.
MY MOVE UPON THE THUNDER-ROAD SEEMED SAFE: TWENTY-TWO YOTTA-CLICKS GALACTIC SOUTH, SEVEN YOTTA-CLICKS GALACTIC WEST INTO AN UN-OCCUPIED SQUARE...
IT WAS OCCUPIED BY ME AND MY WIFE, YOU $%&#, OR DON'T WE COUNT?
LOOK, EVERYBODY CALM DOWN...
I AM CALM.
MY FRIEND, YOUR MATE AND YOURSELF COUNT FOR A GREAT DEAL.
YOUR VALUE IN THE GREAT GAME IS FAR IN EXCESS OF MY OWN.
IT'S NOT A GAME! IT'S NOT A £$%&ING GAME!
IT WAS OUR £$%&ING LIVES, MAN!

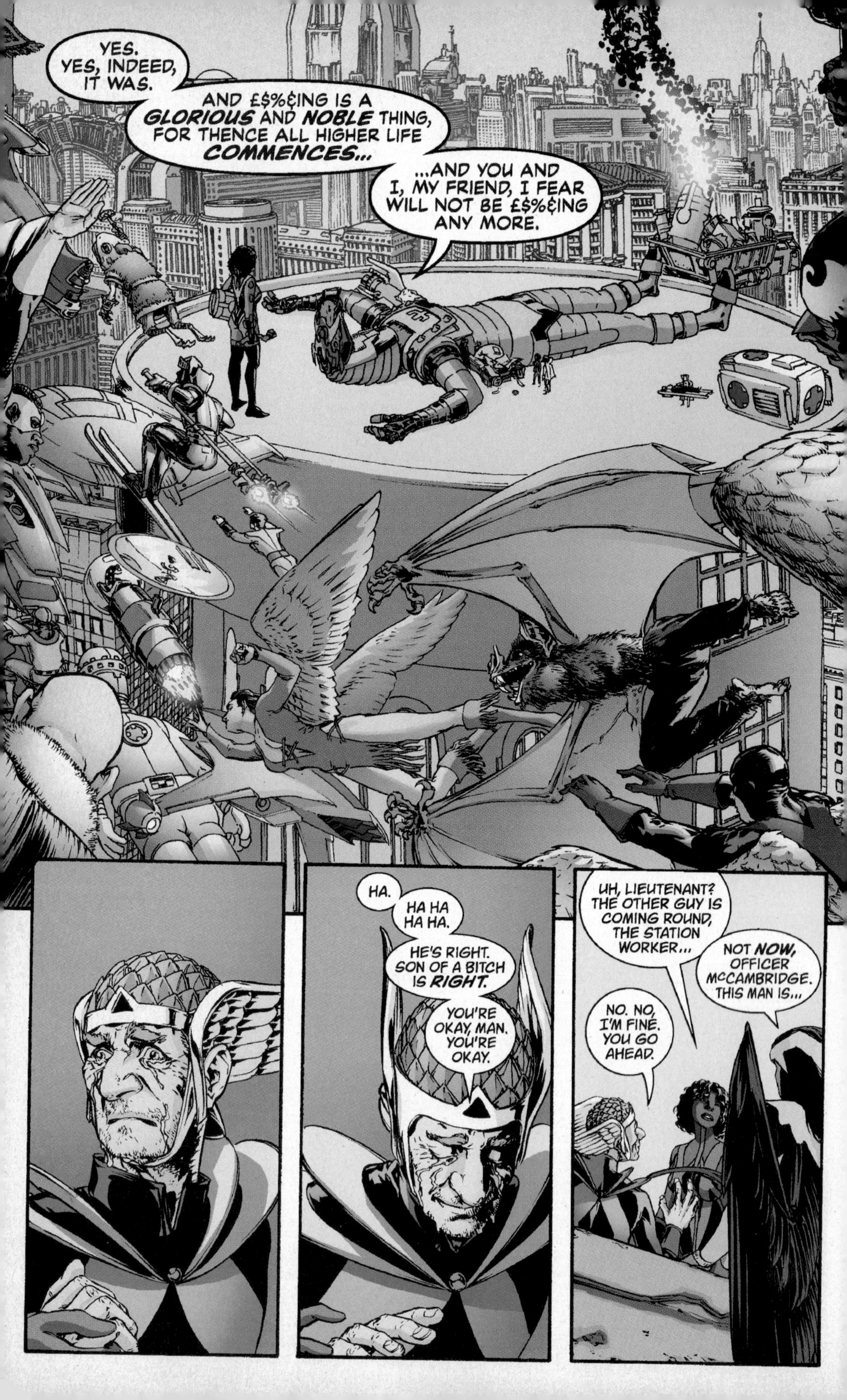
YES. YES, INDEED, IT WAS.
AND £$%&ING IS A **GLORIOUS** AND **NOBLE** THING, FOR THENCE ALL HIGHER LIFE **COMMENCES...**
...AND YOU AND I, MY FRIEND, I FEAR WILL NOT BE £$%&ING ANY MORE.
HA.
HA HA HA HA.
HE'S RIGHT. SON OF A BITCH IS **RIGHT.**
YOU'RE OKAY, MAN. YOU'RE OKAY.
UH, LIEUTENANT? THE OTHER GUY IS COMING ROUND, THE STATION WORKER...
NOT **NOW,** OFFICER McCAMBRIDGE. THIS MAN IS...
NO. NO, I'M FINE. YOU GO AHEAD.

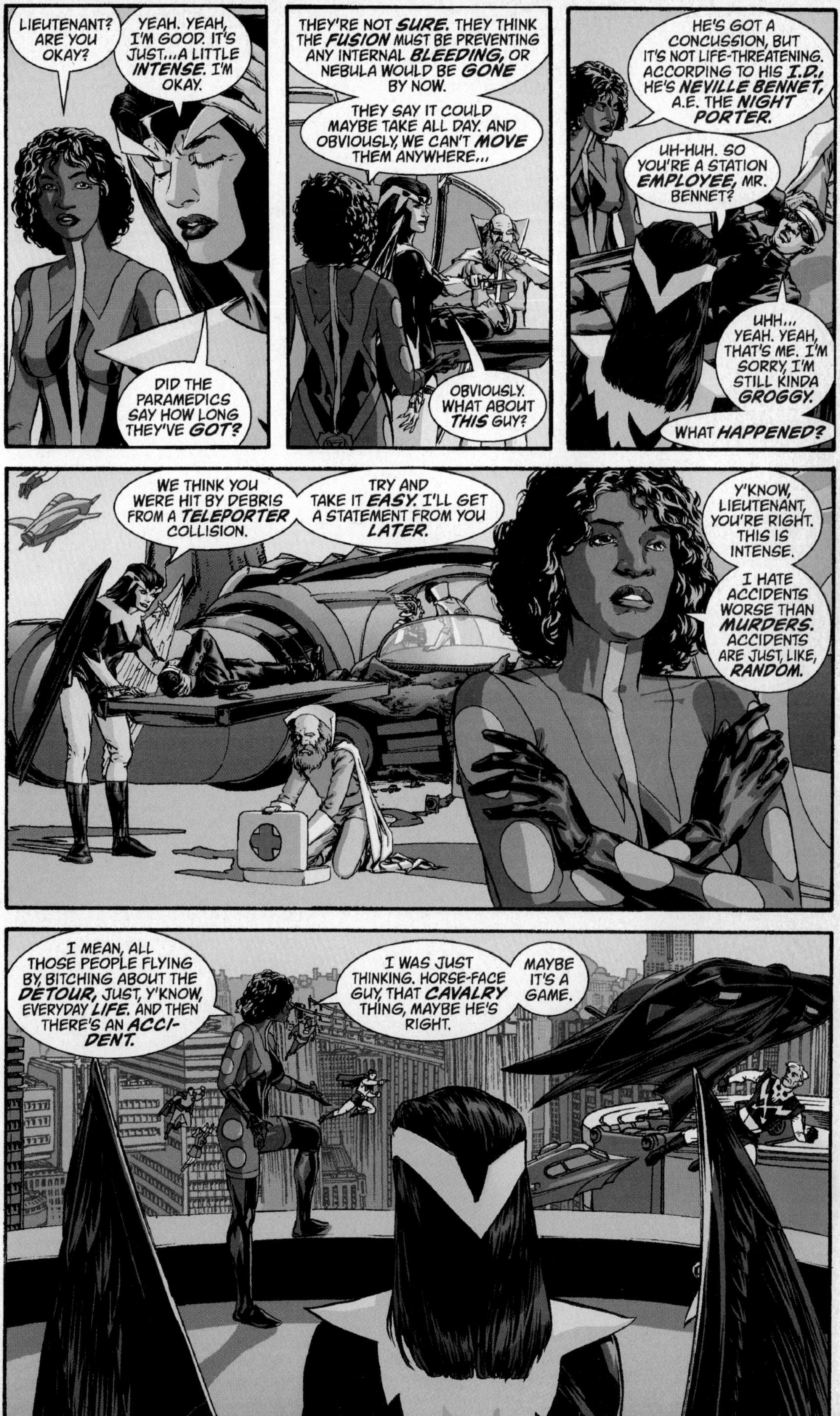
LIEUTENANT? ARE YOU OKAY?
YEAH. YEAH, I'M GOOD. IT'S JUST...A LITTLE INTENSE. I'M OKAY.
DID THE PARAMEDICS SAY HOW LONG THEY'VE GOT?
THEY'RE NOT SURE. THEY THINK THE FUSION MUST BE PREVENTING ANY INTERNAL BLEEDING, OR NEBULA WOULD BE GONE BY NOW.
THEY SAY IT COULD MAYBE TAKE ALL DAY. AND OBVIOUSLY, WE CAN'T MOVE THEM ANYWHERE...
OBVIOUSLY. WHAT ABOUT THIS GUY?
HE'S GOT A CONCUSSION, BUT IT'S NOT LIFE-THREATENING. ACCORDING TO HIS I.D., HE'S NEVILLE BENNET, A.E. THE NIGHT PORTER.
UH-HUH. SO YOU'RE A STATION EMPLOYEE, MR. BENNET?
UHH... YEAH. YEAH, THAT'S ME. I'M SORRY, I'M STILL KINDA GROGGY.
WHAT HAPPENED?
WE THINK YOU WERE HIT BY DEBRIS FROM A TELEPORTER COLLISION.
TRY AND TAKE IT EASY. I'LL GET A STATEMENT FROM YOU LATER.
Y'KNOW, LIEUTENANT, YOU'RE RIGHT. THIS IS INTENSE.
I HATE ACCIDENTS WORSE THAN MURDERS. ACCIDENTS ARE JUST, LIKE, RANDOM.
I MEAN, ALL THOSE PEOPLE FLYING BY, BITCHING ABOUT THE DETOUR, JUST, Y'KNOW, EVERYDAY LIFE. AND THEN THERE'S AN ACCI-DENT.
I WAS JUST THINKING. HORSE-FACE GUY, THAT CAVALRY THING, MAYBE HE'S RIGHT.
MAYBE IT'S A GAME.

MAN, I'M **DEAD** AGAIN! THIS GAME IS A **GYP**! I'M **WAY** BETTER THAN THIS...

HUH. WELL, I THOUGHT IT WAS PRETTY GOOD. **CHERRY** WAS PLAYIN' IT LAST NIGHT. SHE HAD ME NUKE **SOUTH GREEN.**

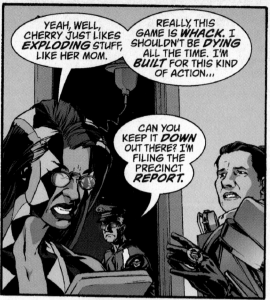

YEAH, WELL, CHERRY JUST LIKES **EXPLODING** STUFF, LIKE HER MOM.

REALLY. THIS GAME IS **WHACK.** I SHOULDN'T BE **DYING** ALL THE TIME. I'M **BUILT** FOR THIS KIND OF ACTION...

CAN YOU KEEP IT **DOWN** OUT THERE? I'M FILING THE PRECINCT **REPORT.**

THERE. SORRY ABOUT THAT, COMMISSIONER ULTIMA. I WAS JUST TELLING YOU ABOUT THE COMPLICATIONS IN THE **QUALTZ** CASE...

YES. WELL, DON'T LET HER RICH **FRIENDS** INTIMIDATE THE **DEPARTMENT.** FIGHT THIS ALL THE **WAY,** TRAYNOR.

NOW, WHAT'S THIS ABOUT **CORBEAU** VISITING GRAND **CENTRAL?**

IT'S THE **GRACZIK/GROMOLKO** CASE, COMMISSIONER. WHEN DETECTIVES RAIDED GRACZIK'S **HIDEOUT,** THEY FOUND A STRANGE RADIOACTIVE **DRUG** AND A **TRANS-WORLD** TICKET.

CORBEAU'S FOLLOWING UP THE **LATTER.**

HMMPH. HOLIDAYING IN **NOVA ROMA,** MORE LIKE.

INCIDENTALLY, TRAYNOR, BE **IN** NEXT WEDNESDAY...

I'M SCHEDULING AN **INSPECTION.**

I'LL LOOK FORWARD TO SEEING YOU THEN, CAPTAIN.

ULTIMA OUT.

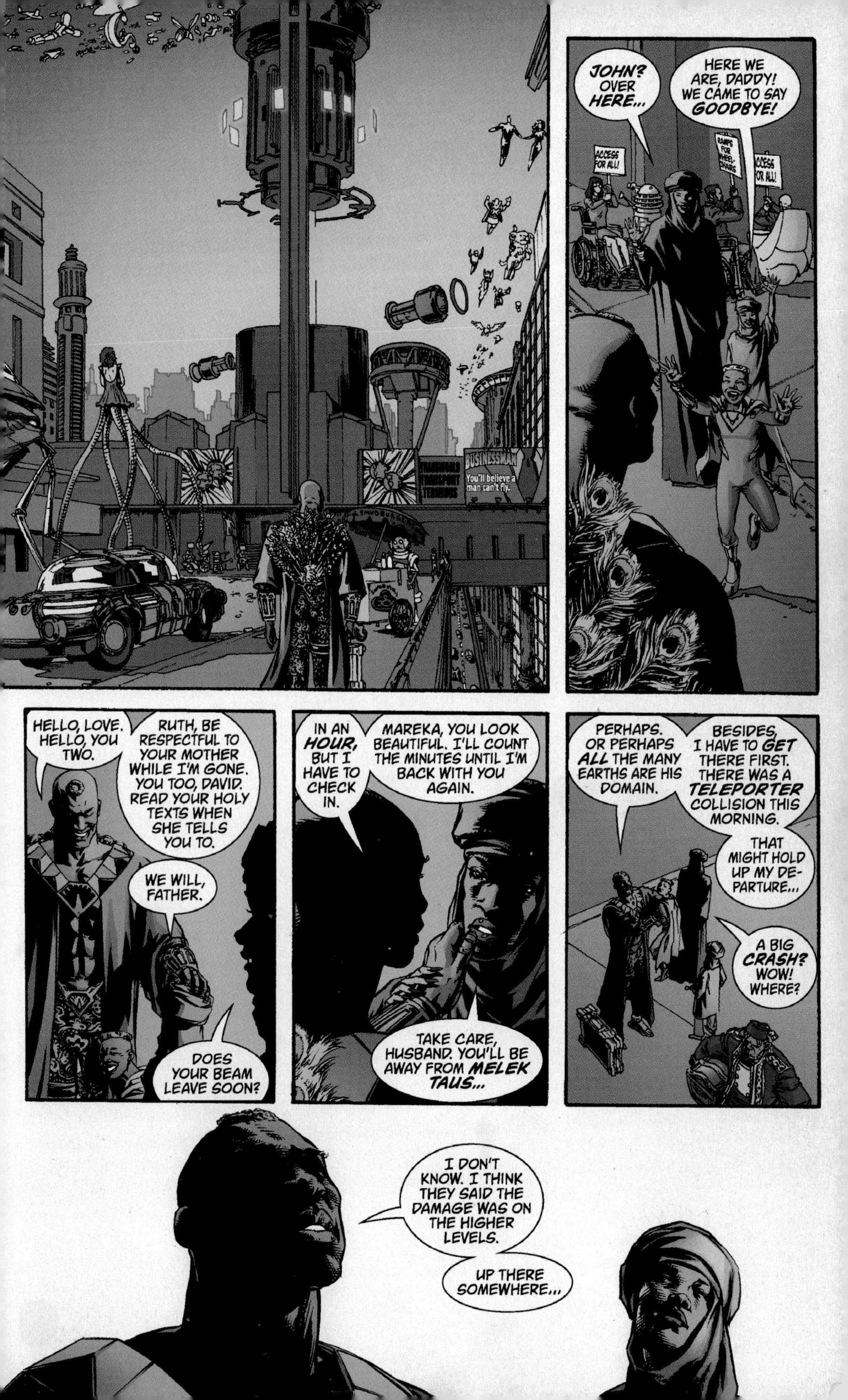
BUSINESSMAN
You'll believe a man can't fly.
JOHN? OVER HERE...
HERE WE ARE, DADDY! WE CAME TO SAY GOODBYE!
ACCESS FOR ALL!
RAMPS FOR WHEEL-CHAIRS
ACCESS FOR ALL!
HELLO, LOVE. HELLO, YOU TWO.
RUTH, BE RESPECTFUL TO YOUR MOTHER WHILE I'M GONE. YOU TOO, DAVID. READ YOUR HOLY TEXTS WHEN SHE TELLS YOU TO.
WE WILL, FATHER.
DOES YOUR BEAM LEAVE SOON?
IN AN HOUR, BUT I HAVE TO CHECK IN.
MAREKA, YOU LOOK BEAUTIFUL. I'LL COUNT THE MINUTES UNTIL I'M BACK WITH YOU AGAIN.
TAKE CARE, HUSBAND. YOU'LL BE AWAY FROM MELEK TAUS...
PERHAPS. OR PERHAPS ALL THE MANY EARTHS ARE HIS DOMAIN.
BESIDES, I HAVE TO GET THERE FIRST. THERE WAS A TELEPORTER COLLISION THIS MORNING.
THAT MIGHT HOLD UP MY DE-PARTURE...
A BIG CRASH? WOW! WHERE?
I DON'T KNOW. I THINK THEY SAID THE DAMAGE WAS ON THE HIGHER LEVELS.
UP THERE SOMEWHERE...

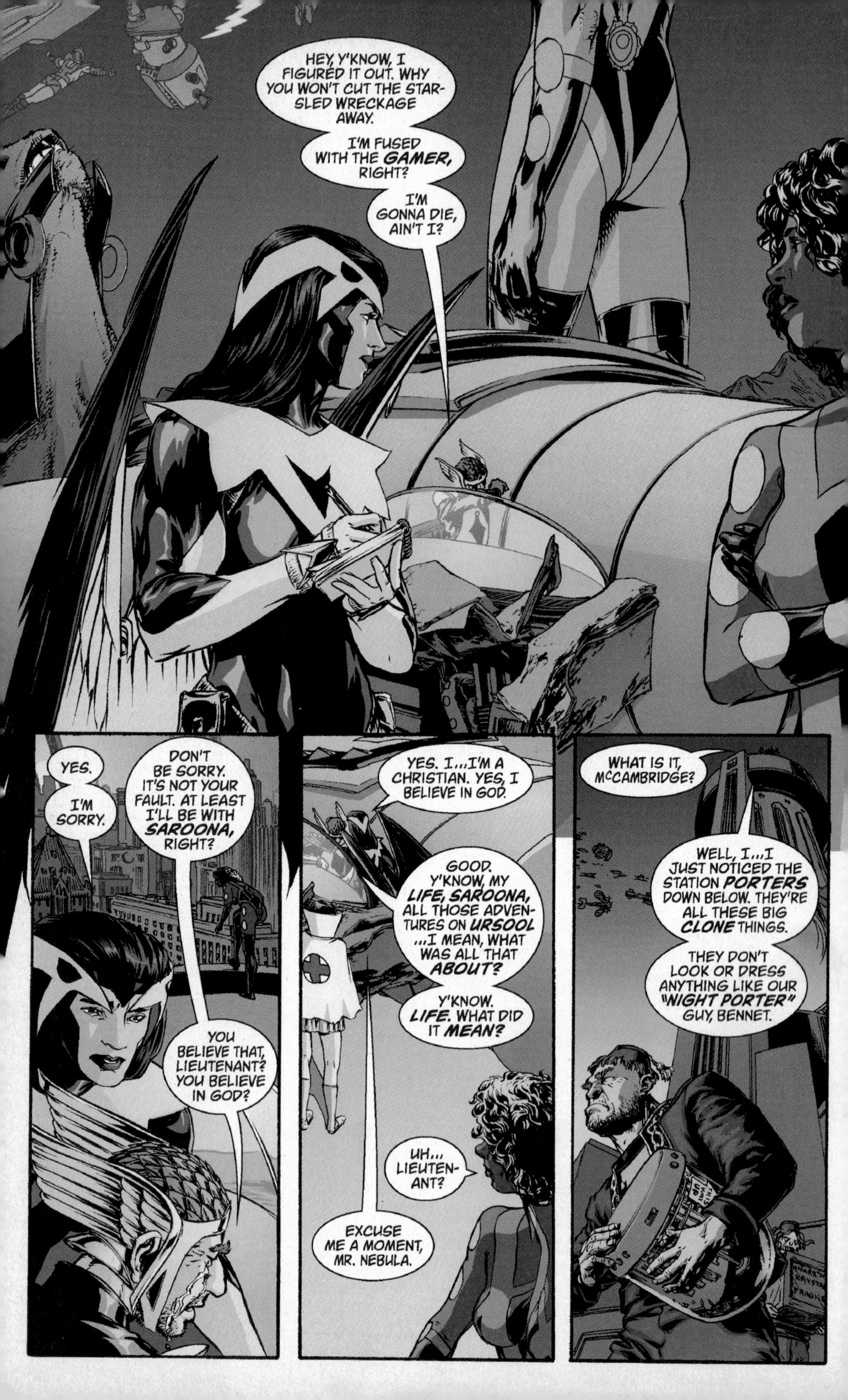
HEY, Y'KNOW, I FIGURED IT OUT. WHY YOU WON'T CUT THE STAR-SLED WRECKAGE AWAY.
I'M FUSED WITH THE GAMER, RIGHT?
I'M GONNA DIE, AIN'T I?
YES.
I'M SORRY.
DON'T BE SORRY. IT'S NOT YOUR FAULT. AT LEAST I'LL BE WITH SAROONA, RIGHT?
YOU BELIEVE THAT, LIEUTENANT? YOU BELIEVE IN GOD?
YES. I...I'M A CHRISTIAN. YES, I BELIEVE IN GOD.
GOOD. Y'KNOW, MY LIFE, SAROONA, ALL THOSE ADVENTURES ON URSOOL ...I MEAN, WHAT WAS ALL THAT ABOUT?
Y'KNOW. LIFE. WHAT DID IT MEAN?
UH... LIEUTENANT?
EXCUSE ME A MOMENT, MR. NEBULA.
WHAT IS IT, McCAMBRIDGE?
WELL, I...I JUST NOTICED THE STATION PORTERS DOWN BELOW. THEY'RE ALL THESE BIG CLONE THINGS.
THEY DON'T LOOK OR DRESS ANYTHING LIKE OUR "NIGHT PORTER" GUY, BENNET.

NO. NO, THEY DON'T. YOU'RE RIGHT.

CHECK OUT BENNET'S *I.D.* AGAIN. YOU'RE *SURE* IT SAYS HE'S A PORTER?

YEAH. IT...NO, WAIT. THAT'S NOT HIS *OCCUPATION*, THAT'S HIS *A.E.!* AND IT'S SPELLED WITH AN *APOSTROPHE*.

WHAT DO YOU MEAN?

LOOK...SEE *HERE*? IT'S, LIKE, "*WIGHT-'PORTER*," WITH AN APOSTROPHE BEFORE *PORTER*.

'PORTER. TELEPORTER...OUR GUY'S A *JUMPER*, LIEUTENANT.

UH-OH...

OKAY, I GET IT.

BOTH *NEBULA* AND THE *GAMER* REPORTED SEEING A HUMAN FIGURE WHILE IN *TRANSIT*, JUST BEFORE THEY *CRASHED*.

HEY! *YOU!* I WANT A *WORD!*

OH GOD. COME *ON*, COME *ON!* TAHITI, *ANY-WHERE*...

YOU LITTLE *WRETCH!*

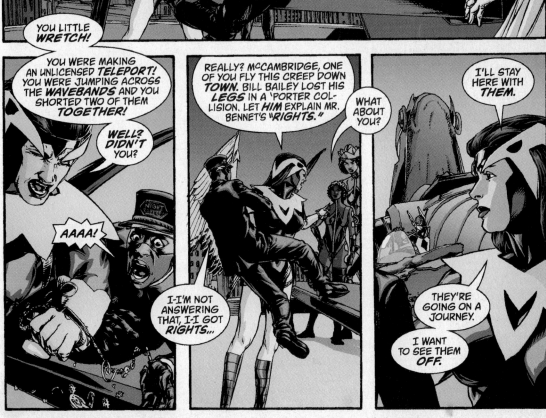

YOU WERE MAKING AN UNLICENSED *TELEPORT!* YOU WERE JUMPING ACROSS THE *WAVEBANDS* AND YOU SHORTED TWO OF THEM *TOGETHER!*

WELL? *DIDN'T* YOU?

AAAA!

I-I'M NOT ANSWERING THAT, I-I GOT *RIGHTS*...

REALLY? McCAMBRIDGE, ONE OF YOU FLY THIS CREEP DOWN *TOWN*. BILL BAILEY LOST HIS *LEGS* IN A 'PORTER COLLISION. LET *HIM* EXPLAIN MR. BENNET'S "*RIGHTS*."

WHAT ABOUT YOU?

I'LL STAY HERE WITH *THEM*.

THEY'RE GOING ON A JOURNEY.

I WANT TO SEE THEM *OFF*.

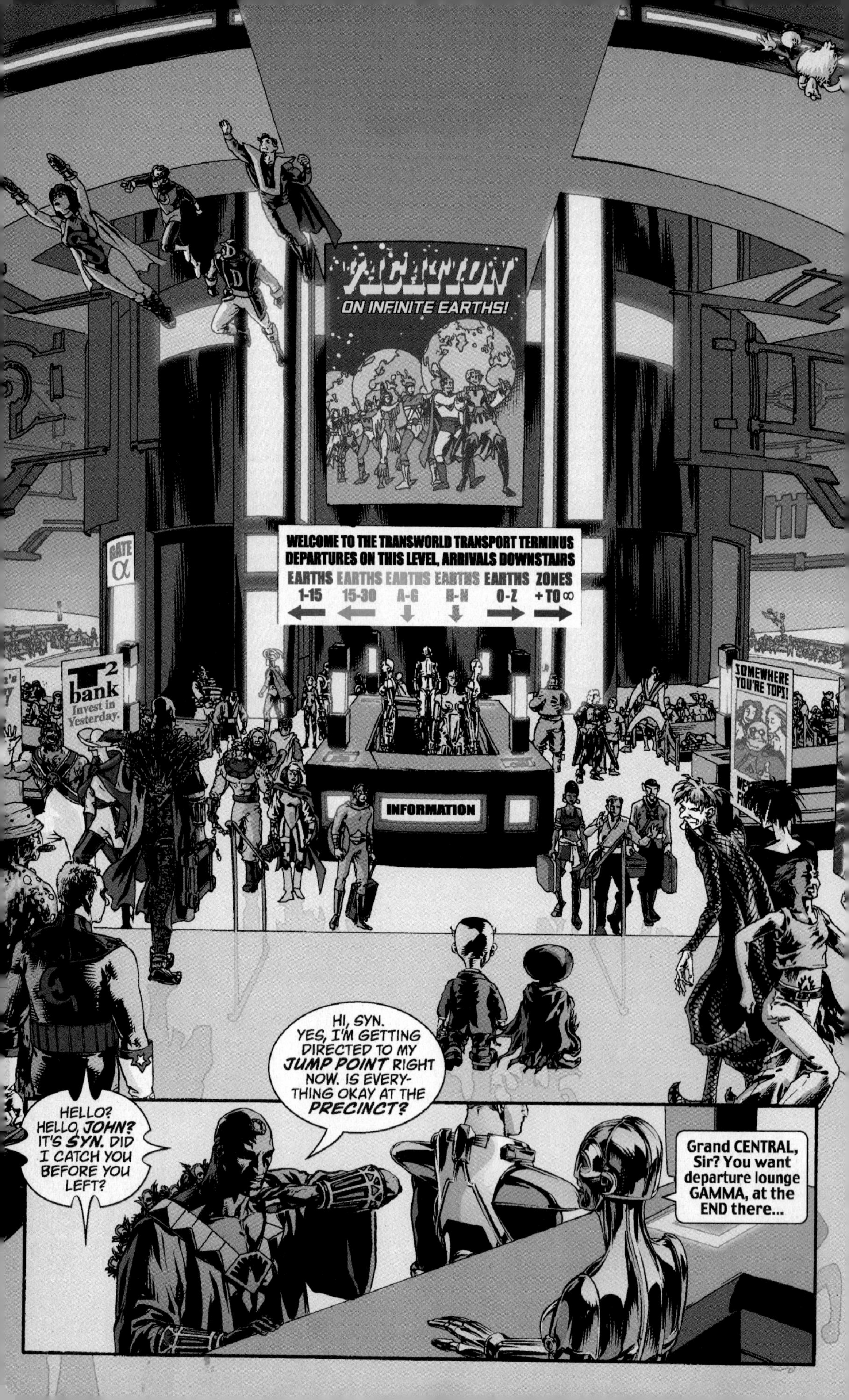
VACATION
ON INFINITE EARTHS!
WELCOME TO THE TRANSWORLD TRANSPORT TERMINUS
DEPARTURES ON THIS LEVEL, ARRIVALS DOWNSTAIRS
EARTHS 1-15
EARTHS 15-30
EARTHS A-G
EARTHS H-N
EARTHS O-Z
ZONES + TO ∞
GATE α
T² bank Invest in Yesterday.
INFORMATION
SOMEWHERE YOU'RE TOPS!
HELLO? HELLO, JOHN? IT'S SYN. DID I CATCH YOU BEFORE YOU LEFT?
HI, SYN. YES, I'M GETTING DIRECTED TO MY JUMP POINT RIGHT NOW. IS EVERYTHING OKAY AT THE PRECINCT?
Grand CENTRAL, Sir? You want departure lounge GAMMA, at the END there...

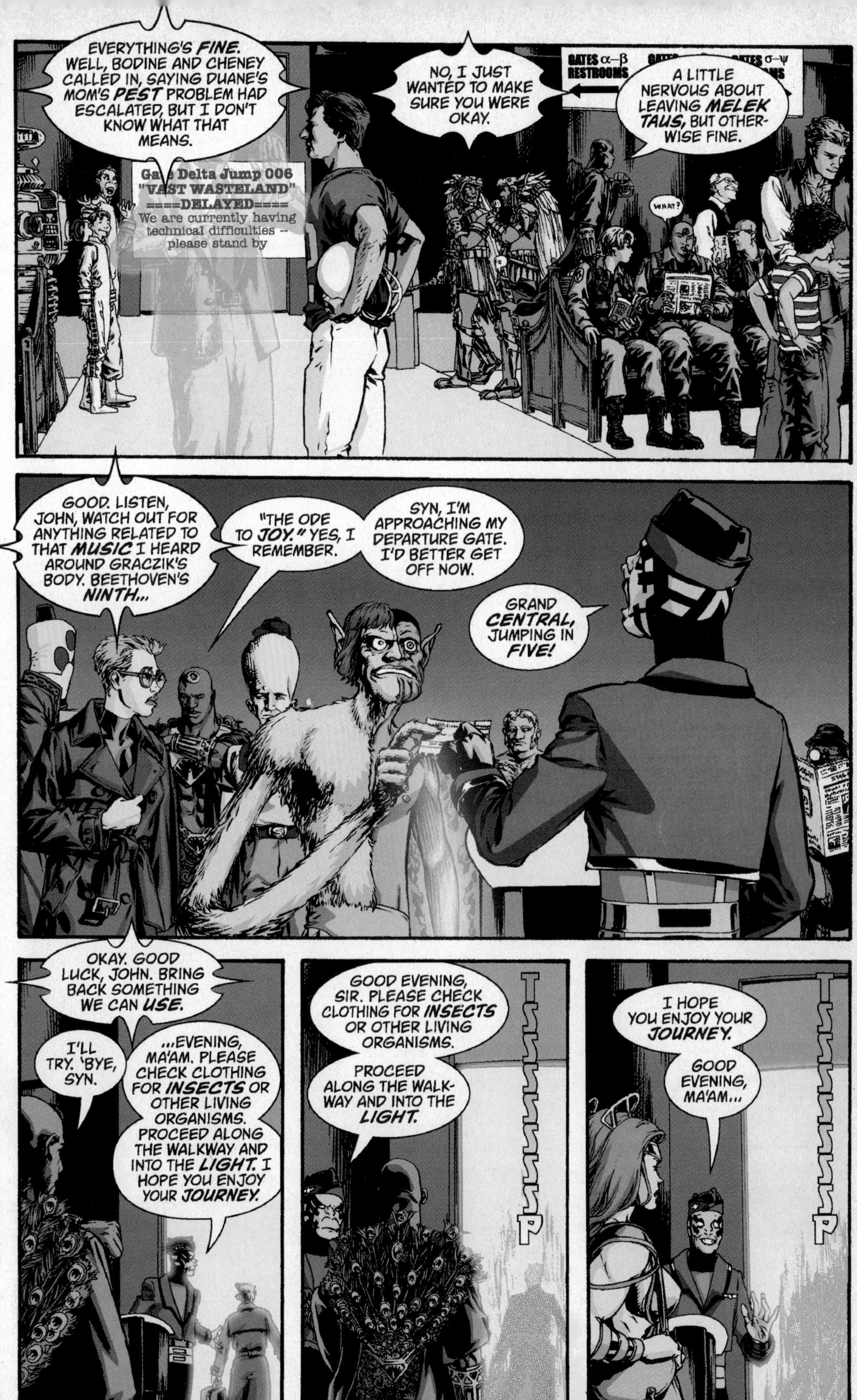
EVERYTHING'S FINE. WELL, BODINE AND CHENEY CALLED IN, SAYING DUANE'S MOM'S PEST PROBLEM HAD ESCALATED, BUT I DON'T KNOW WHAT THAT MEANS.
Gate Delta Jump 006 "VAST WASTELAND" ====DELAYED==== We are currently having technical difficulties -- please stand by
NO, I JUST WANTED TO MAKE SURE YOU WERE OKAY.
GATES α–β RESTROOMS
A LITTLE NERVOUS ABOUT LEAVING MELEK TAUS, BUT OTHER-WISE FINE.
WHAT?
GOOD. LISTEN, JOHN, WATCH OUT FOR ANYTHING RELATED TO THAT MUSIC I HEARD AROUND GRACZIK'S BODY. BEETHOVEN'S NINTH...
"THE ODE TO JOY." YES, I REMEMBER.
SYN, I'M APPROACHING MY DEPARTURE GATE. I'D BETTER GET OFF NOW.
GRAND CENTRAL, JUMPING IN FIVE!
OKAY. GOOD LUCK, JOHN. BRING BACK SOMETHING WE CAN USE.
I'LL TRY. 'BYE, SYN.
...EVENING, MA'AM. PLEASE CHECK CLOTHING FOR INSECTS OR OTHER LIVING ORGANISMS. PROCEED ALONG THE WALKWAY AND INTO THE LIGHT. I HOPE YOU ENJOY YOUR JOURNEY.
GOOD EVENING, SIR. PLEASE CHECK CLOTHING FOR INSECTS OR OTHER LIVING ORGANISMS.
PROCEED ALONG THE WALK-WAY AND INTO THE LIGHT.
TSSSSSSP
I HOPE YOU ENJOY YOUR JOURNEY.
GOOD EVENING, MA'AM...
TSSSSSSP

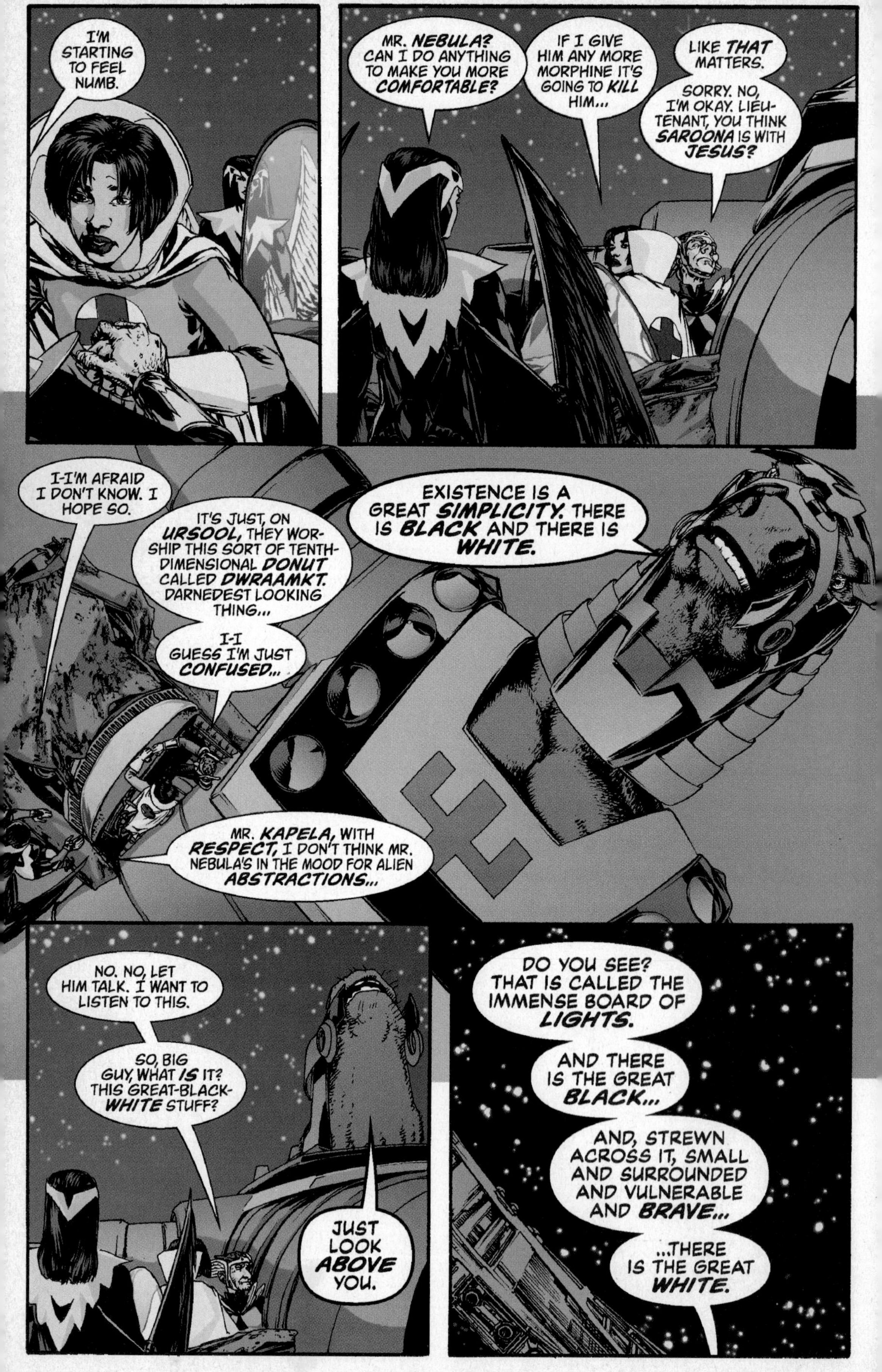
I'M STARTING TO FEEL NUMB.
MR. NEBULA? CAN I DO ANYTHING TO MAKE YOU MORE COMFORTABLE?
IF I GIVE HIM ANY MORE MORPHINE IT'S GOING TO KILL HIM...
LIKE THAT MATTERS.
SORRY. NO, I'M OKAY. LIEUTENANT, YOU THINK SAROONA IS WITH JESUS?
I-I'M AFRAID I DON'T KNOW. I HOPE SO.
IT'S JUST, ON URSOOL, THEY WORSHIP THIS SORT OF TENTH-DIMENSIONAL DONUT CALLED DWRAAMKT. DARNEDEST LOOKING THING...
I-I GUESS I'M JUST CONFUSED...
EXISTENCE IS A GREAT SIMPLICITY. THERE IS BLACK AND THERE IS WHITE.
MR. KAPELA, WITH RESPECT, I DON'T THINK MR. NEBULA'S IN THE MOOD FOR ALIEN ABSTRACTIONS...
NO. NO, LET HIM TALK. I WANT TO LISTEN TO THIS.
SO, BIG GUY, WHAT IS IT? THIS GREAT-BLACK-WHITE STUFF?
JUST LOOK ABOVE YOU.
DO YOU SEE? THAT IS CALLED THE IMMENSE BOARD OF LIGHTS.
AND THERE IS THE GREAT BLACK...
AND, STREWN ACROSS IT, SMALL AND SURROUNDED AND VULNERABLE AND BRAVE...
...THERE IS THE GREAT WHITE.

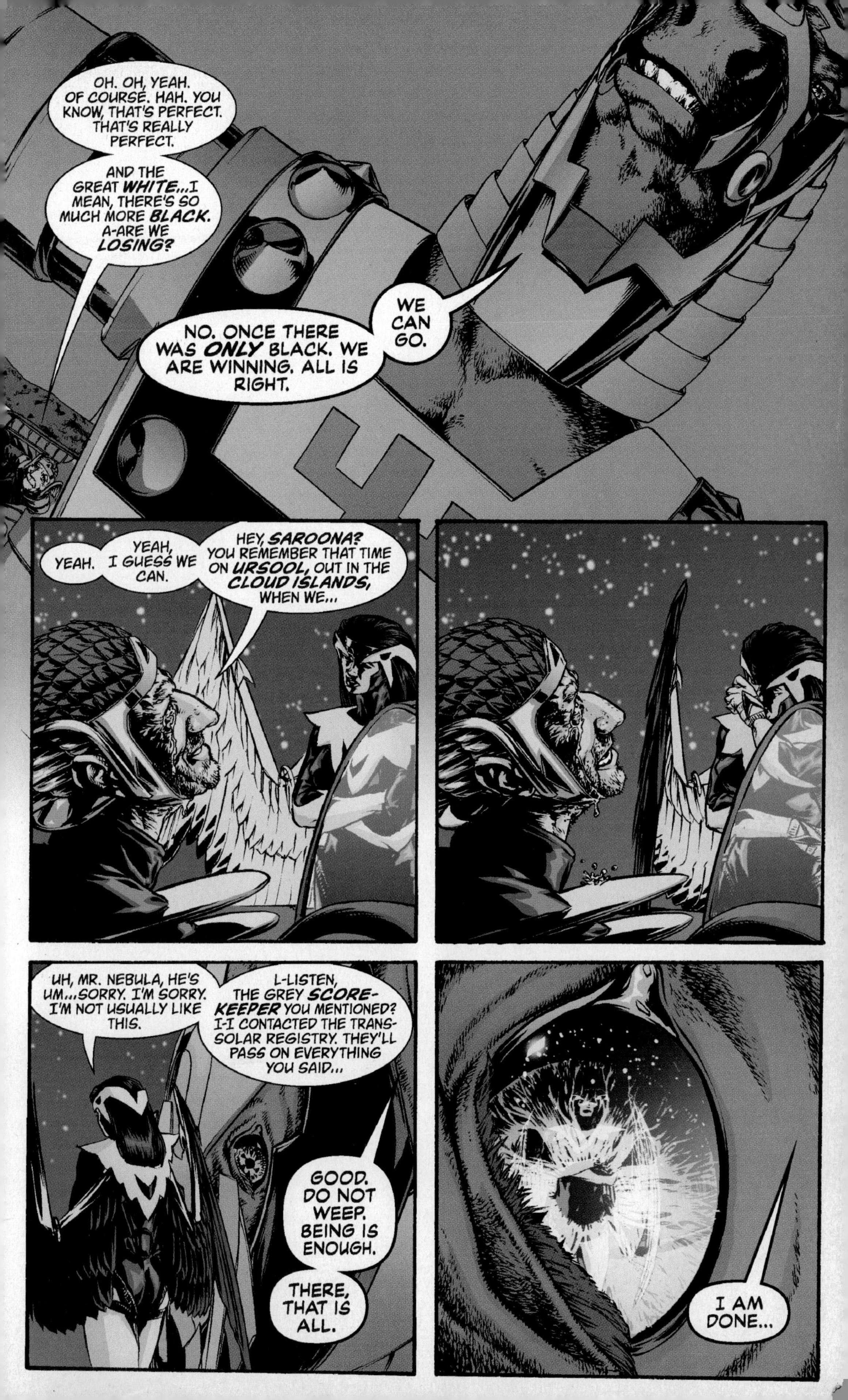
OH. OH, YEAH. OF COURSE. HAH. YOU KNOW, THAT'S PERFECT. THAT'S REALLY PERFECT.
AND THE GREAT WHITE...I MEAN, THERE'S SO MUCH MORE BLACK. A-ARE WE LOSING?
NO. ONCE THERE WAS ONLY BLACK. WE ARE WINNING. ALL IS RIGHT.
WE CAN GO.
YEAH.
YEAH, I GUESS WE CAN.
HEY, SAROONA? YOU REMEMBER THAT TIME ON URSOOL, OUT IN THE CLOUD ISLANDS, WHEN WE...
UH, MR. NEBULA, HE'S UM...SORRY. I'M SORRY. I'M NOT USUALLY LIKE THIS.
L-LISTEN, THE GREY SCORE-KEEPER YOU MENTIONED? I-I CONTACTED THE TRANS-SOLAR REGISTRY. THEY'LL PASS ON EVERYTHING YOU SAID...
GOOD. DO NOT WEEP. BEING IS ENOUGH.
THERE, THAT IS ALL.
I AM DONE...

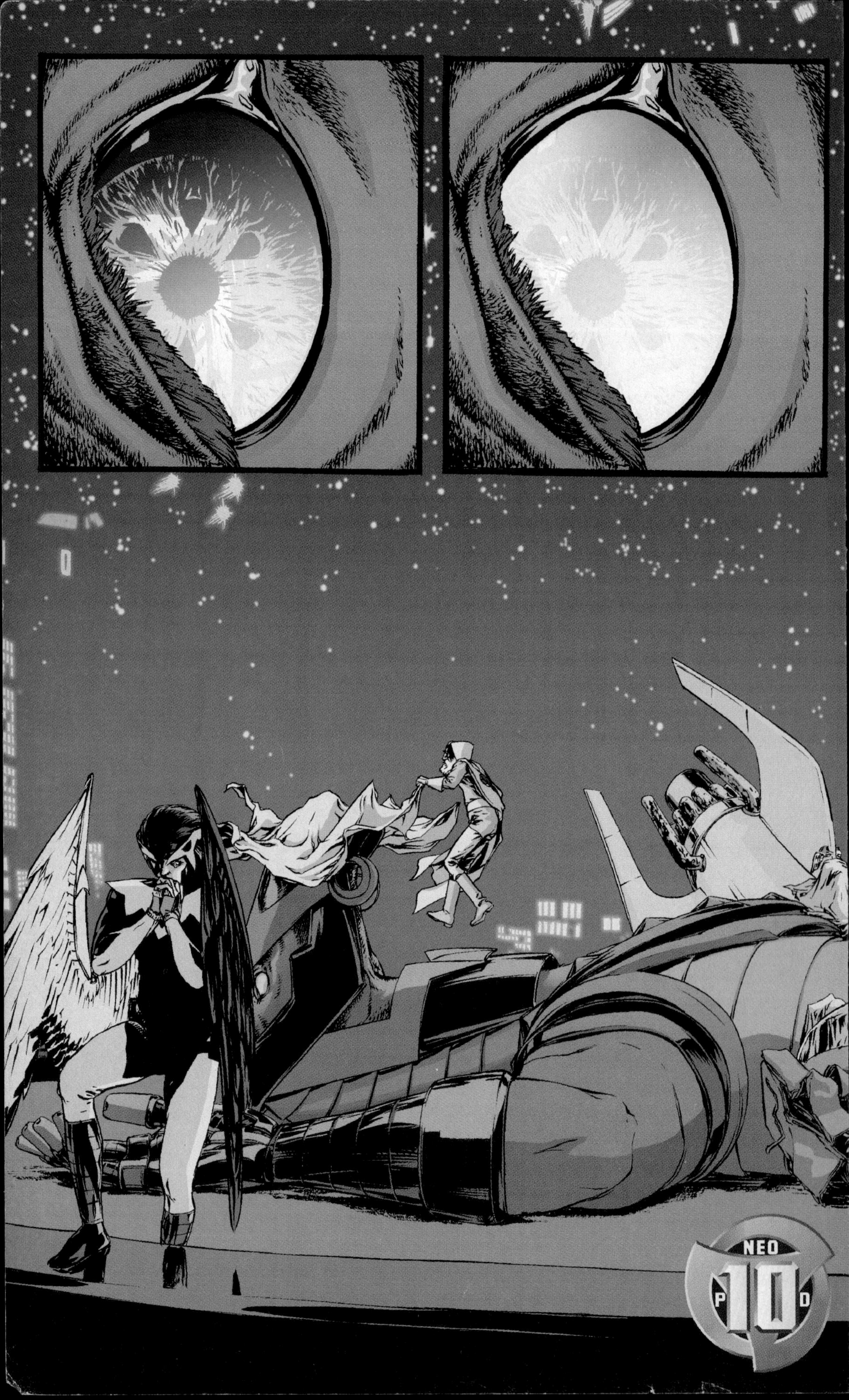

CHAPTER TWO

ON THE DOCKET:
Dust Devil faces powerful vermin,
Detective Jackson gets in early,
and King Peacock goes on assignment.

Cover art:
Gene Ha and
Zander Cannon

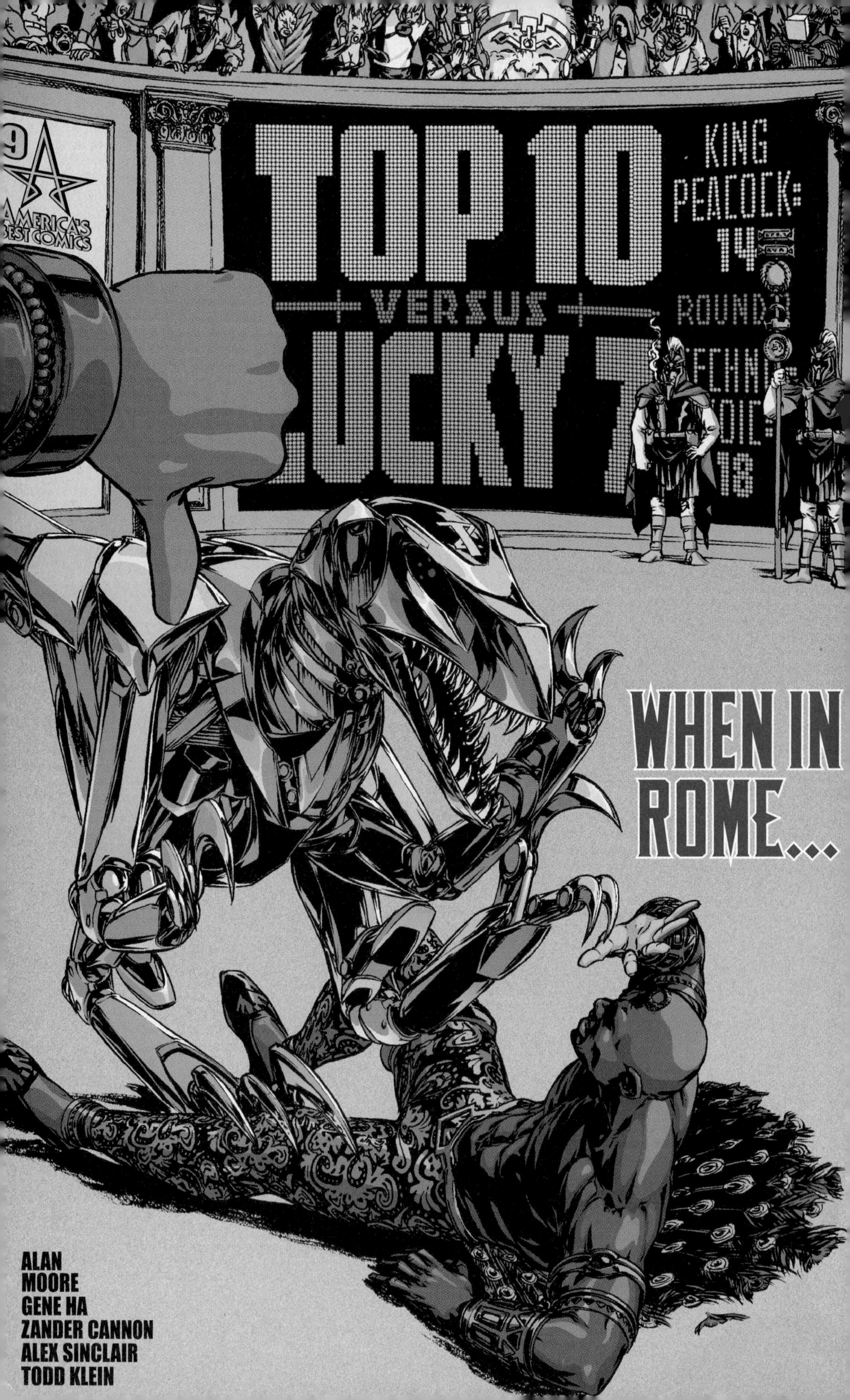
9
AMERICA'S BEST COMICS
TOP 10
VERSUS
KING PEACOCK: 14
ROUND
18
WHEN IN ROME...
ALAN MOORE
GENE HA
ZANDER CANNON
ALEX SINCLAIR
TODD KLEIN

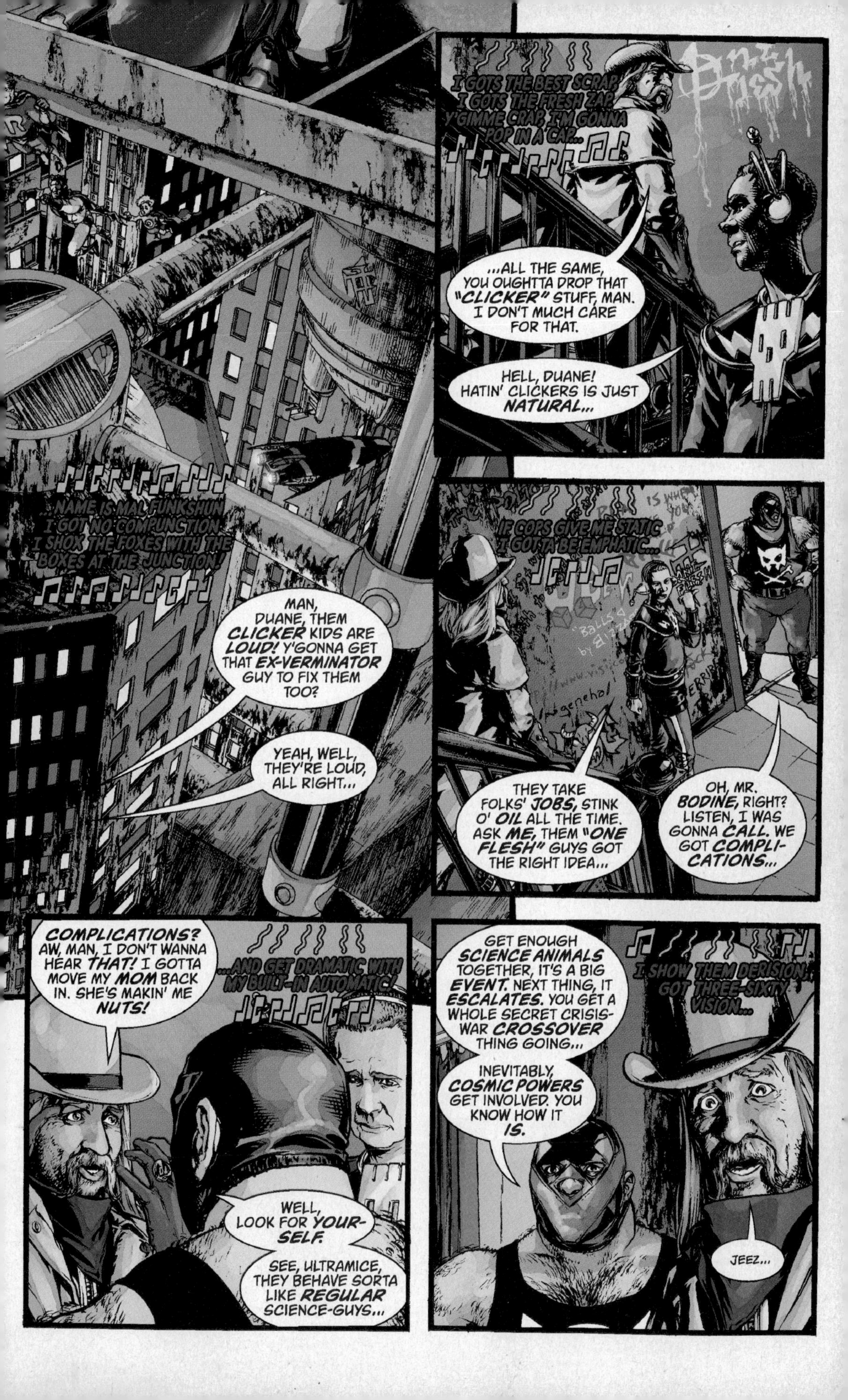
...NAME IS MAL FUNKSHUN I GOT NO COMPUNCTION I SHOX THE FOXES WITH THE BOXES AT THE JUNCTION!
MAN, DUANE, THEM CLICKER KIDS ARE LOUD! Y'GONNA GET THAT EX-VERMINATOR GUY TO FIX THEM TOO?
YEAH, WELL, THEY'RE LOUD, ALL RIGHT...
I GOTS THE BEST SCRAP, I GOTS THE FRESH ZAP. Y'GIMME CRAP, I'M GONNA POP IN A CAP...
ONE FLESH
...ALL THE SAME, YOU OUGHTTA DROP THAT "CLICKER" STUFF, MAN. I DON'T MUCH CARE FOR THAT.
HELL, DUANE! HATIN' CLICKERS IS JUST NATURAL...
IF COPS GIVE ME STATIC I GOTTA BE EMPHATIC...
THEY TAKE FOLKS' JOBS, STINK O' OIL ALL THE TIME. ASK ME, THEM "ONE FLESH" GUYS GOT THE RIGHT IDEA...
OH, MR. BODINE, RIGHT? LISTEN, I WAS GONNA CALL. WE GOT COMPLICATIONS...
COMPLICATIONS? AW, MAN, I DON'T WANNA HEAR THAT! I GOTTA MOVE MY MOM BACK IN. SHE'S MAKIN' ME NUTS!
...AND GET DRAMATIC WITH MY BUILT-IN AUTOMATIC!
WELL, LOOK FOR YOURSELF.
SEE, ULTRAMICE, THEY BEHAVE SORTA LIKE REGULAR SCIENCE-GUYS...
GET ENOUGH SCIENCE ANIMALS TOGETHER, IT'S A BIG EVENT. NEXT THING, IT ESCALATES. YOU GET A WHOLE SECRET CRISIS-WAR CROSSOVER THING GOING...
INEVITABLY, COSMIC POWERS GET INVOLVED. YOU KNOW HOW IT IS.
I SHOW THEM DERISION, GOT THREE-SIXTY VISION...
JEEZ...

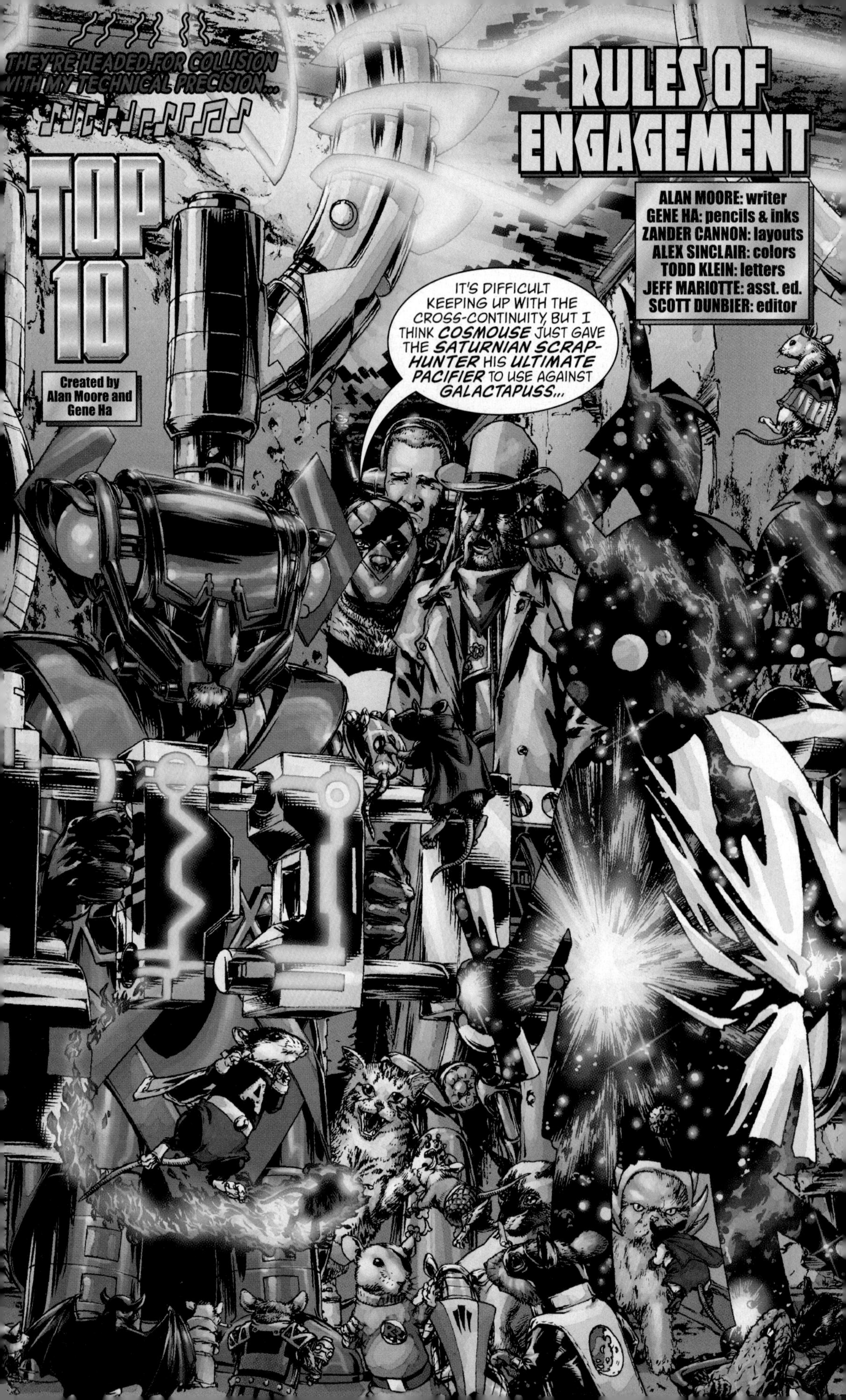
THEY'RE HEADED FOR COLLISION WITH MY TECHNICAL PRECISION...
RULES OF ENGAGEMENT
TOP 10
Created by Alan Moore and Gene Ha
ALAN MOORE: writer
GENE HA: pencils & inks
ZANDER CANNON: layouts
ALEX SINCLAIR: colors
TODD KLEIN: letters
JEFF MARIOTTE: asst. ed.
SCOTT DUNBIER: editor
IT'S DIFFICULT KEEPING UP WITH THE CROSS-CONTINUITY, BUT I THINK COSMOUSE JUST GAVE THE SATURNIAN SCRAP-HUNTER HIS ULTIMATE PACIFIER TO USE AGAINST GALACTAPUSS...

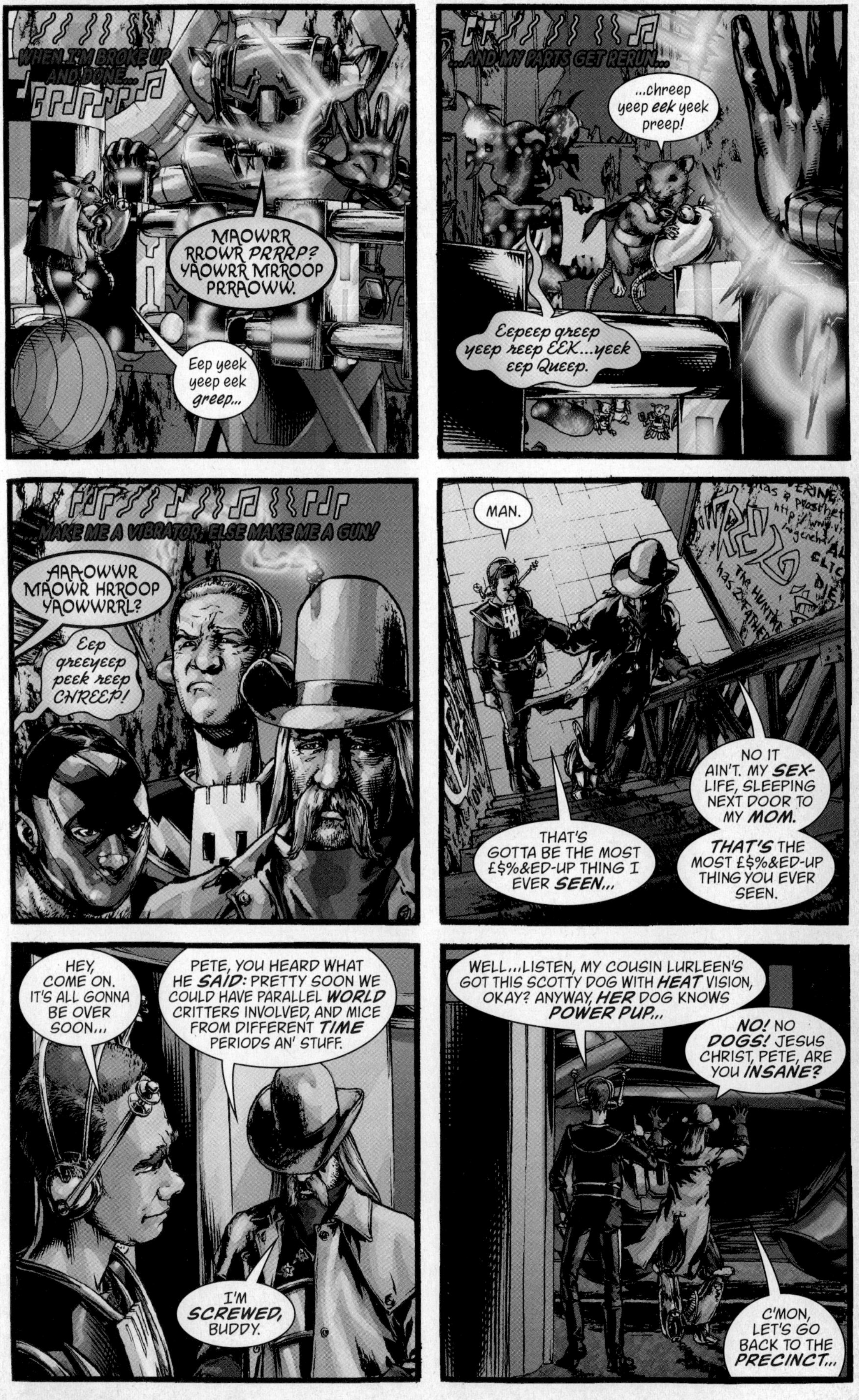
WHEN I'M BROKE UP AND DONE...
MAOWRR RROWR PRRRP? YAOWRR MRROOP PRRAOWW.
Eep yeek yeep eek greep...
...AND MY PARTS GET RERUN...
...chreep yeep eek yeek preep!
Eepeep greep yeep reep EEK...yeek eep Queep.
...MAKE ME A VIBRATOR, ELSE MAKE ME A GUN!
AAAOWWR MAOWR HRROOP YAOWWRRL?
Eep greeyeep peek reep CHREEP!
MAN.
THAT'S GOTTA BE THE MOST £$%&ED-UP THING I EVER SEEN...
NO IT AIN'T. MY SEX-LIFE, SLEEPING NEXT DOOR TO MY MOM. THAT'S THE MOST £$%&ED-UP THING YOU EVER SEEN.
HEY, COME ON. IT'S ALL GONNA BE OVER SOON...
PETE, YOU HEARD WHAT HE SAID: PRETTY SOON WE COULD HAVE PARALLEL WORLD CRITTERS INVOLVED, AND MICE FROM DIFFERENT TIME PERIODS AN' STUFF.
I'M SCREWED, BUDDY.
WELL...LISTEN, MY COUSIN LURLEEN'S GOT THIS SCOTTY DOG WITH HEAT VISION, OKAY? ANYWAY, HER DOG KNOWS POWER PUP...
NO! NO DOGS! JESUS CHRIST, PETE, ARE YOU INSANE?
C'MON, LET'S GO BACK TO THE PRECINCT...

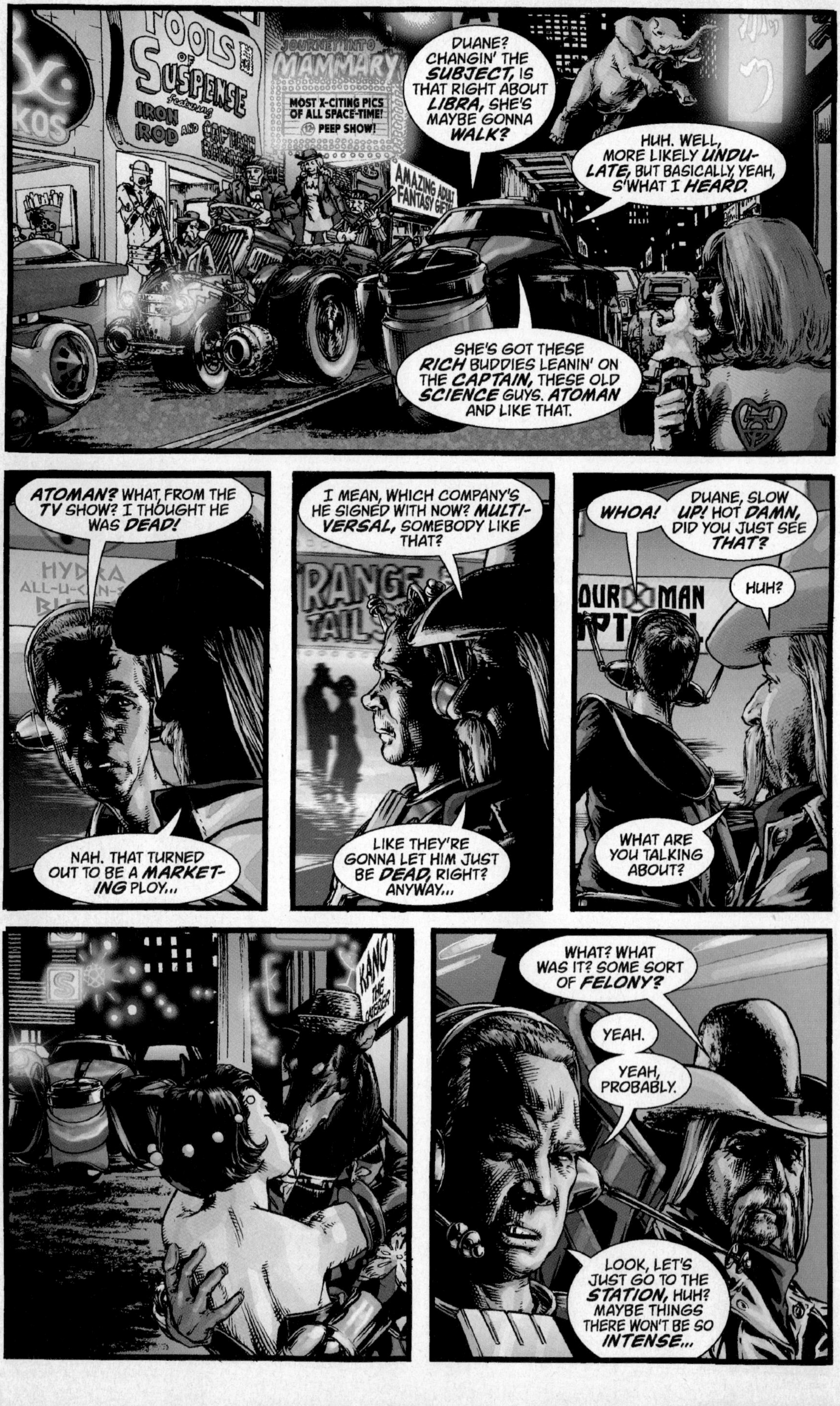

FOOLS OF SUSPENSE
IRON ROD AND
JOURNEY INTO MAMMARY
MOST X-CITING PICS OF ALL SPACE-TIME!
PEEP SHOW!
DUANE? CHANGIN' THE **SUBJECT,** IS THAT RIGHT ABOUT **LIBRA,** SHE'S MAYBE GONNA **WALK?**
HUH. WELL, MORE LIKELY **UNDULATE,** BUT BASICALLY, YEAH, S'WHAT I **HEARD.**
SHE'S GOT THESE **RICH** BUDDIES LEANIN' ON THE **CAPTAIN,** THESE OLD **SCIENCE** GUYS. **ATOMAN** AND LIKE THAT.
ATOMAN? WHAT, FROM THE **TV** SHOW? I THOUGHT HE WAS **DEAD!**
NAH. THAT TURNED OUT TO BE A **MARKETING** PLOY...
I MEAN, WHICH COMPANY'S HE SIGNED WITH NOW? **MULTIVERSAL,** SOMEBODY LIKE THAT?
LIKE THEY'RE GONNA LET HIM JUST BE **DEAD,** RIGHT? ANYWAY...
WHOA!
DUANE, SLOW **UP!** HOT **DAMN,** DID YOU JUST SEE **THAT?**
HUH?
WHAT ARE YOU TALKING ABOUT?
WHAT? WHAT WAS IT? SOME SORT OF **FELONY?**
YEAH.
YEAH, PROBABLY.
LOOK, LET'S JUST GO TO THE **STATION,** HUH? MAYBE THINGS THERE WON'T BE SO **INTENSE...**

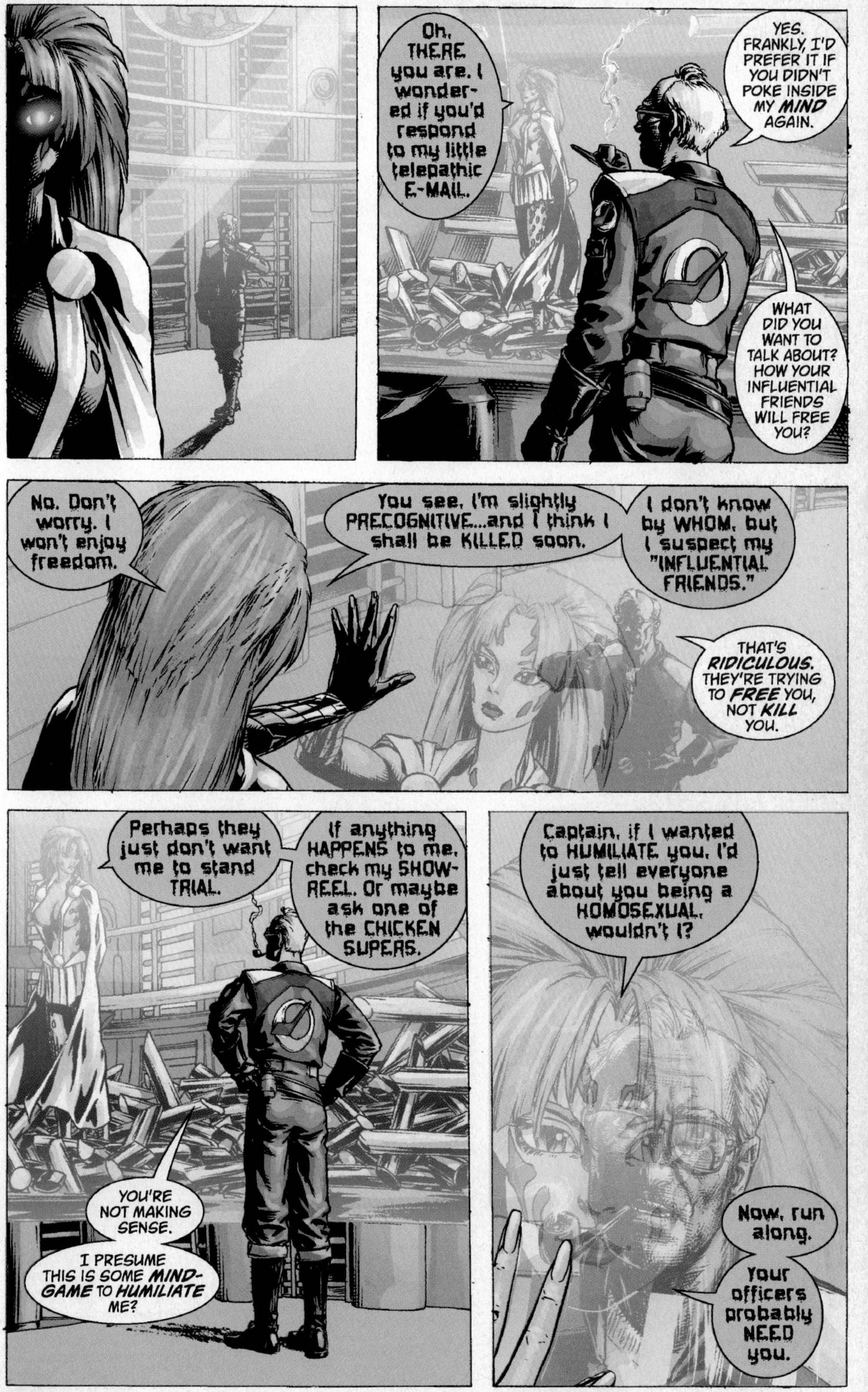

Oh, THERE you are. I wondered if you'd respond to my little telepathic E-MAIL.
YES. FRANKLY, I'D PREFER IT IF YOU DIDN'T POKE INSIDE MY *MIND* AGAIN.
WHAT DID YOU WANT TO TALK ABOUT? HOW YOUR INFLUENTIAL FRIENDS WILL FREE YOU?
No. Don't worry. I won't enjoy freedom.
You see, I'm slightly PRECOGNITIVE...and I think I shall be KILLED soon.
I don't know by WHOM, but I suspect my "INFLUENTIAL FRIENDS."
THAT'S *RIDICULOUS.* THEY'RE TRYING TO *FREE* YOU, NOT *KILL* YOU.
Perhaps they just don't want me to stand TRIAL.
If anything HAPPENS to me, check my SHOW-REEL. Or maybe ask one of the CHICKEN SUPERS.
YOU'RE NOT MAKING SENSE.
I PRESUME THIS IS SOME *MIND-GAME* TO *HUMILIATE* ME?
Captain, if I wanted to HUMILIATE you, I'd just tell everyone about you being a HOMOSEXUAL, wouldn't I?
Now, run along.
Your officers probably NEED you.

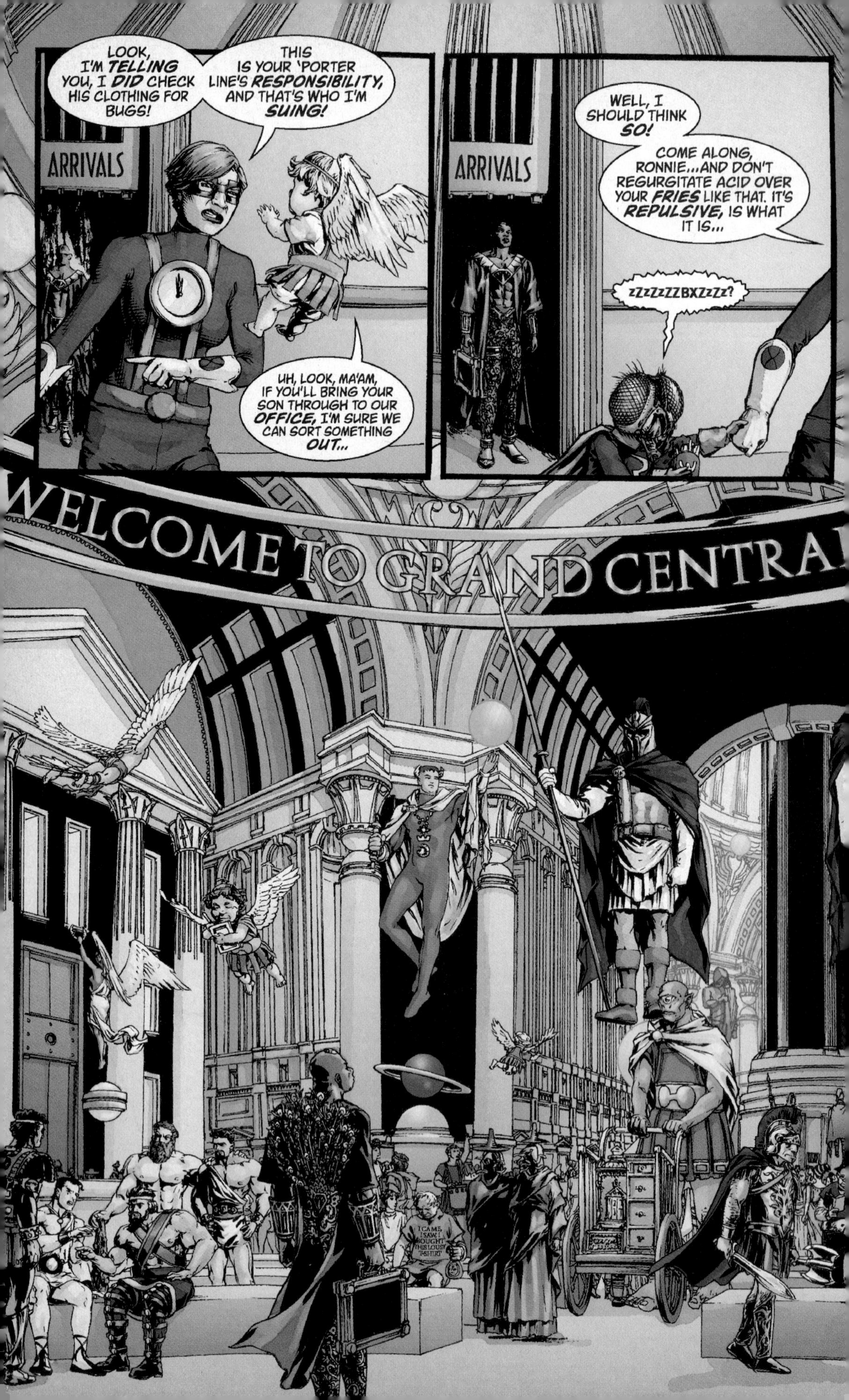
ARRIVALS
LOOK, I'M TELLING YOU, I DID CHECK HIS CLOTHING FOR BUGS!
THIS IS YOUR 'PORTER LINE'S RESPONSIBILITY, AND THAT'S WHO I'M SUING!
UH, LOOK, MA'AM, IF YOU'LL BRING YOUR SON THROUGH TO OUR OFFICE, I'M SURE WE CAN SORT SOMETHING OUT...
ARRIVALS
WELL, I SHOULD THINK SO!
COME ALONG, RONNIE...AND DON'T REGURGITATE ACID OVER YOUR FRIES LIKE THAT. IT'S REPULSIVE, IS WHAT IT IS...
zZzZzZZBXZzZzZ?
WELCOME TO GRAND CENTRA
I CAME, I SAW, I BOUGHT THIS LOUSY T-SHIRT

NO. NO, I'M NOT IMPORTING ANY PORNOGRAPHIC *VASES,* SEMI-PRECIOUS *FLEECES,* OR...WHAT WAS THE LAST ONE AGAIN?

"STRANGE GODS." IMPORTING STRANGE GODS IS A *HEMLOCK* OFFENSE.

OKAY, YOUR PASSPORT'S IN ORDER. ENJOY YOUR STAY.

B-BUT... LISTEN. I HAD *SHOTS...*

I DON'T WANNA *HEAR* IT. KEEP *MOVING.*

DETECTIVE JOHN *CORBEAU,* FROM *NEOPOLIS* ON PARALLEL *TEN.* I'M HERE ON *POLICE BUSINESS...*

YEAH? WELL, I'LL BE THE JUDGE OF THAT, NUBIE.

ANY *PORNO-POTTERY,* GOLD *GOATSKINS,* STRANGE *GODS?*

NO.

I THINK YOU'LL FIND MY DEPARTMENT CONTACTED *PRECINCT ONE* TO LET THEM KNOW I WAS *COMING.*

OH... YEAH, THAT'S RIGHT.

HEY, TONY, DIDN'T THOSE *PRAETS* CALL EARLIER, ASKING ABOUT SOME OUT-OF-*WORLDER?*

YEAH. I'LL GO *FIND* 'EM.

THANK YOU.

SO, *GRAND CENTRAL* IS A PARALLEL UPON WHICH THE ROMAN EMPIRE NEVER *FELL?*

BZZZT

NO. *YOUR* &%$£-HOLE WORLD IS SOME *FREAK* PARALLEL WHERE IT *DID.*

I SEE THEY EVEN LET *NUBIES* IN THEIR PRAETORIAN *GUARD.*

AAH. TONY'S *FOUND* 'EM.

AVE! I'M LEGIONNAIRE *BRIAREUS,* THIS IS LEGIONNAIRE *HERCULA.*

AVE! YOU MUST BE *CORBEAU* FROM PARALLEL *TEN.* I SEE YOU'VE ALREADY ENCOUNTERED OUR *BARBARIC CUSTOMS...*

EHHH. YOU *PRAETS,* YOU *SLAY* ME.

PLEASED TO *MEET* YOU. CLEARLY, YOU WERE EXPECTING ME.

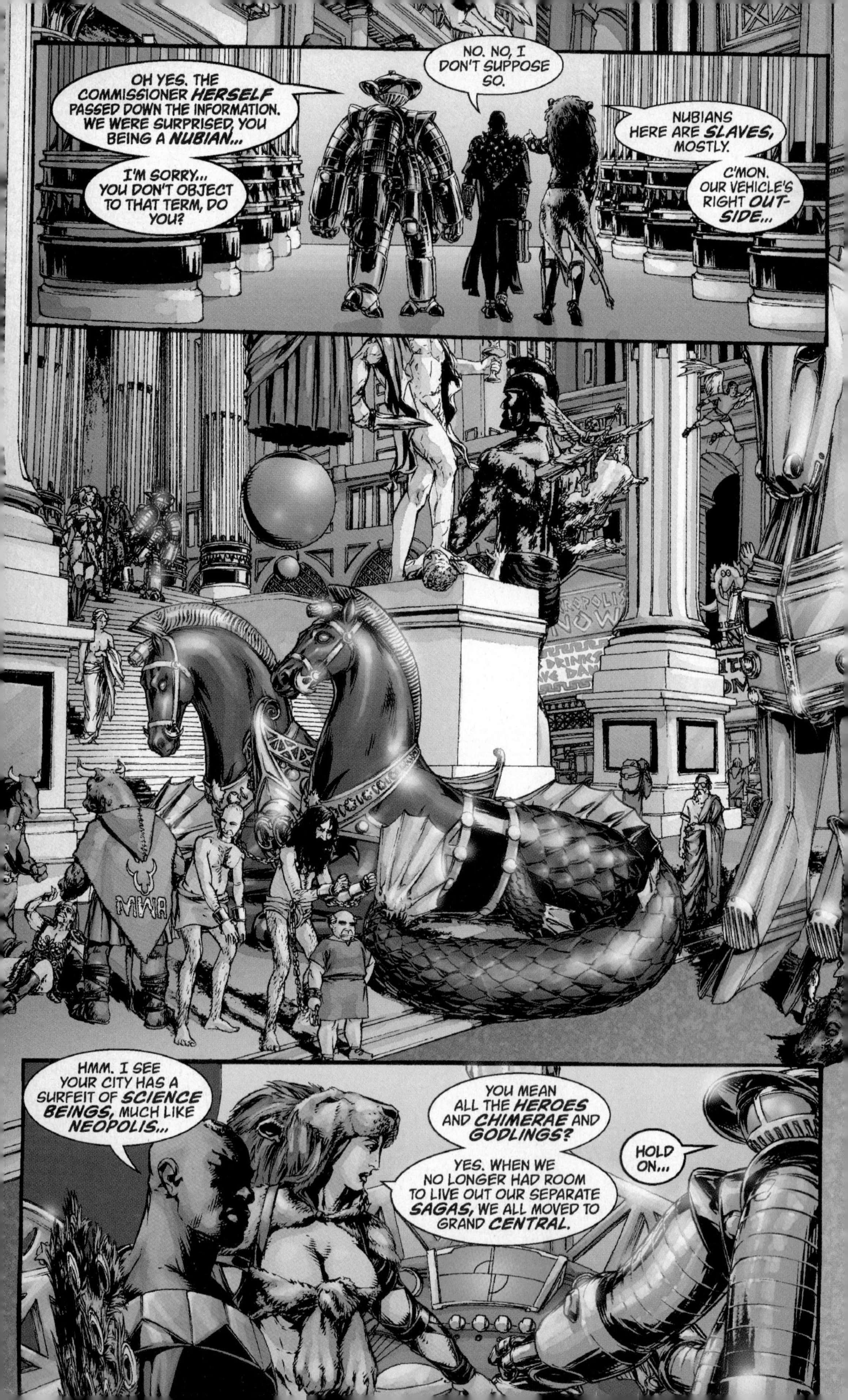
OH YES. THE COMMISSIONER HERSELF PASSED DOWN THE INFORMATION. WE WERE SURPRISED, YOU BEING A NUBIAN...
I'M SORRY... YOU DON'T OBJECT TO THAT TERM, DO YOU?
NO. NO, I DON'T SUPPOSE SO.
NUBIANS HERE ARE SLAVES, MOSTLY.
C'MON. OUR VEHICLE'S RIGHT OUTSIDE...
MWR
HMM. I SEE YOUR CITY HAS A SURFEIT OF SCIENCE BEINGS, MUCH LIKE NEOPOLIS...
YOU MEAN ALL THE HEROES AND CHIMERAE AND GODLINGS?
YES. WHEN WE NO LONGER HAD ROOM TO LIVE OUT OUR SEPARATE SAGAS, WE ALL MOVED TO GRAND CENTRAL.
HOLD ON...

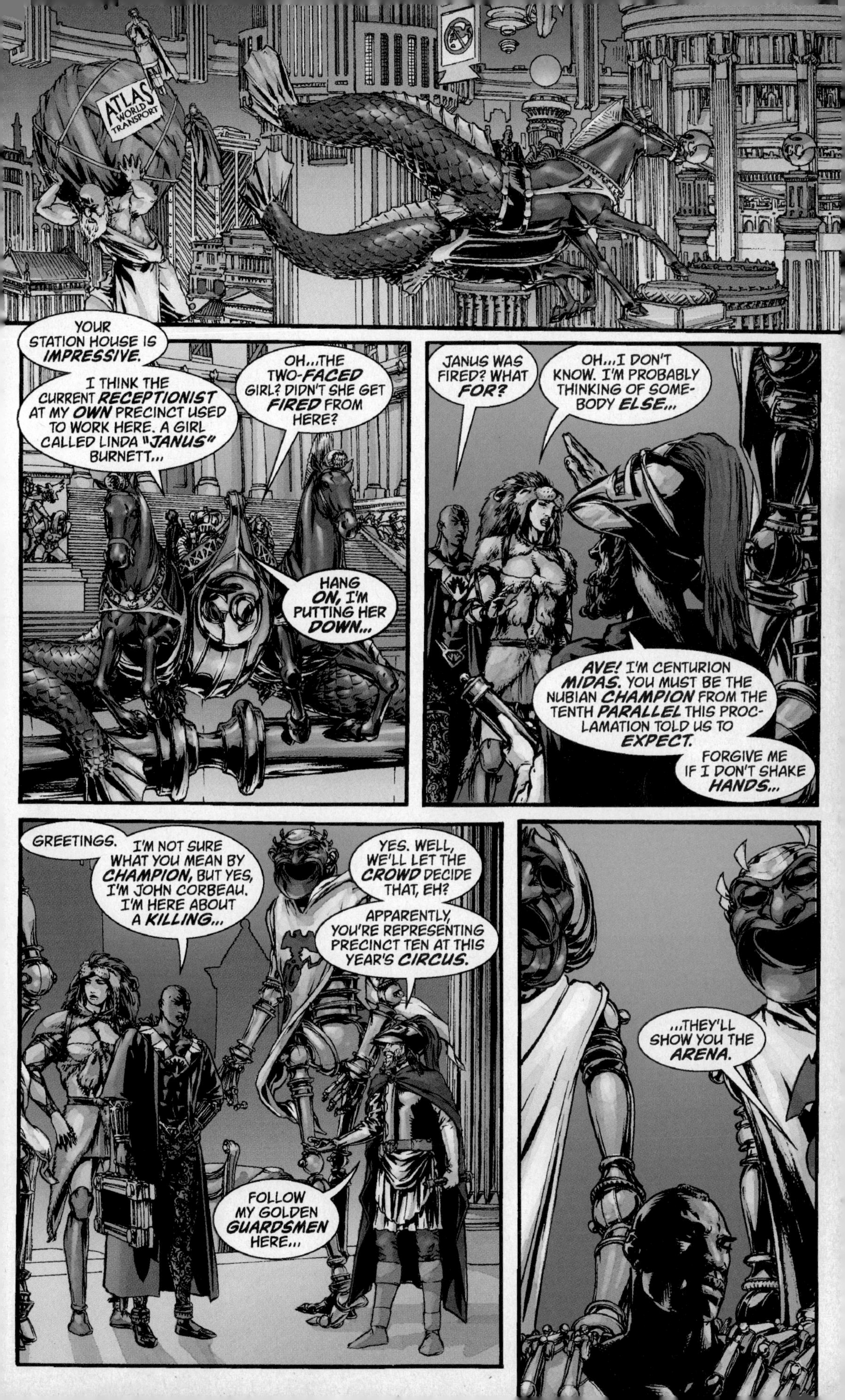
ATLAS WORLD TRANSPORT
YOUR STATION HOUSE IS IMPRESSIVE.
I THINK THE CURRENT RECEPTIONIST AT MY OWN PRECINCT USED TO WORK HERE. A GIRL CALLED LINDA "JANUS" BURNETT...
OH...THE TWO-FACED GIRL? DIDN'T SHE GET FIRED FROM HERE?
HANG ON, I'M PUTTING HER DOWN...
JANUS WAS FIRED? WHAT FOR?
OH...I DON'T KNOW. I'M PROBABLY THINKING OF SOME-BODY ELSE...
AVE! I'M CENTURION MIDAS. YOU MUST BE THE NUBIAN CHAMPION FROM THE TENTH PARALLEL THIS PROC-LAMATION TOLD US TO EXPECT.
FORGIVE ME IF I DON'T SHAKE HANDS...
GREETINGS.
I'M NOT SURE WHAT YOU MEAN BY CHAMPION, BUT YES, I'M JOHN CORBEAU. I'M HERE ABOUT A KILLING...
YES. WELL, WE'LL LET THE CROWD DECIDE THAT, EH?
APPARENTLY, YOU'RE REPRESENTING PRECINCT TEN AT THIS YEAR'S CIRCUS.
FOLLOW MY GOLDEN GUARDSMEN HERE...
...THEY'LL SHOW YOU THE ARENA.

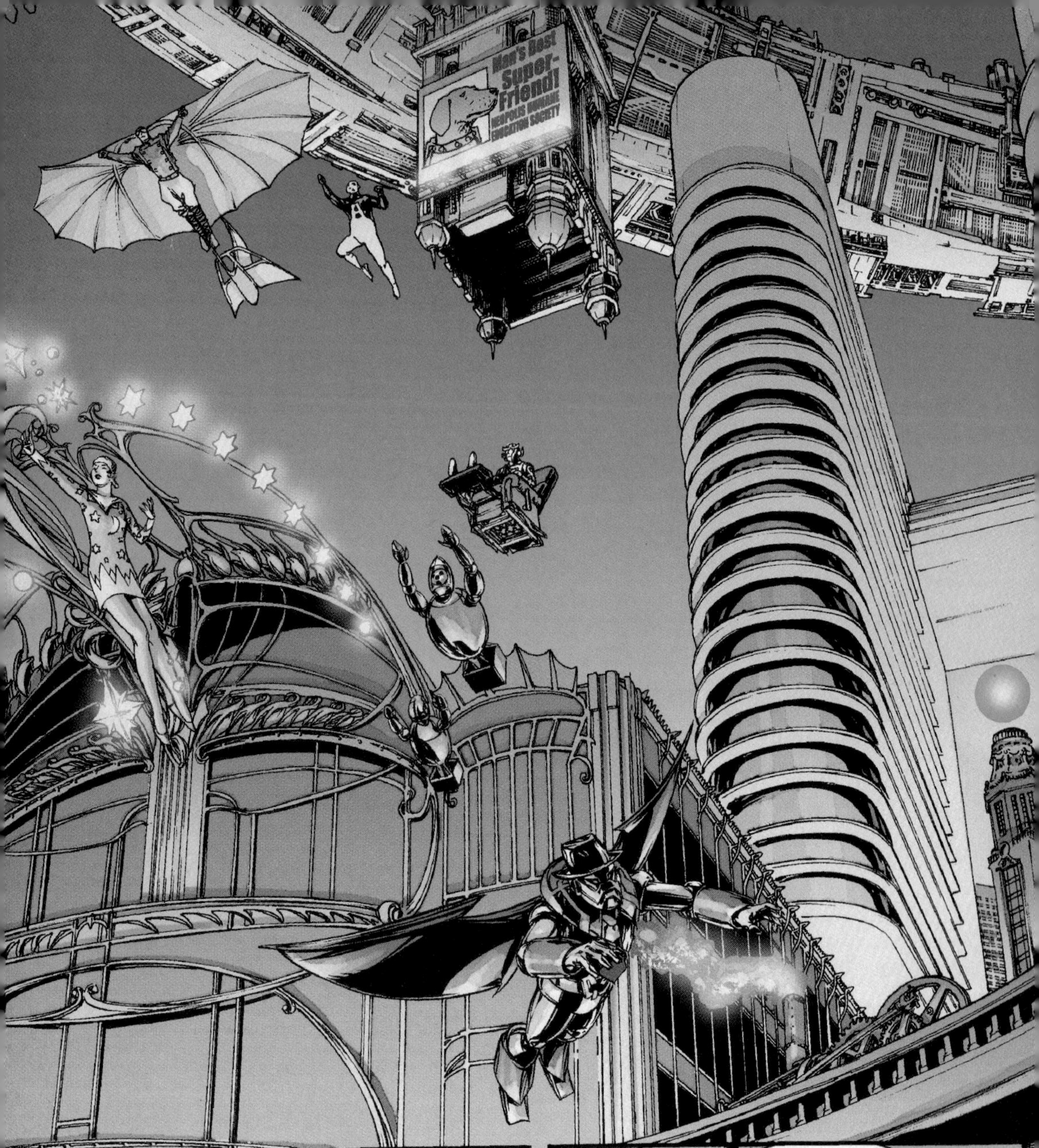
Man's Best Super-Friend!

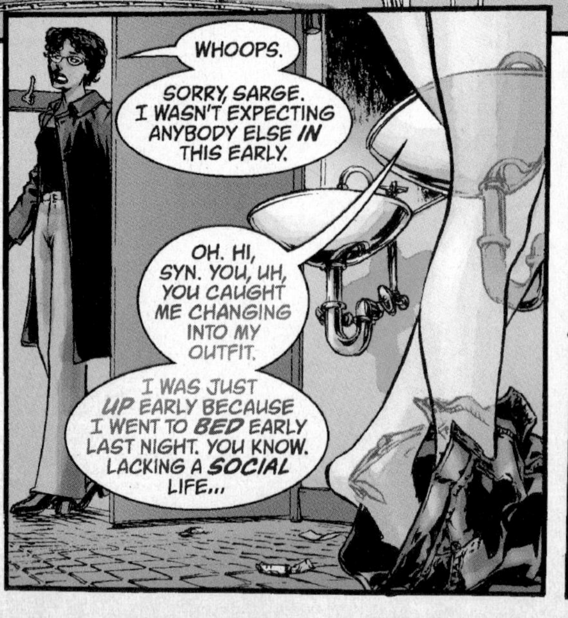
WHOOPS.
SORRY, SARGE. I WASN'T EXPECTING ANYBODY ELSE IN THIS EARLY.
OH. HI, SYN. YOU, UH, YOU CAUGHT ME CHANGING INTO MY OUTFIT.
I WAS JUST UP EARLY BECAUSE I WENT TO BED EARLY LAST NIGHT. YOU KNOW. LACKING A SOCIAL LIFE...

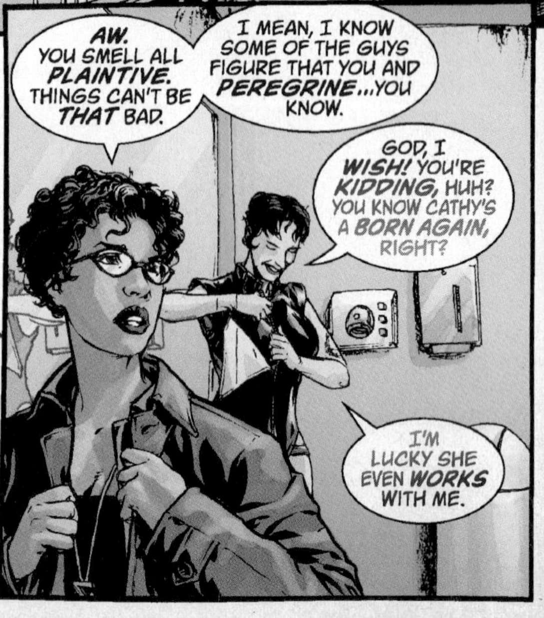
AW. YOU SMELL ALL PLAINTIVE. THINGS CAN'T BE THAT BAD.
I MEAN, I KNOW SOME OF THE GUYS FIGURE THAT YOU AND PEREGRINE...YOU KNOW.
GOD, I WISH! YOU'RE KIDDING, HUH? YOU KNOW CATHY'S A BORN AGAIN, RIGHT?
I'M LUCKY SHE EVEN WORKS WITH ME.

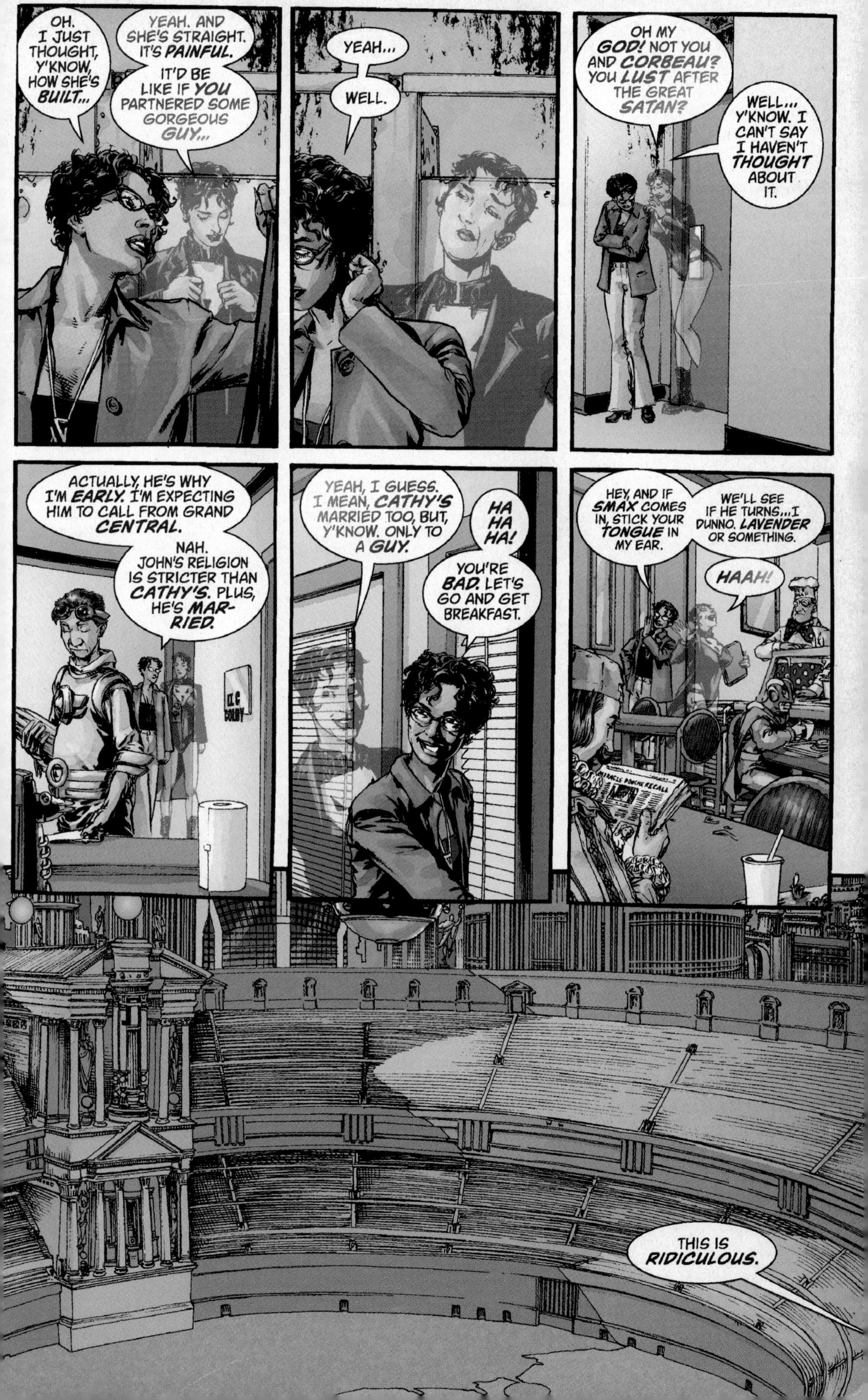
OH. I JUST THOUGHT, Y'KNOW, HOW SHE'S BUILT...
YEAH. AND SHE'S STRAIGHT. IT'S PAINFUL.
IT'D BE LIKE IF YOU PARTNERED SOME GORGEOUS GUY...
YEAH...
WELL.
OH MY GOD! NOT YOU AND CORBEAU? YOU LUST AFTER THE GREAT SATAN?
WELL... Y'KNOW. I CAN'T SAY I HAVEN'T THOUGHT ABOUT IT.
ACTUALLY, HE'S WHY I'M EARLY. I'M EXPECTING HIM TO CALL FROM GRAND CENTRAL.
NAH. JOHN'S RELIGION IS STRICTER THAN CATHY'S. PLUS, HE'S MARRIED.
YEAH, I GUESS. I MEAN, CATHY'S MARRIED TOO, BUT, Y'KNOW. ONLY TO A GUY.
HA HA HA!
YOU'RE BAD. LET'S GO AND GET BREAKFAST.
HEY, AND IF SMAX COMES IN, STICK YOUR TONGUE IN MY EAR.
WE'LL SEE IF HE TURNS...I DUNNO. LAVENDER OR SOMETHING.
HAAH!
THIS IS RIDICULOUS.

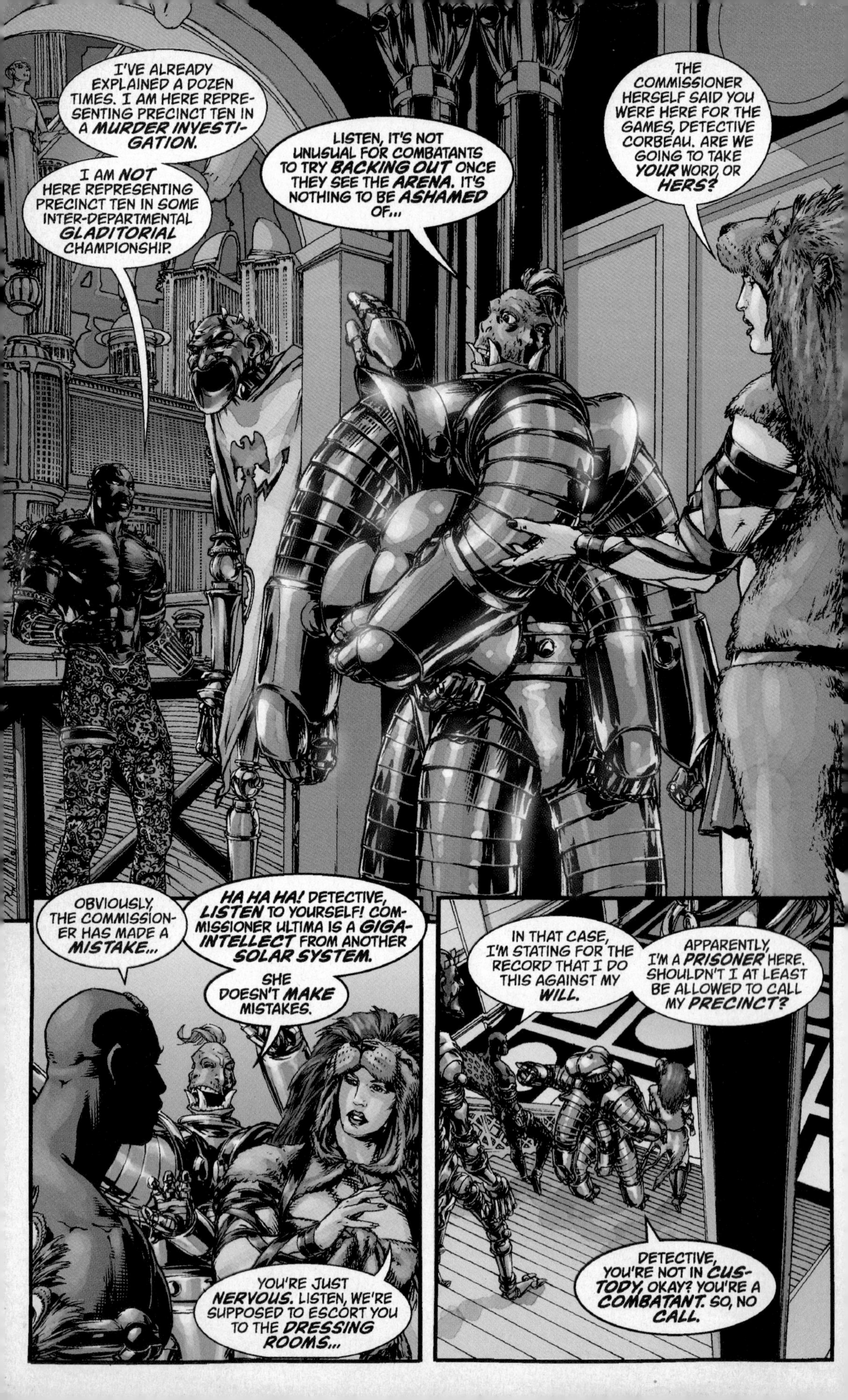
I'VE ALREADY EXPLAINED A DOZEN TIMES. I AM HERE REPRESENTING PRECINCT TEN IN A MURDER INVESTIGATION.
I AM NOT HERE REPRESENTING PRECINCT TEN IN SOME INTER-DEPARTMENTAL GLADITORIAL CHAMPIONSHIP.
LISTEN, IT'S NOT UNUSUAL FOR COMBATANTS TO TRY BACKING OUT ONCE THEY SEE THE ARENA. IT'S NOTHING TO BE ASHAMED OF...
THE COMMISSIONER HERSELF SAID YOU WERE HERE FOR THE GAMES, DETECTIVE CORBEAU. ARE WE GOING TO TAKE YOUR WORD, OR HERS?
OBVIOUSLY, THE COMMISSIONER HAS MADE A MISTAKE...
HA HA HA! DETECTIVE, LISTEN TO YOURSELF! COMMISSIONER ULTIMA IS A GIGA-INTELLECT FROM ANOTHER SOLAR SYSTEM.
SHE DOESN'T MAKE MISTAKES.
YOU'RE JUST NERVOUS. LISTEN, WE'RE SUPPOSED TO ESCORT YOU TO THE DRESSING ROOMS...
IN THAT CASE, I'M STATING FOR THE RECORD THAT I DO THIS AGAINST MY WILL.
APPARENTLY, I'M A PRISONER HERE. SHOULDN'T I AT LEAST BE ALLOWED TO CALL MY PRECINCT?
DETECTIVE, YOU'RE NOT IN CUSTODY, OKAY? YOU'RE A COMBATANT. SO, NO CALL.

HMM. ACTUALLY, CASS, THAT *DOES* SEEM STRANGE, THAT PHONE CALL THING.

DETECTIVE, LET ME CHECK ON THAT AND GET *BACK* TO YOU, OKAY?

I...I SUPPOSE SO. BUT I'D BE GRATEFUL IF YOU'D MAKE IT A *PRIORITY*.

NATURALLY. THIS WAY, DETECTIVE...

AND THESE ARE MY FELLOW *COMBATANTS*?

THAT'S RIGHT. LISTEN, WE'LL LEAVE YOU TO GET *ACQUAINTED*... AND I WON'T FORGET THAT *PHONE CALL* REQUEST, ALL RIGHT?

HI. JUST IN, HUH? SO, WHICH PRECINCT YOU REPRESENT?

I'M TECHNOZOIC, INCIDENTALLY, FROM PRECINCT SEVEN.

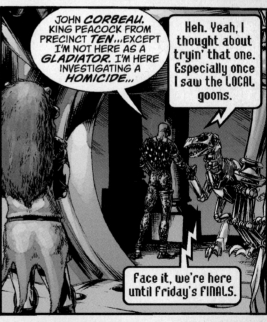

JOHN *CORBEAU*. KING PEACOCK FROM PRECINCT *TEN*...EXCEPT I'M NOT HERE AS A *GLADIATOR*. I'M HERE INVESTIGATING A *HOMICIDE*...

Heh. Yeah, I thought about tryin' that one. Especially once I saw the LOCAL goons.

Face it, we're here until Friday's FINALS.

Always assumin' we live through the PRELIMINARIES, that is.

Here, y'wanna be a bud and spray some o' this on the back o' my HEAD? It's just I can't REACH.

Goddamn tiny ARMS. Ehh, whaddaya gonna do?

CHROME DOME METAL POLISH NON-ABRASIVE NON-TOXIC

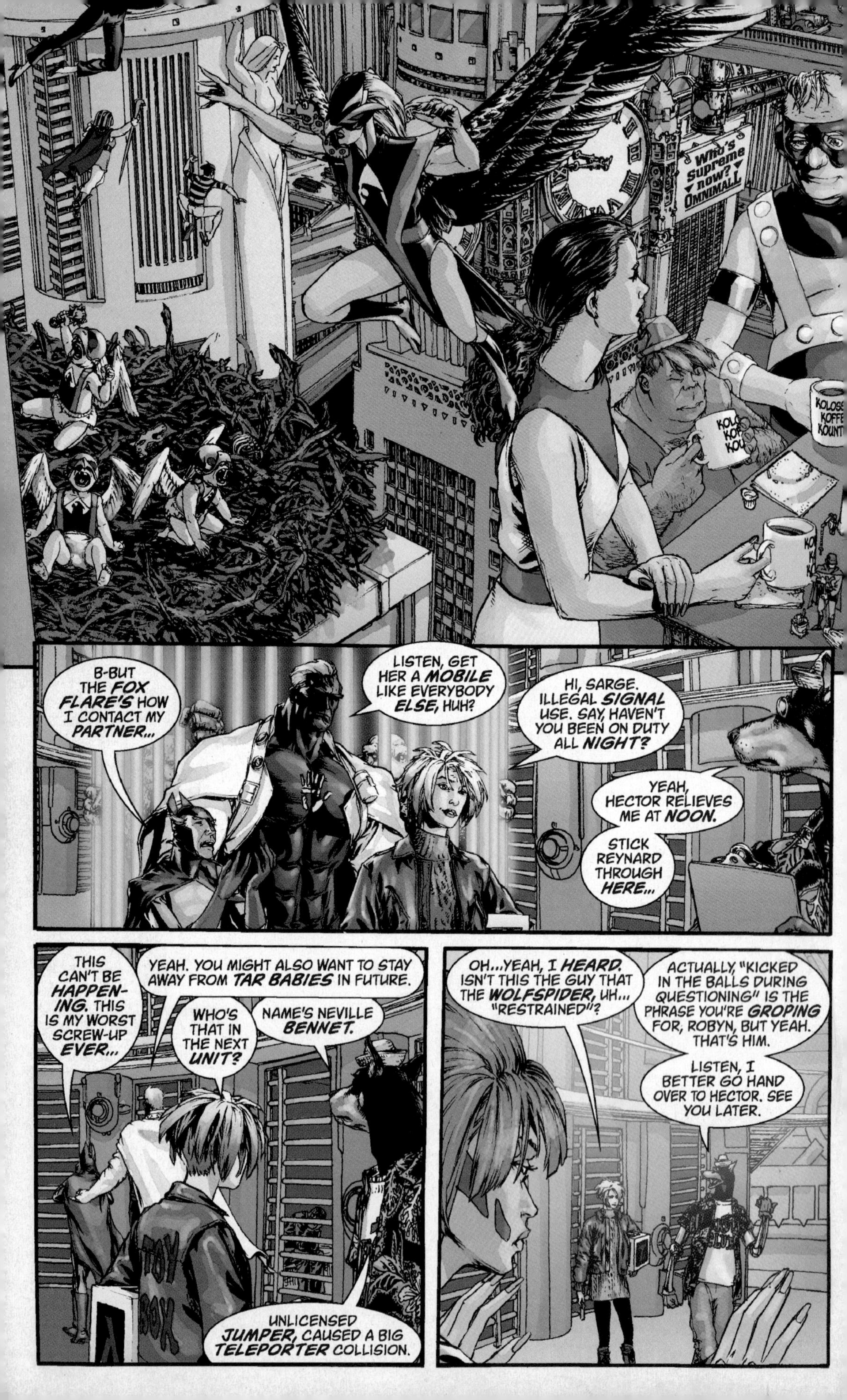

Who's Supreme now?
OMNIMALL
B-BUT THE FOX FLARE'S HOW I CONTACT MY PARTNER...
LISTEN, GET HER A MOBILE LIKE EVERYBODY ELSE, HUH?
HI, SARGE. ILLEGAL SIGNAL USE. SAY, HAVEN'T YOU BEEN ON DUTY ALL NIGHT?
YEAH, HECTOR RELIEVES ME AT NOON.
STICK REYNARD THROUGH HERE...
THIS CAN'T BE HAPPENING. THIS IS MY WORST SCREW-UP EVER...
YEAH. YOU MIGHT ALSO WANT TO STAY AWAY FROM TAR BABIES IN FUTURE.
WHO'S THAT IN THE NEXT UNIT?
NAME'S NEVILLE BENNET.
UNLICENSED JUMPER, CAUSED A BIG TELEPORTER COLLISION.
OH...YEAH, I HEARD. ISN'T THIS THE GUY THAT THE WOLFSPIDER, UH... "RESTRAINED"?
ACTUALLY, "KICKED IN THE BALLS DURING QUESTIONING" IS THE PHRASE YOU'RE GROPING FOR, ROBYN, BUT YEAH. THAT'S HIM.
LISTEN, I BETTER GO HAND OVER TO HECTOR. SEE YOU LATER.

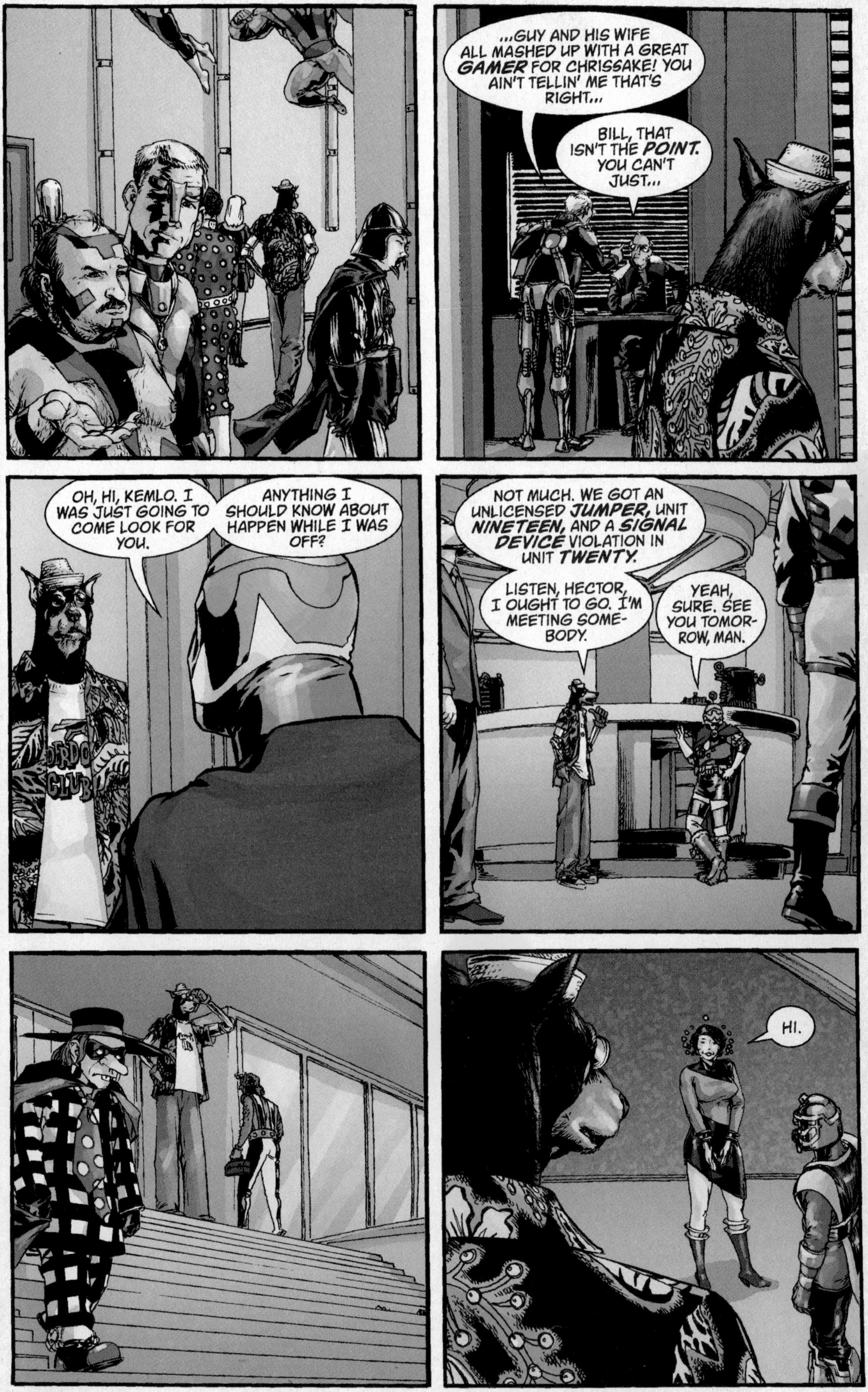
...GUY AND HIS WIFE ALL MASHED UP WITH A GREAT GAMER FOR CHRISSAKE! YOU AIN'T TELLIN' ME THAT'S RIGHT...
BILL, THAT ISN'T THE POINT. YOU CAN'T JUST...
OH, HI, KEMLO. I WAS JUST GOING TO COME LOOK FOR YOU.
ANYTHING I SHOULD KNOW ABOUT HAPPEN WHILE I WAS OFF?
NOT MUCH. WE GOT AN UNLICENSED JUMPER, UNIT NINETEEN, AND A SIGNAL DEVICE VIOLATION IN UNIT TWENTY.
LISTEN, HECTOR, I OUGHT TO GO. I'M MEETING SOMEBODY.
YEAH, SURE. SEE YOU TOMORROW, MAN.
HI.

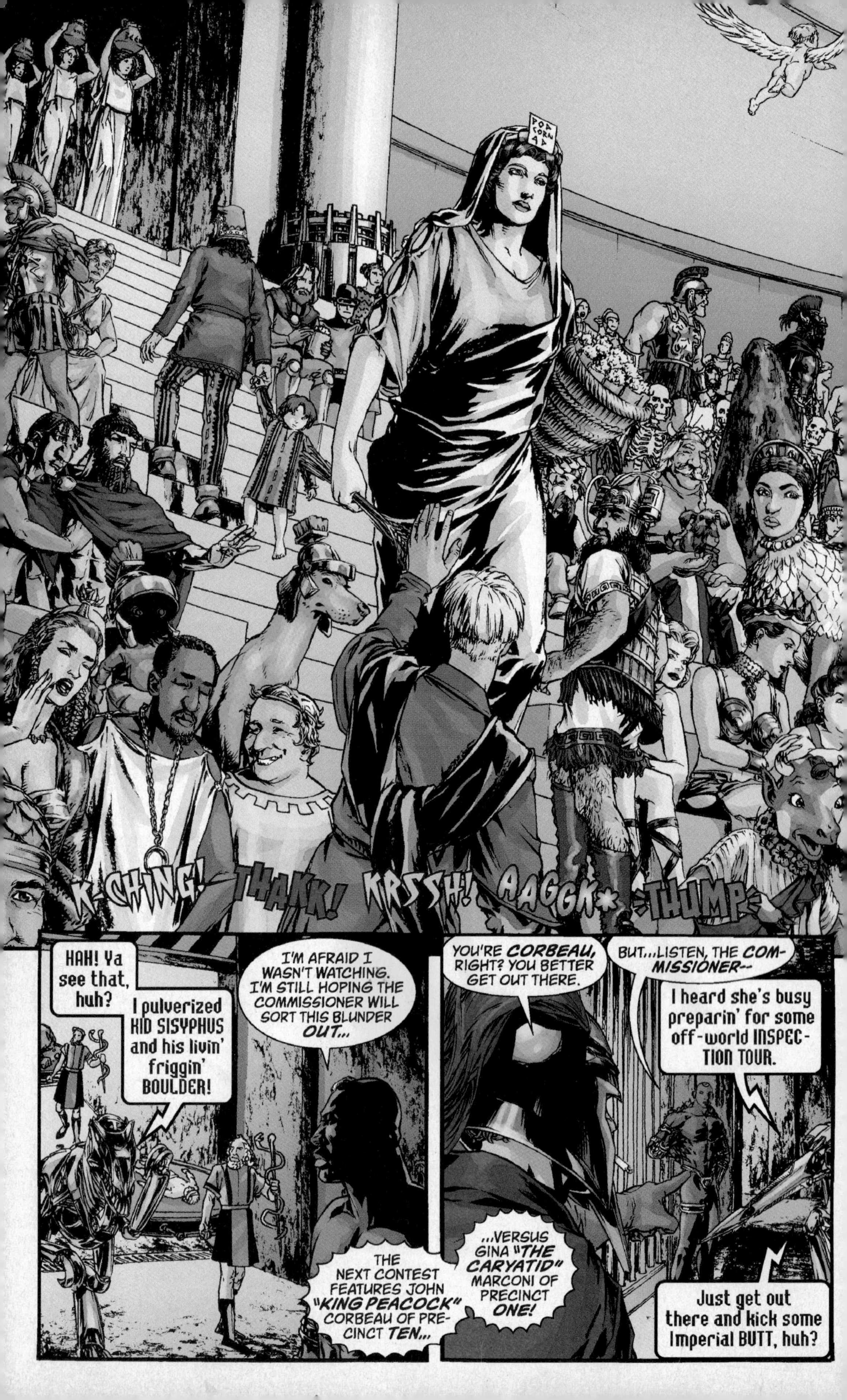
K-CHING!
THAKK!
KRSSH!
AAGGK
THUMP
HAH! Ya see that, huh?
I pulverized KID SISYPHUS and his livin' friggin' BOULDER!
I'M AFRAID I WASN'T WATCHING. I'M STILL HOPING THE COMMISSIONER WILL SORT THIS BLUNDER OUT...
THE NEXT CONTEST FEATURES JOHN "KING PEACOCK" CORBEAU OF PRECINCT TEN...
...VERSUS GINA "THE CARYATID" MARCONI OF PRECINCT ONE!
YOU'RE CORBEAU, RIGHT? YOU BETTER GET OUT THERE.
BUT...LISTEN, THE COMMISSIONER--
I heard she's busy preparin' for some off-world INSPECTION TOUR.
Just get out there and kick some Imperial BUTT, huh?

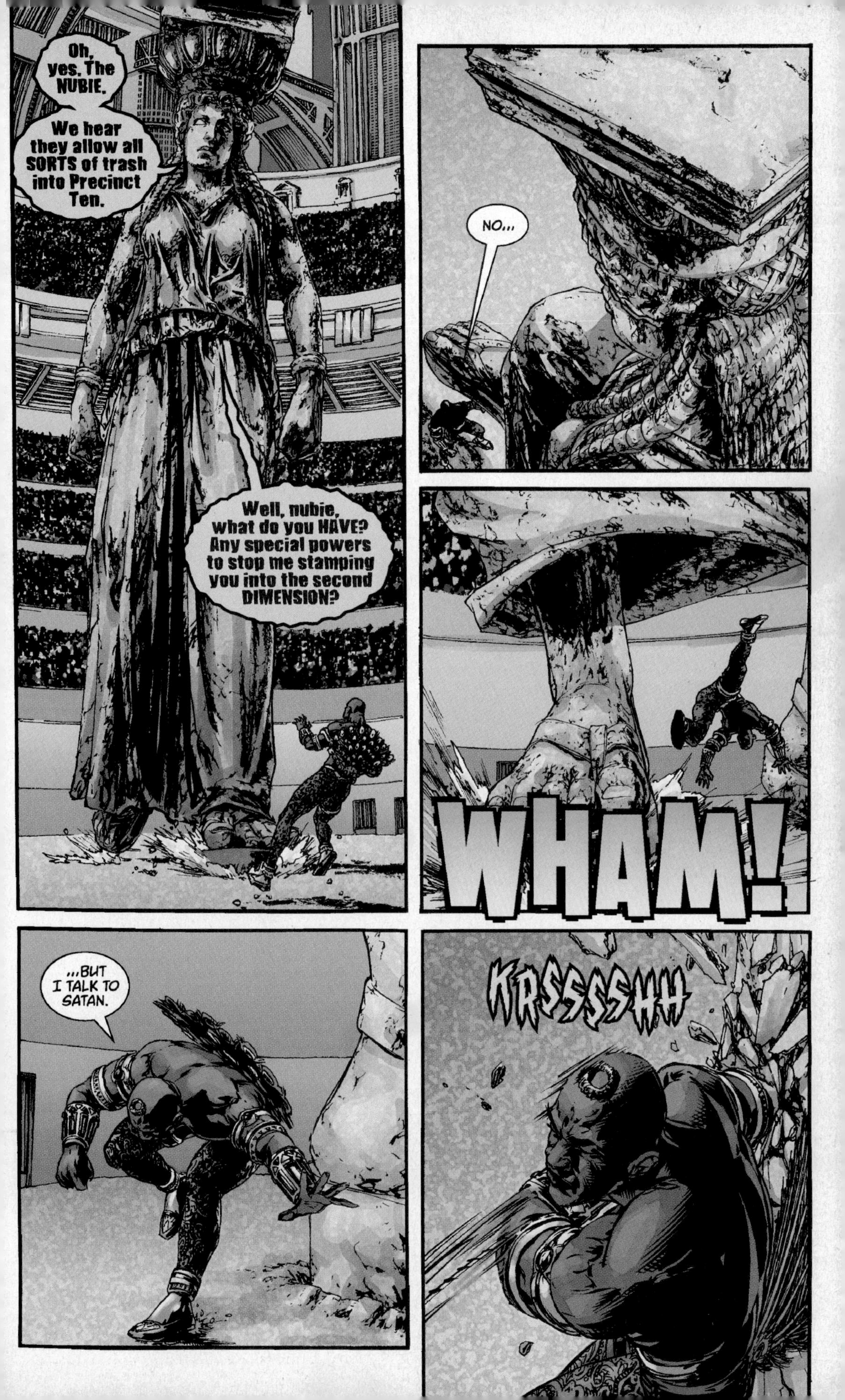
Oh, yes. The NUBIE.
We hear they allow all SORTS of trash into Precinct Ten.
Well, nubie, what do you HAVE? Any special powers to stop me stamping you into the second DIMENSION?
NO...
WHAM!
...BUT I TALK TO SATAN.
KRSSSSHH

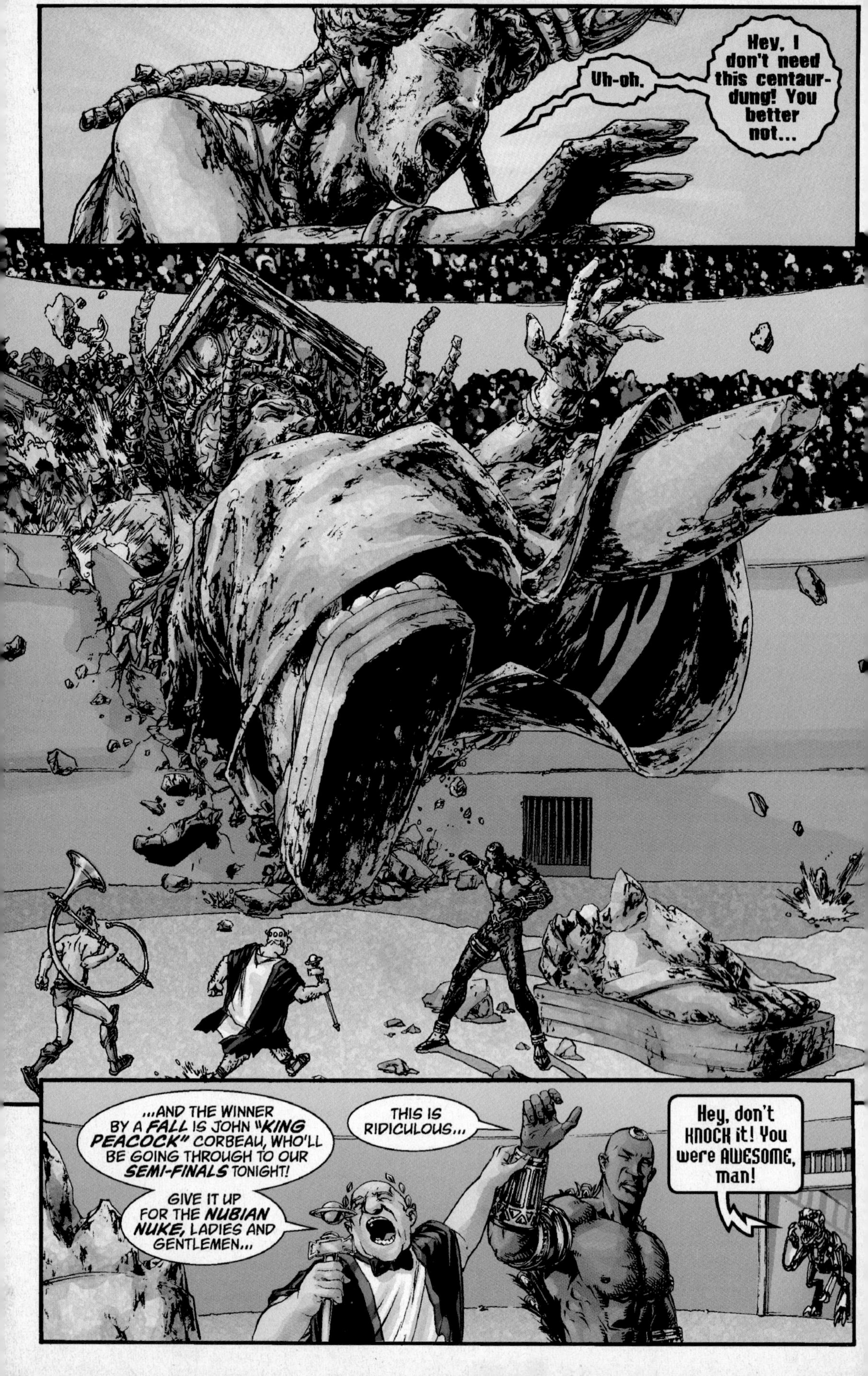
Uh-oh.
Hey, I don't need this centaur-dung! You better not...
...AND THE WINNER BY A FALL IS JOHN "KING PEACOCK" CORBEAU, WHO'LL BE GOING THROUGH TO OUR SEMI-FINALS TONIGHT!
GIVE IT UP FOR THE NUBIAN NUKE, LADIES AND GENTLEMEN...
THIS IS RIDICULOUS...
Hey, don't KNOCK it! You were AWESOME, man!

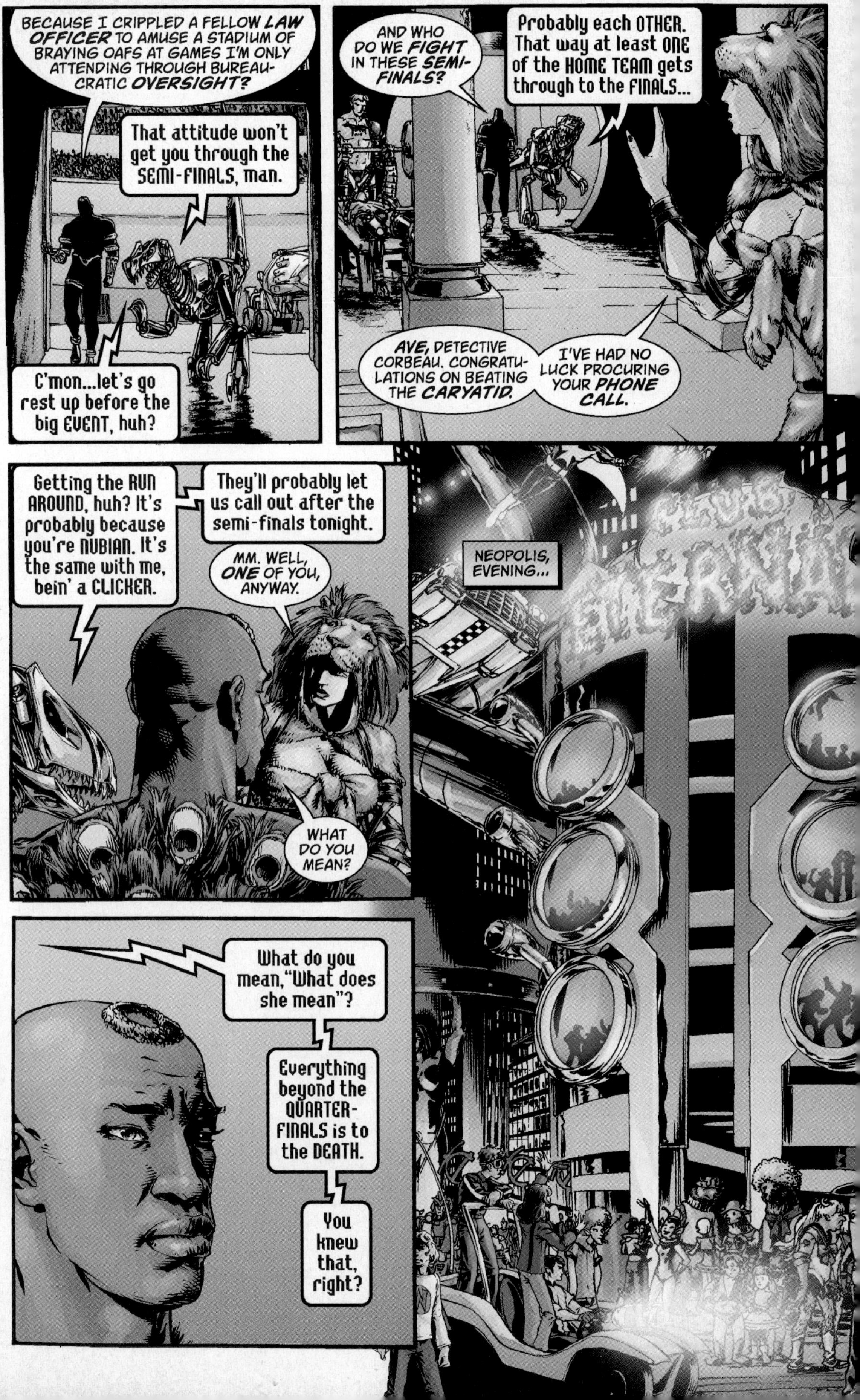
BECAUSE I CRIPPLED A FELLOW LAW OFFICER TO AMUSE A STADIUM OF BRAYING OAFS AT GAMES I'M ONLY ATTENDING THROUGH BUREAU-CRATIC OVERSIGHT?
That attitude won't get you through the SEMI-FINALS, man.
C'mon...let's go rest up before the big EVENT, huh?
AND WHO DO WE FIGHT IN THESE SEMI-FINALS?
Probably each OTHER. That way at least ONE of the HOME TEAM gets through to the FINALS...
AVE, DETECTIVE CORBEAU. CONGRATU-LATIONS ON BEATING THE CARYATID.
I'VE HAD NO LUCK PROCURING YOUR PHONE CALL.
Getting the RUN AROUND, huh? It's probably because you're NUBIAN. It's the same with me, bein' a CLICKER.
They'll probably let us call out after the semi-finals tonight.
MM. WELL, ONE OF YOU, ANYWAY.
WHAT DO YOU MEAN?
What do you mean,"What does she mean"?
Everything beyond the QUARTER-FINALS is to the DEATH.
You knew that, right?
NEOPOLIS, EVENING...

UH... CAPTAIN?

OH... I'M SORRY, DETECTIVE JACKSON. PLEASE COME IN. I WAS...

OH, I WAS JUST THINKING STUFF OVER. THIS AND THAT. WHAT CAN I DO FOR YOU?

I-IT'S DETECTIVE CORBEAU. I STILL HAVEN'T HEARD FROM HIM.

I WONDERED IF THERE WERE MAYBE PARTICLE STORMS MESSING UP INTER-WORLD COMMUNICATIONS OR WHATEVER...

HM. WELL, COMMISSIONER ULTIMA'S OFFICE ON GRAND CENTRAL FAXED ME EARLIER CONCERNING TOMORROW'S INSPECTION.

THAT SEEMED TO GET THROUGH OKAY.

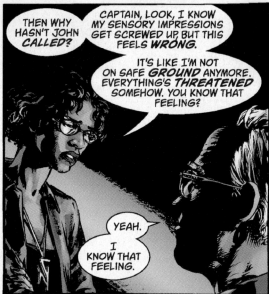

THEN WHY HASN'T JOHN CALLED?

CAPTAIN, LOOK, I KNOW MY SENSORY IMPRESSIONS GET SCREWED UP, BUT THIS FEELS WRONG.

IT'S LIKE I'M NOT ON SAFE GROUND ANYMORE. EVERYTHING'S THREATENED SOMEHOW. YOU KNOW THAT FEELING?

YEAH. I KNOW THAT FEELING.

LISTEN, I'LL CALL GRAND CENTRAL ABOUT CORBEAU. MEANWHILE, YOU SHOULD GO HOME AND GET SOME SLEEP. WE'VE ALL GOT A HEAVY DAY TOMORROW...

...ALWAYS ASSUMING WE GET THROUGH TONIGHT.

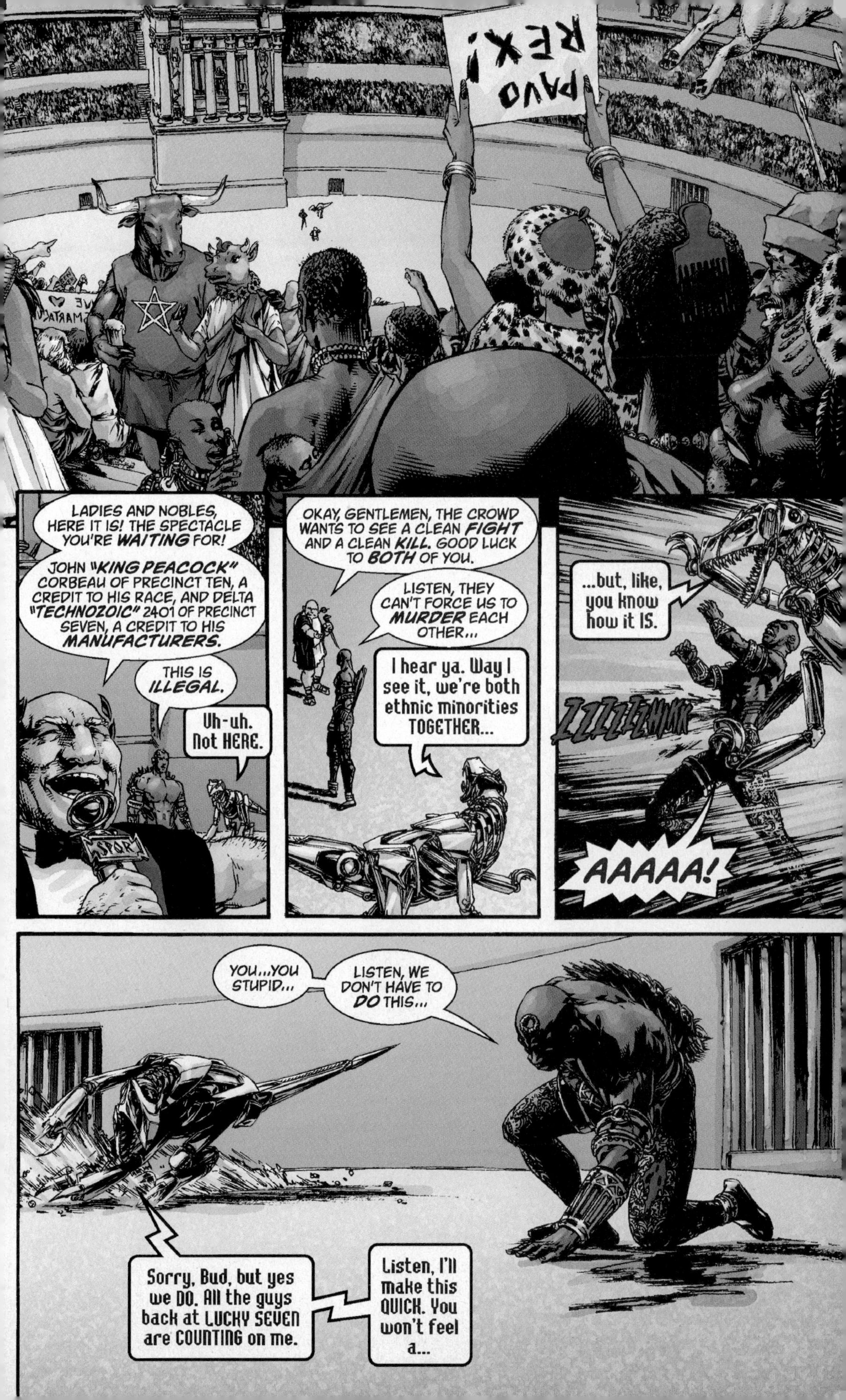
PAVO REX!
LADIES AND NOBLES, HERE IT IS! THE SPECTACLE YOU'RE WAITING FOR!
JOHN "KING PEACOCK" CORBEAU OF PRECINCT TEN, A CREDIT TO HIS RACE, AND DELTA "TECHNOZOIC" 2401 OF PRECINCT SEVEN, A CREDIT TO HIS MANUFACTURERS.
THIS IS ILLEGAL.
Uh-uh. Not HERE.
SPQR
OKAY, GENTLEMEN, THE CROWD WANTS TO SEE A CLEAN FIGHT AND A CLEAN KILL. GOOD LUCK TO BOTH OF YOU.
LISTEN, THEY CAN'T FORCE US TO MURDER EACH OTHER...
I hear ya. Way I see it, we're both ethnic minorities TOGETHER...
...but, like, you know how it IS.
ZZZZZHKKK
AAAAA!
YOU...YOU STUPID...
LISTEN, WE DON'T HAVE TO DO THIS...
Sorry, Bud, but yes we DO. All the guys back at LUCKY SEVEN are COUNTING on me.
Listen, I'll make this QUICK. You won't feel a...

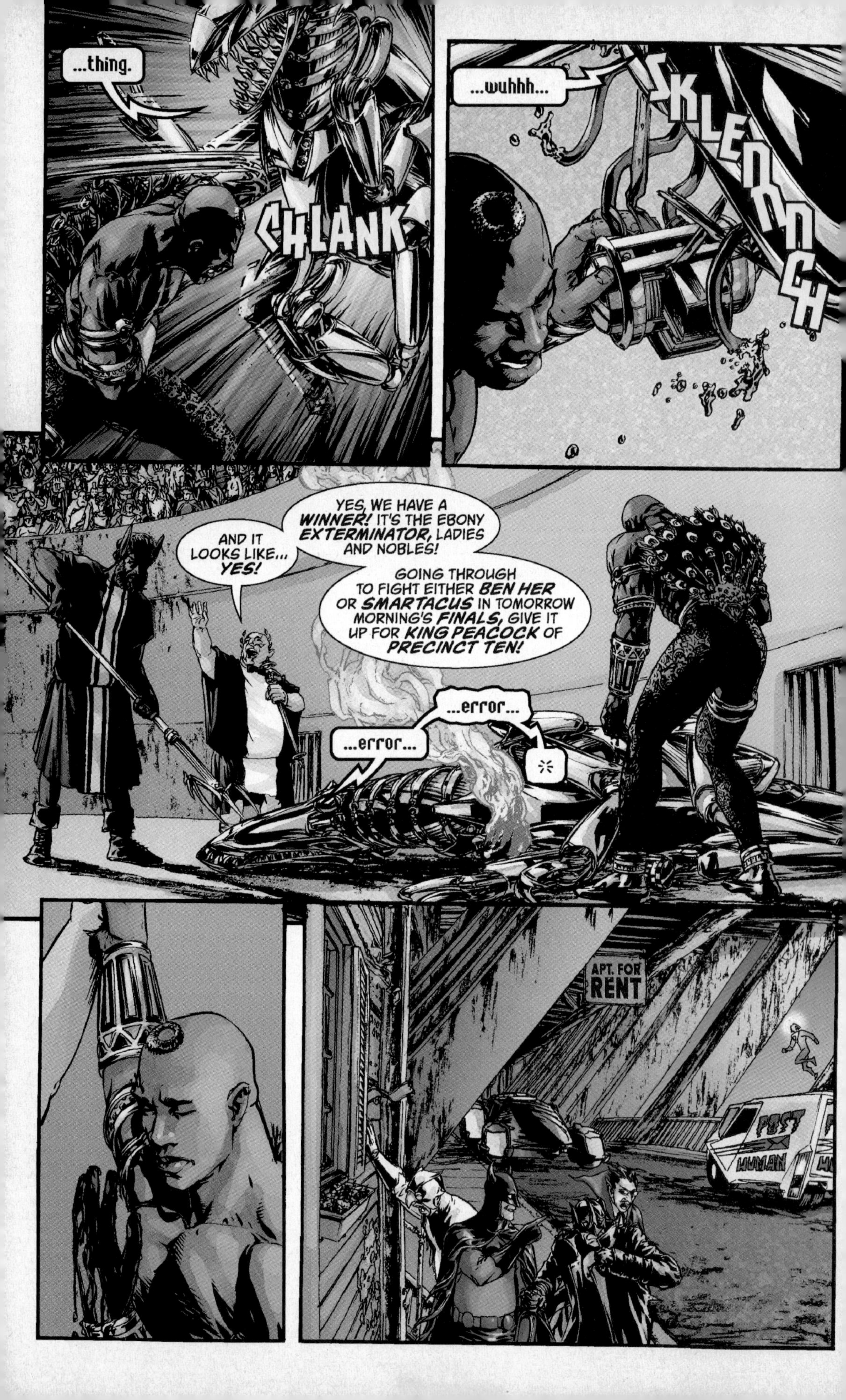
...thing.
CHLANK
...wuhhh...
SKLENNNCH
AND IT LOOKS LIKE... YES!
YES, WE HAVE A WINNER! IT'S THE EBONY EXTERMINATOR, LADIES AND NOBLES!
GOING THROUGH TO FIGHT EITHER BEN HER OR SMARTACUS IN TOMORROW MORNING'S FINALS, GIVE IT UP FOR KING PEACOCK OF PRECINCT TEN!
...error...
...error...
APT. FOR RENT
HUMAN

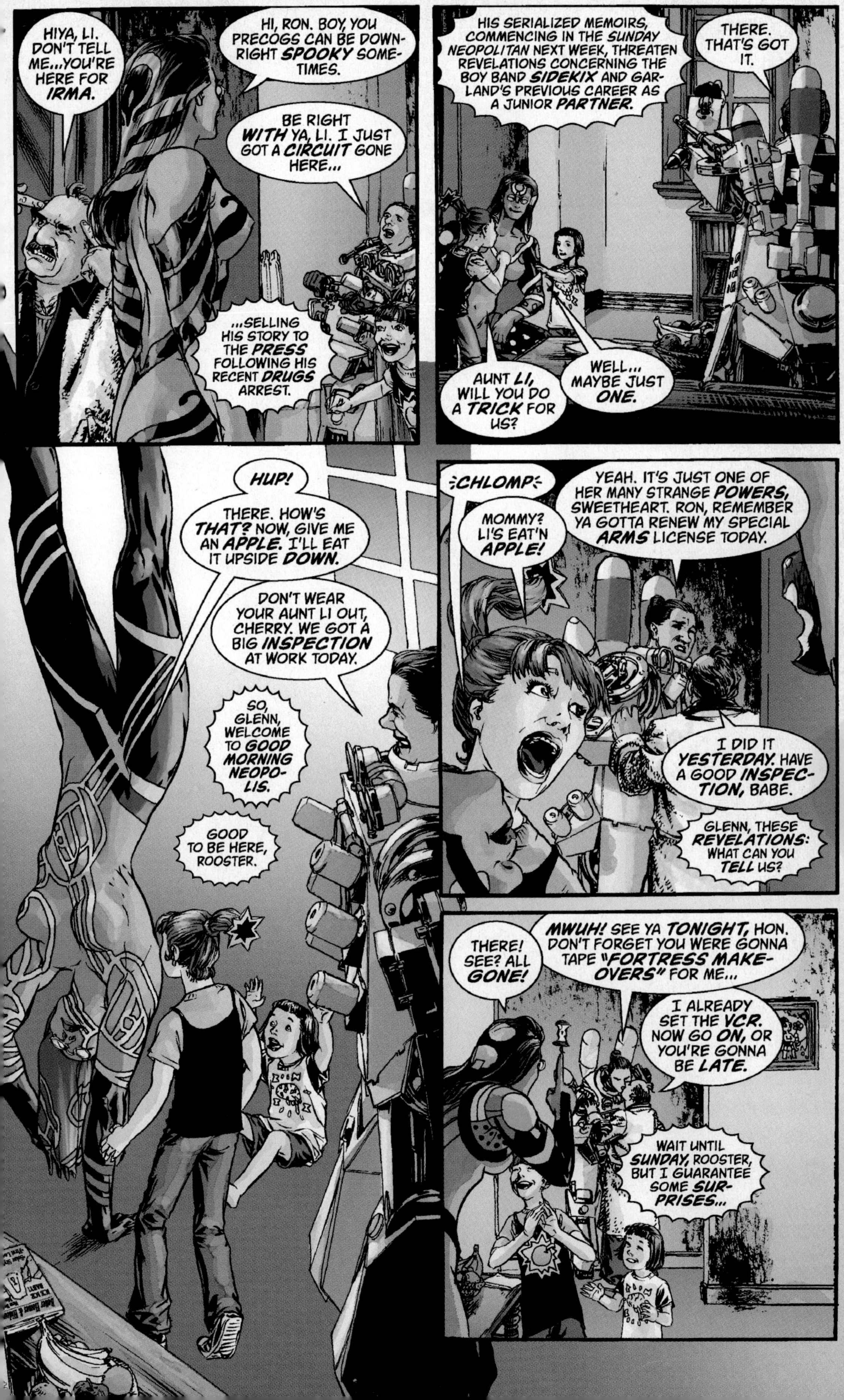
HIYA, LI. DON'T TELL ME...YOU'RE HERE FOR IRMA.
HI, RON. BOY, YOU PRECOGS CAN BE DOWN-RIGHT SPOOKY SOME-TIMES.
BE RIGHT WITH YA, LI. I JUST GOT A CIRCUIT GONE HERE...
...SELLING HIS STORY TO THE PRESS FOLLOWING HIS RECENT DRUGS ARREST.
HIS SERIALIZED MEMOIRS, COMMENCING IN THE SUNDAY NEOPOLITAN NEXT WEEK, THREATEN REVELATIONS CONCERNING THE BOY BAND SIDEKIX AND GAR-LAND'S PREVIOUS CAREER AS A JUNIOR PARTNER.
THERE. THAT'S GOT IT.
AUNT LI, WILL YOU DO A TRICK FOR US?
WELL... MAYBE JUST ONE.
HUP!
THERE. HOW'S THAT? NOW, GIVE ME AN APPLE. I'LL EAT IT UPSIDE DOWN.
DON'T WEAR YOUR AUNT LI OUT, CHERRY. WE GOT A BIG INSPECTION AT WORK TODAY.
SO, GLENN, WELCOME TO GOOD MORNING NEOPO-LIS.
GOOD TO BE HERE, ROOSTER.
CHLOMP
MOMMY? LI'S EAT'N APPLE!
YEAH. IT'S JUST ONE OF HER MANY STRANGE POWERS, SWEETHEART. RON, REMEMBER YA GOTTA RENEW MY SPECIAL ARMS LICENSE TODAY.
I DID IT YESTERDAY. HAVE A GOOD INSPEC-TION, BABE.
GLENN, THESE REVELATIONS: WHAT CAN YOU TELL US?
THERE! SEE? ALL GONE!
MWUH! SEE YA TONIGHT, HON. DON'T FORGET YOU WERE GONNA TAPE "FORTRESS MAKE-OVERS" FOR ME...
I ALREADY SET THE VCR. NOW GO ON, OR YOU'RE GONNA BE LATE.
WAIT UNTIL SUNDAY, ROOSTER, BUT I GUARANTEE SOME SUR-PRISES...

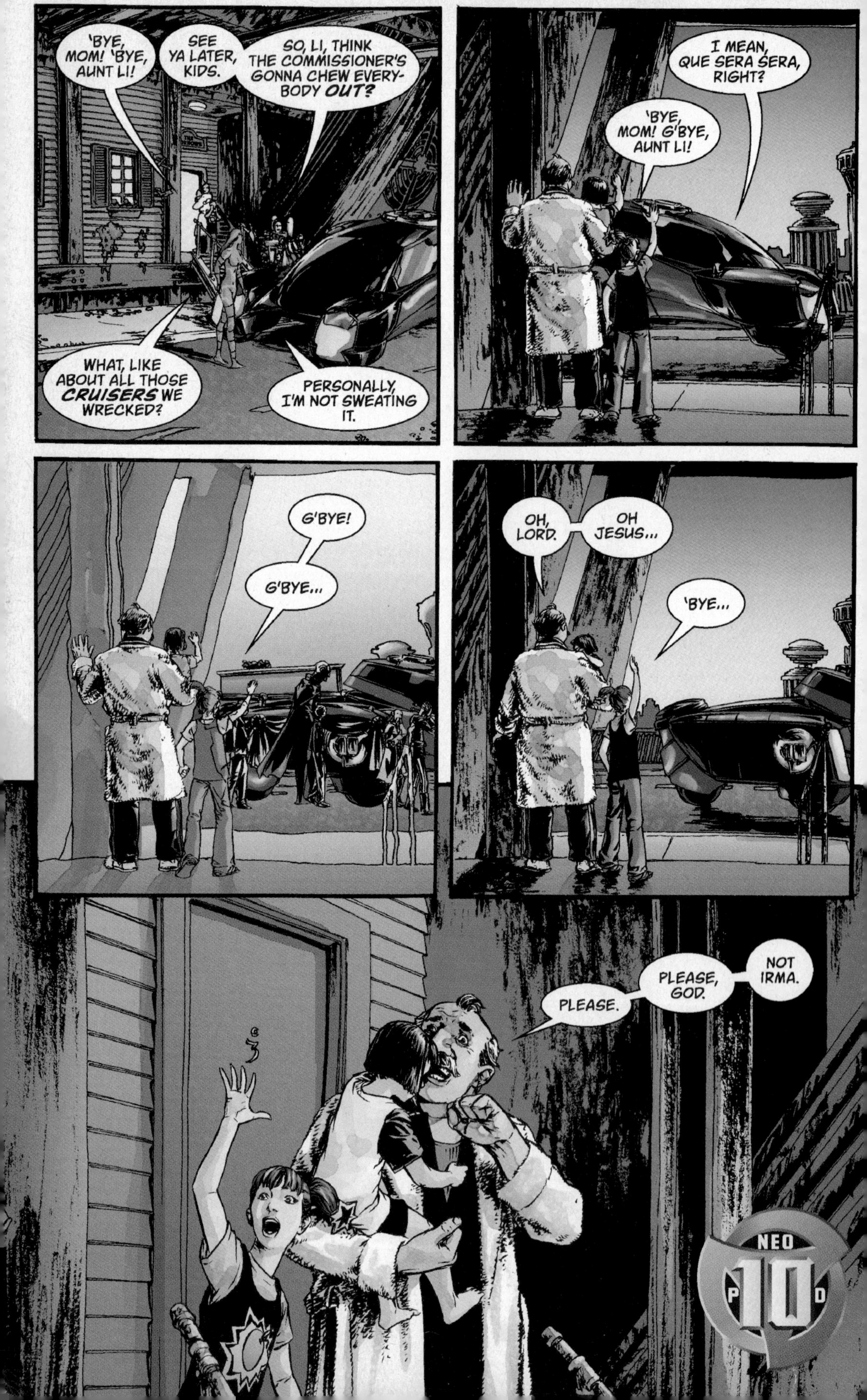

'BYE, MOM! 'BYE, AUNT LI!
SEE YA LATER, KIDS.
SO, LI, THINK THE COMMISSIONER'S GONNA CHEW EVERY-BODY OUT?
WHAT, LIKE ABOUT ALL THOSE CRUISERS WE WRECKED?
PERSONALLY, I'M NOT SWEATING IT.
I MEAN, QUE SERA SERA, RIGHT?
'BYE, MOM! G'BYE, AUNT LI!
G'BYE!
G'BYE...
OH, LORD.
OH JESUS...
'BYE...
PLEASE.
PLEASE, GOD.
NOT IRMA.
NEO P 10 D

CHAPTER THREE

ON THE DOCKET:
Smax investigates a homicide,
the squad gets a high-rank inspection,
and Toybox hears the latest rumor.

Cover art:
Gene Ha and
Zander Cannon

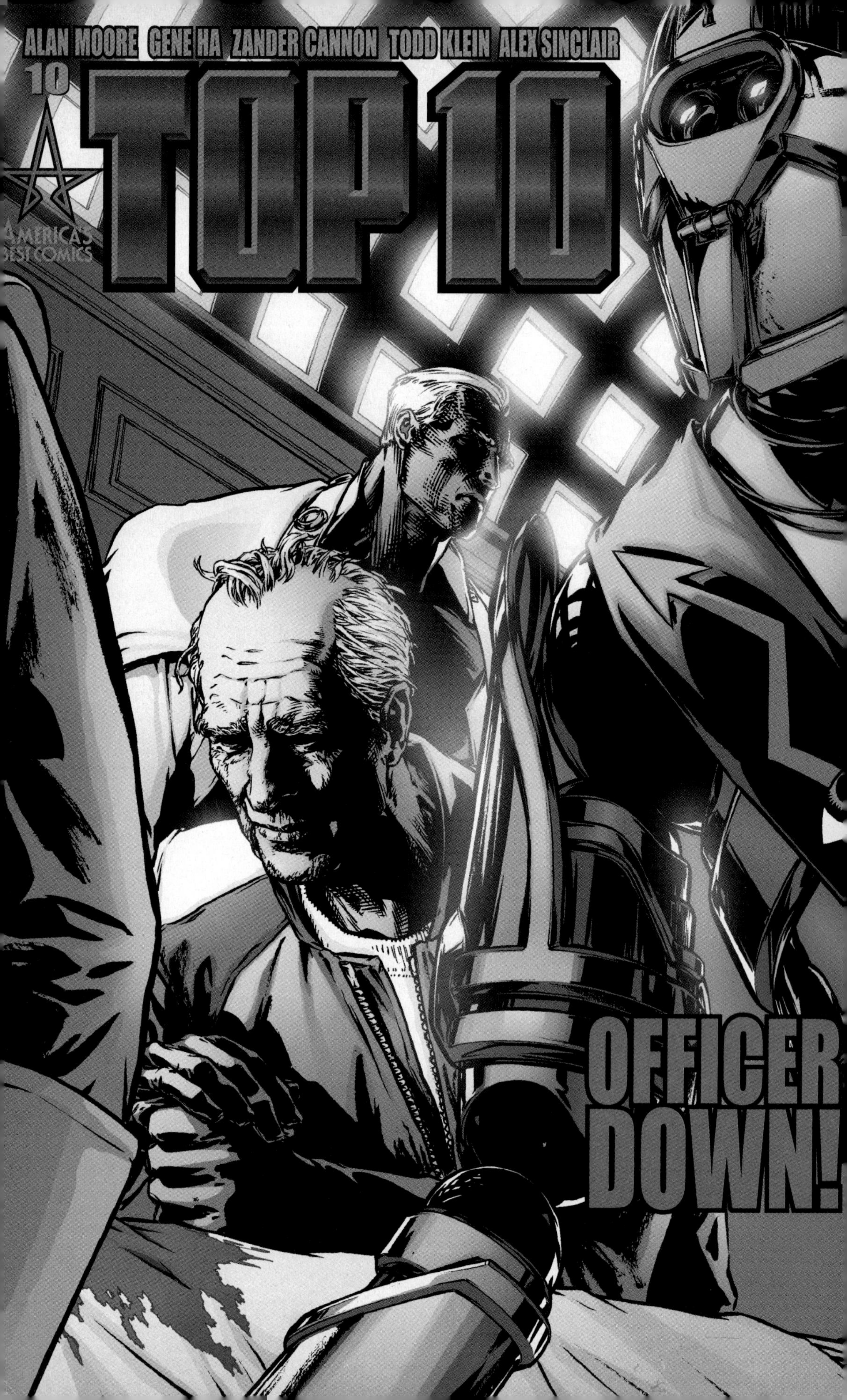
ALAN MOORE GENE HA ZANDER CANNON TODD KLEIN ALEX SINCLAIR
10
TOP 10
AMERICA'S BEST COMICS
OFFICER DOWN!

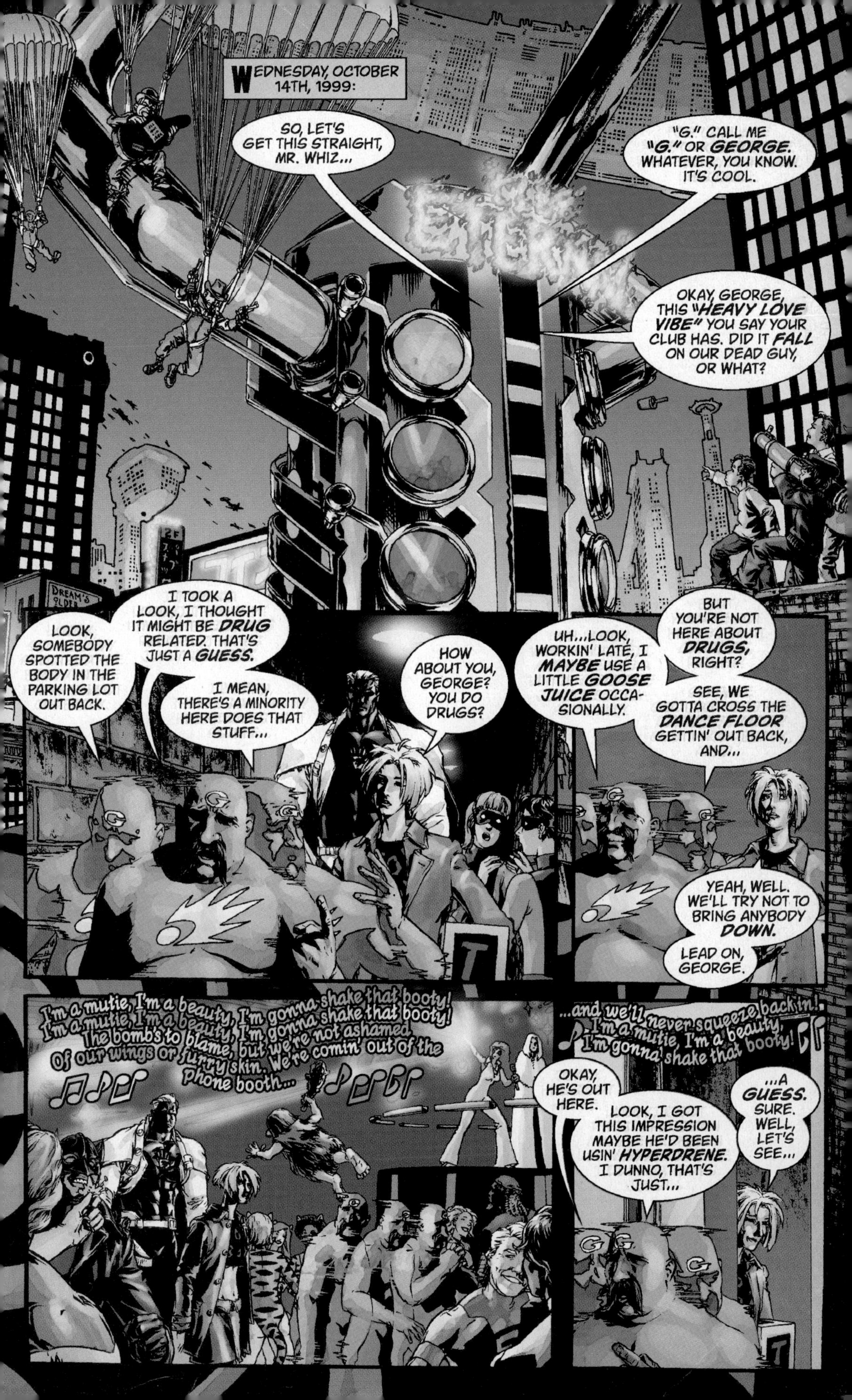
WEDNESDAY, OCTOBER 14TH, 1999:
SO, LET'S GET THIS STRAIGHT, MR. WHIZ...
"G." CALL ME "G." OR GEORGE. WHATEVER, YOU KNOW. IT'S COOL.
OKAY, GEORGE, THIS "HEAVY LOVE VIBE" YOU SAY YOUR CLUB HAS. DID IT FALL ON OUR DEAD GUY, OR WHAT?
LOOK, SOMEBODY SPOTTED THE BODY IN THE PARKING LOT OUT BACK.
I TOOK A LOOK, I THOUGHT IT MIGHT BE DRUG RELATED. THAT'S JUST A GUESS.
I MEAN, THERE'S A MINORITY HERE DOES THAT STUFF...
HOW ABOUT YOU, GEORGE? YOU DO DRUGS?
UH...LOOK, WORKIN' LATE, I MAYBE USE A LITTLE GOOSE JUICE OCCASIONALLY.
BUT YOU'RE NOT HERE ABOUT DRUGS, RIGHT?
SEE, WE GOTTA CROSS THE DANCE FLOOR GETTIN' OUT BACK, AND...
YEAH, WELL. WE'LL TRY NOT TO BRING ANYBODY DOWN.
LEAD ON, GEORGE.
I'm a mutie, I'm a beauty, I'm gonna shake that booty! I'm a mutie, I'm a beauty, I'm gonna shake that booty! The bomb's to blame, but we're not ashamed of our wings or furry skin. We're comin' out of the phone booth...
...and we'll never squeeze back in! I'm a mutie, I'm a beauty, I'm gonna shake that booty!
OKAY, HE'S OUT HERE.
LOOK, I GOT THIS IMPRESSION MAYBE HE'D BEEN USIN' HYPERDRENE. I DUNNO, THAT'S JUST...
...A GUESS. SURE. WELL, LET'S SEE...

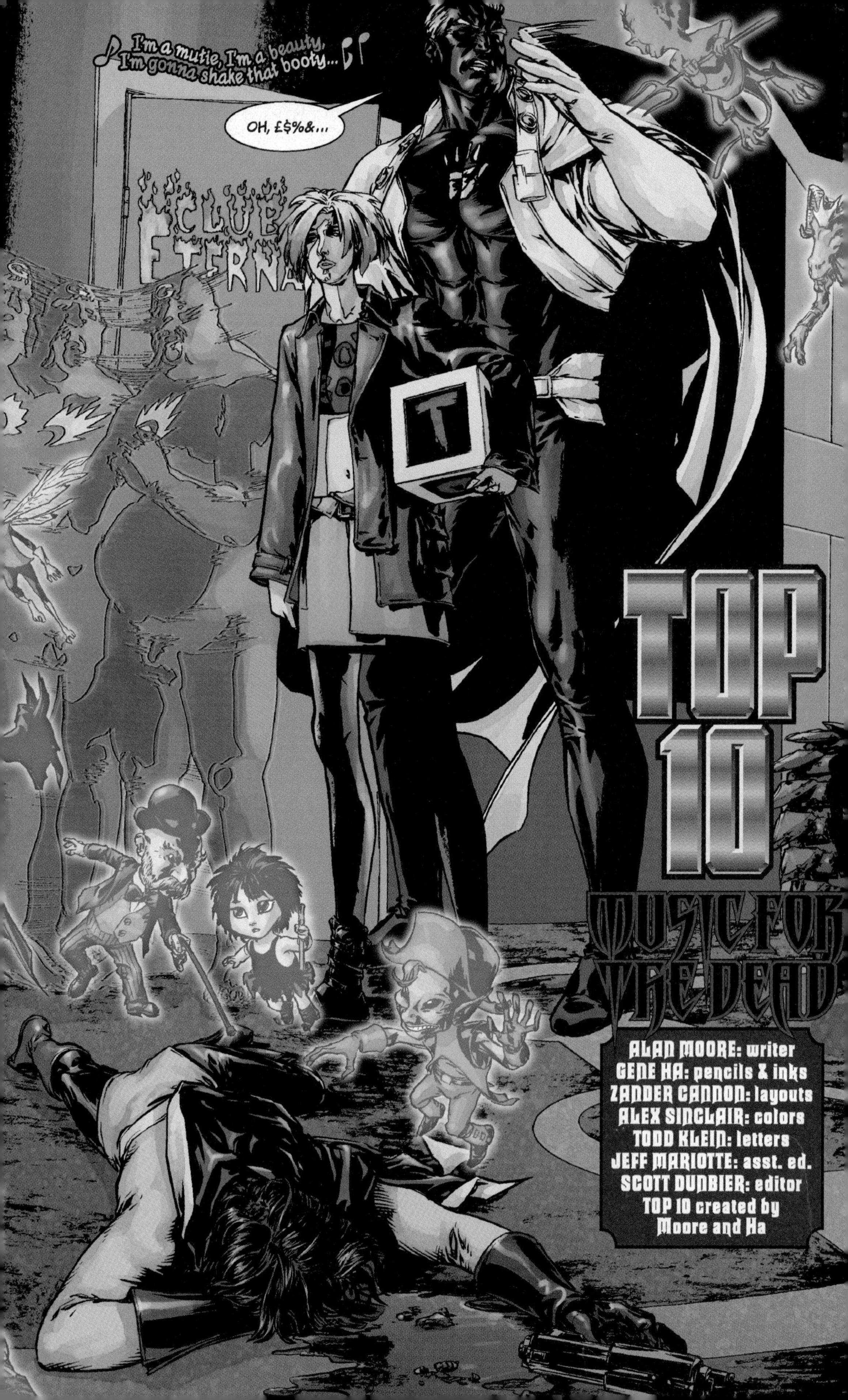

I'm a mutie, I'm a beauty,
I'm gonna shake that booty...
OH, £$%&...
CLUB
ETERNA
TOP 10
MUSIC FOR THE DEAD
ALAN MOORE: writer
GENE HA: pencils & inks
ZANDER CANNON: layouts
ALEX SINCLAIR: colors
TODD KLEIN: letters
JEFF MARIOTTE: asst. ed.
SCOTT DUNBIER: editor
TOP 10 created by
Moore and Ha

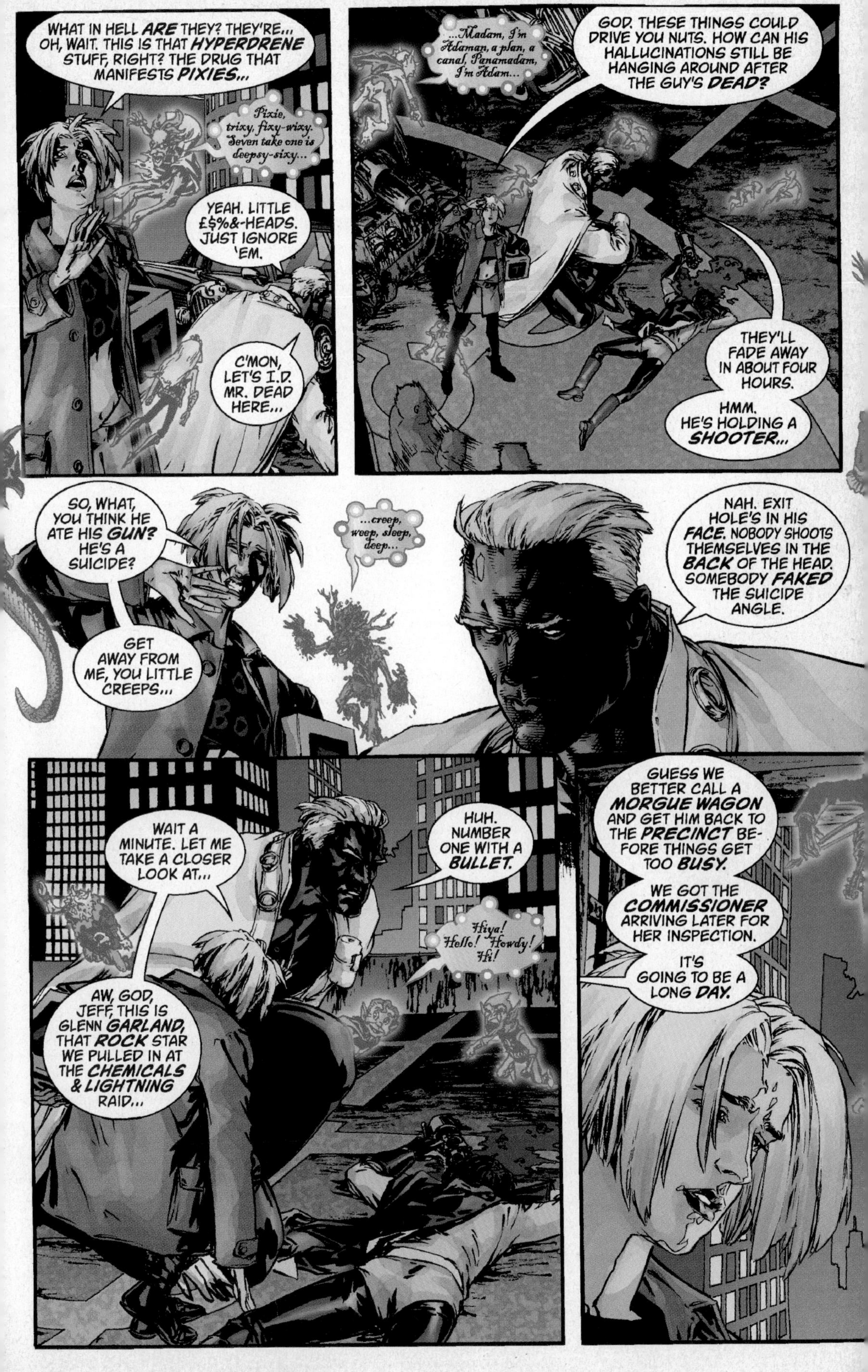
WHAT IN HELL ARE THEY? THEY'RE... OH, WAIT. THIS IS THAT HYPERDRENE STUFF, RIGHT? THE DRUG THAT MANIFESTS PIXIES...
Pixie, trixy, fixy-wixy. Seven take one is deepsy-sixy...
YEAH. LITTLE £$%&-HEADS. JUST IGNORE 'EM.
C'MON, LET'S I.D. MR. DEAD HERE...
...Madam, I'm Adaman, a plan, a canal, Panamadam, I'm Adam...
GOD. THESE THINGS COULD DRIVE YOU NUTS. HOW CAN HIS HALLUCINATIONS STILL BE HANGING AROUND AFTER THE GUY'S DEAD?
THEY'LL FADE AWAY IN ABOUT FOUR HOURS.
HMM. HE'S HOLDING A SHOOTER...
SO, WHAT, YOU THINK HE ATE HIS GUN? HE'S A SUICIDE?
...creep, weep, sleep, deep...
NAH. EXIT HOLE'S IN HIS FACE. NOBODY SHOOTS THEMSELVES IN THE BACK OF THE HEAD. SOMEBODY FAKED THE SUICIDE ANGLE.
GET AWAY FROM ME, YOU LITTLE CREEPS...
WAIT A MINUTE. LET ME TAKE A CLOSER LOOK AT...
HUH. NUMBER ONE WITH A BULLET.
Hiya! Hello! Howdy! Hi!
AW, GOD, JEFF, THIS IS GLENN GARLAND, THAT ROCK STAR WE PULLED IN AT THE CHEMICALS & LIGHTNING RAID...
GUESS WE BETTER CALL A MORGUE WAGON AND GET HIM BACK TO THE PRECINCT BE-FORE THINGS GET TOO BUSY.
WE GOT THE COMMISSIONER ARRIVING LATER FOR HER INSPECTION.
IT'S GOING TO BE A LONG DAY.

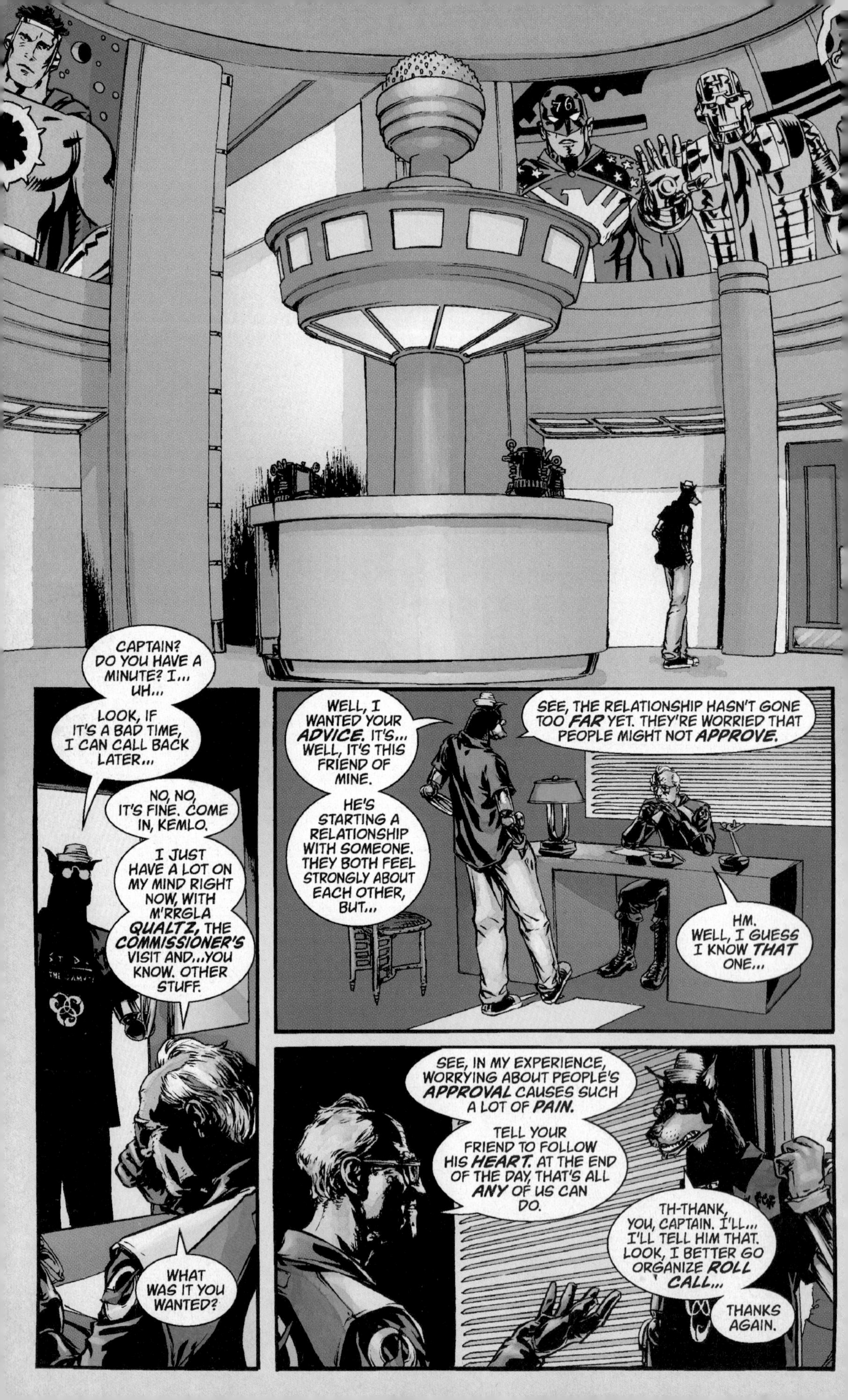
CAPTAIN? DO YOU HAVE A MINUTE? I... UH...
LOOK, IF IT'S A BAD TIME, I CAN CALL BACK LATER...
NO, NO, IT'S FINE. COME IN, KEMLO.
I JUST HAVE A LOT ON MY MIND RIGHT NOW, WITH M'RRGLA QUALTZ, THE COMMISSIONER'S VISIT AND...YOU KNOW. OTHER STUFF.
WHAT WAS IT YOU WANTED?
WELL, I WANTED YOUR ADVICE. IT'S... WELL, IT'S THIS FRIEND OF MINE.
HE'S STARTING A RELATIONSHIP WITH SOMEONE. THEY BOTH FEEL STRONGLY ABOUT EACH OTHER, BUT...
SEE, THE RELATIONSHIP HASN'T GONE TOO FAR YET. THEY'RE WORRIED THAT PEOPLE MIGHT NOT APPROVE.
HM. WELL, I GUESS I KNOW THAT ONE...
SEE, IN MY EXPERIENCE, WORRYING ABOUT PEOPLE'S APPROVAL CAUSES SUCH A LOT OF PAIN.
TELL YOUR FRIEND TO FOLLOW HIS HEART. AT THE END OF THE DAY, THAT'S ALL ANY OF US CAN DO.
TH-THANK, YOU, CAPTAIN. I'LL... I'LL TELL HIM THAT. LOOK, I BETTER GO ORGANIZE ROLL CALL...
THANKS AGAIN.

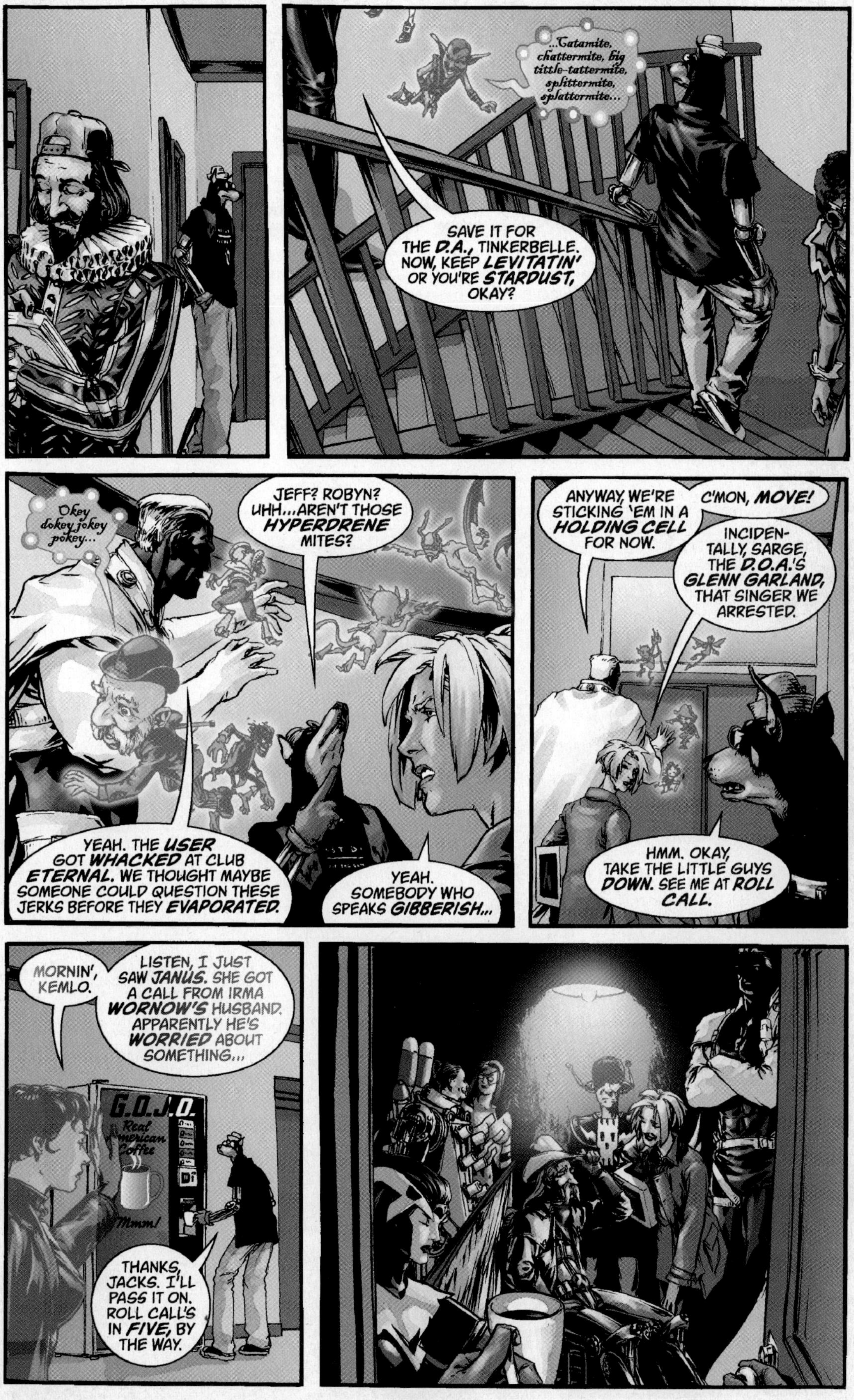
...Catamite, chattermite, big tittle-tattermite, splittermite, splattermite...
SAVE IT FOR THE D.A., TINKERBELLE. NOW, KEEP LEVITATIN' OR YOU'RE STARDUST, OKAY?
Okey dokey jokey pokey...
JEFF? ROBYN? UHH...AREN'T THOSE HYPERDRENE MITES?
YEAH. THE USER GOT WHACKED AT CLUB ETERNAL. WE THOUGHT MAYBE SOMEONE COULD QUESTION THESE JERKS BEFORE THEY EVAPORATED.
YEAH. SOMEBODY WHO SPEAKS GIBBERISH...
ANYWAY, WE'RE STICKING 'EM IN A HOLDING CELL FOR NOW.
C'MON, MOVE!
INCIDENTALLY, SARGE, THE D.O.A.'S GLENN GARLAND, THAT SINGER WE ARRESTED.
HMM. OKAY, TAKE THE LITTLE GUYS DOWN. SEE ME AT ROLL CALL.
MORNIN', KEMLO.
LISTEN, I JUST SAW JANUS. SHE GOT A CALL FROM IRMA WORNOW'S HUSBAND. APPARENTLY HE'S WORRIED ABOUT SOMETHING...
G.O.J.O.
Real American Coffee
Mmm!
THANKS, JACKS. I'LL PASS IT ON. ROLL CALL'S IN FIVE, BY THE WAY.

MORNIN', EVERYONE.

WELL, WE GOT THE FULL COMBO PLATTER TODAY. TOP OF THE LIST, AS WE'RE ALL AWARE, IS COMMISSIONER ULTIMA'S *VISIT*.

LET'S MAKE THIS AS SMOOTH AS POSSIBLE, OKAY? I WANT EVERYBODY LOOKING THEIR *BEST*.

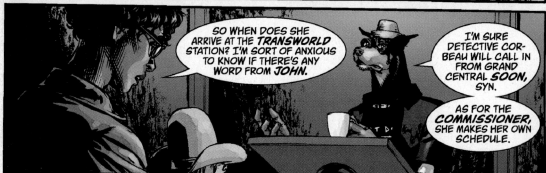

SO WHEN DOES SHE ARRIVE AT THE *TRANSWORLD* STATION? I'M SORT OF ANXIOUS TO KNOW IF THERE'S ANY WORD FROM *JOHN*.

I'M SURE DETECTIVE CORBEAU WILL CALL IN FROM GRAND CENTRAL *SOON*, SYN.

AS FOR THE *COMMISSIONER*, SHE MAKES HER OWN SCHEDULE.

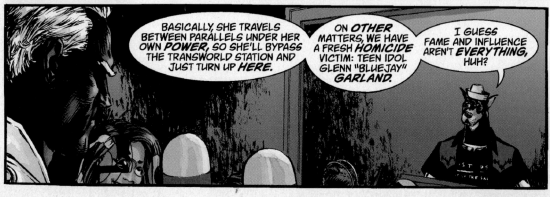

BASICALLY, SHE TRAVELS BETWEEN PARALLELS UNDER HER OWN *POWER*, SO SHE'LL BYPASS THE TRANSWORLD STATION AND JUST TURN UP *HERE*.

ON *OTHER* MATTERS, WE HAVE A FRESH *HOMICIDE* VICTIM: TEEN IDOL GLENN "BLUEJAY" *GARLAND*.

I GUESS FAME AND INFLUENCE AREN'T *EVERYTHING*, HUH?

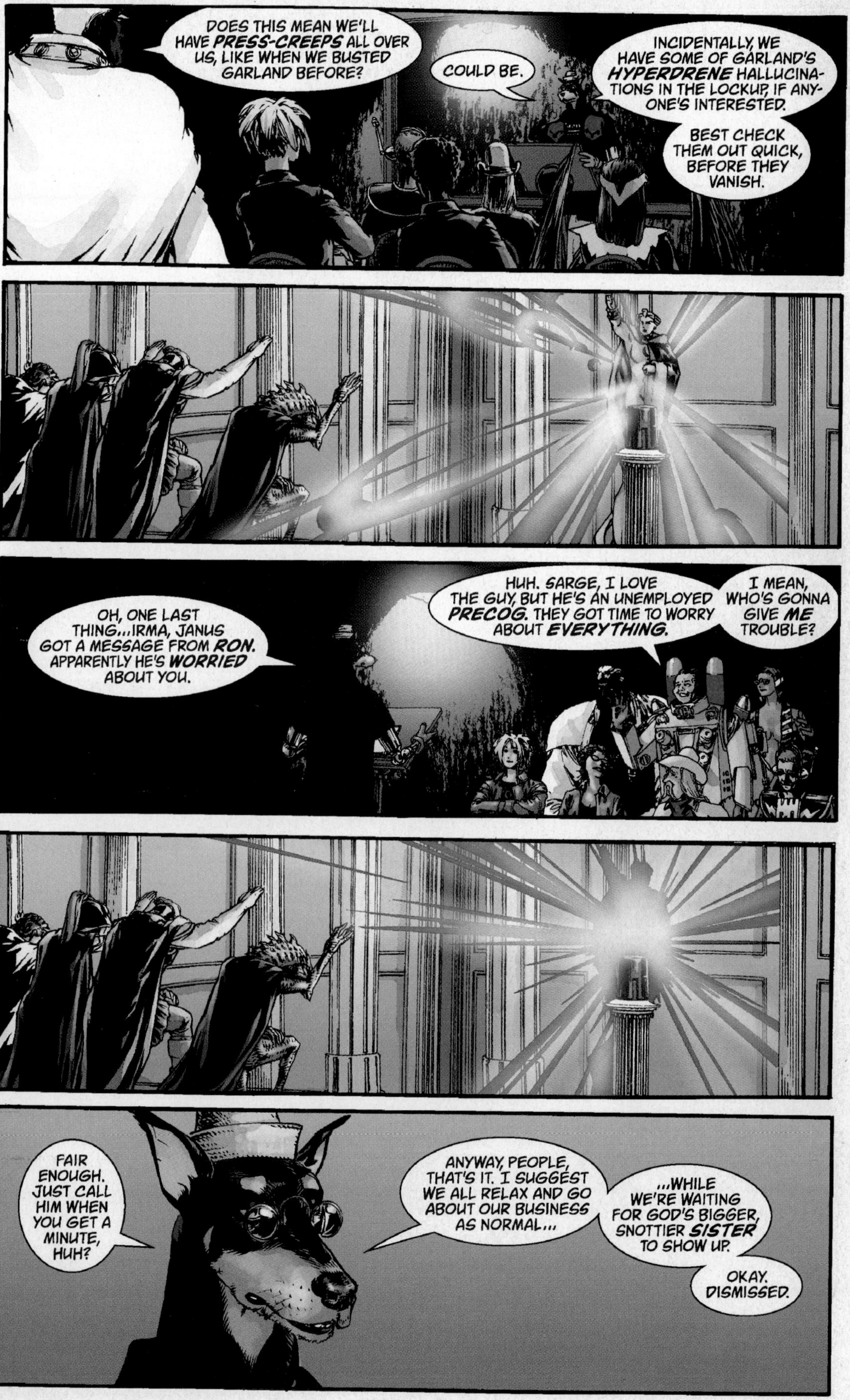
DOES THIS MEAN WE'LL HAVE PRESS-CREEPS ALL OVER US, LIKE WHEN WE BUSTED GARLAND BEFORE?
COULD BE.
INCIDENTALLY, WE HAVE SOME OF GARLAND'S HYPERDRENE HALLUCINATIONS IN THE LOCKUP, IF ANYONE'S INTERESTED.
BEST CHECK THEM OUT QUICK, BEFORE THEY VANISH.
OH, ONE LAST THING...IRMA, JANUS GOT A MESSAGE FROM RON. APPARENTLY HE'S WORRIED ABOUT YOU.
HUH. SARGE, I LOVE THE GUY, BUT HE'S AN UNEMPLOYED PRECOG. THEY GOT TIME TO WORRY ABOUT EVERYTHING.
I MEAN, WHO'S GONNA GIVE ME TROUBLE?
FAIR ENOUGH. JUST CALL HIM WHEN YOU GET A MINUTE, HUH?
ANYWAY, PEOPLE, THAT'S IT. I SUGGEST WE ALL RELAX AND GO ABOUT OUR BUSINESS AS NORMAL...
...WHILE WE'RE WAITING FOR GOD'S BIGGER, SNOTTIER SISTER TO SHOW UP.
OKAY. DISMISSED.

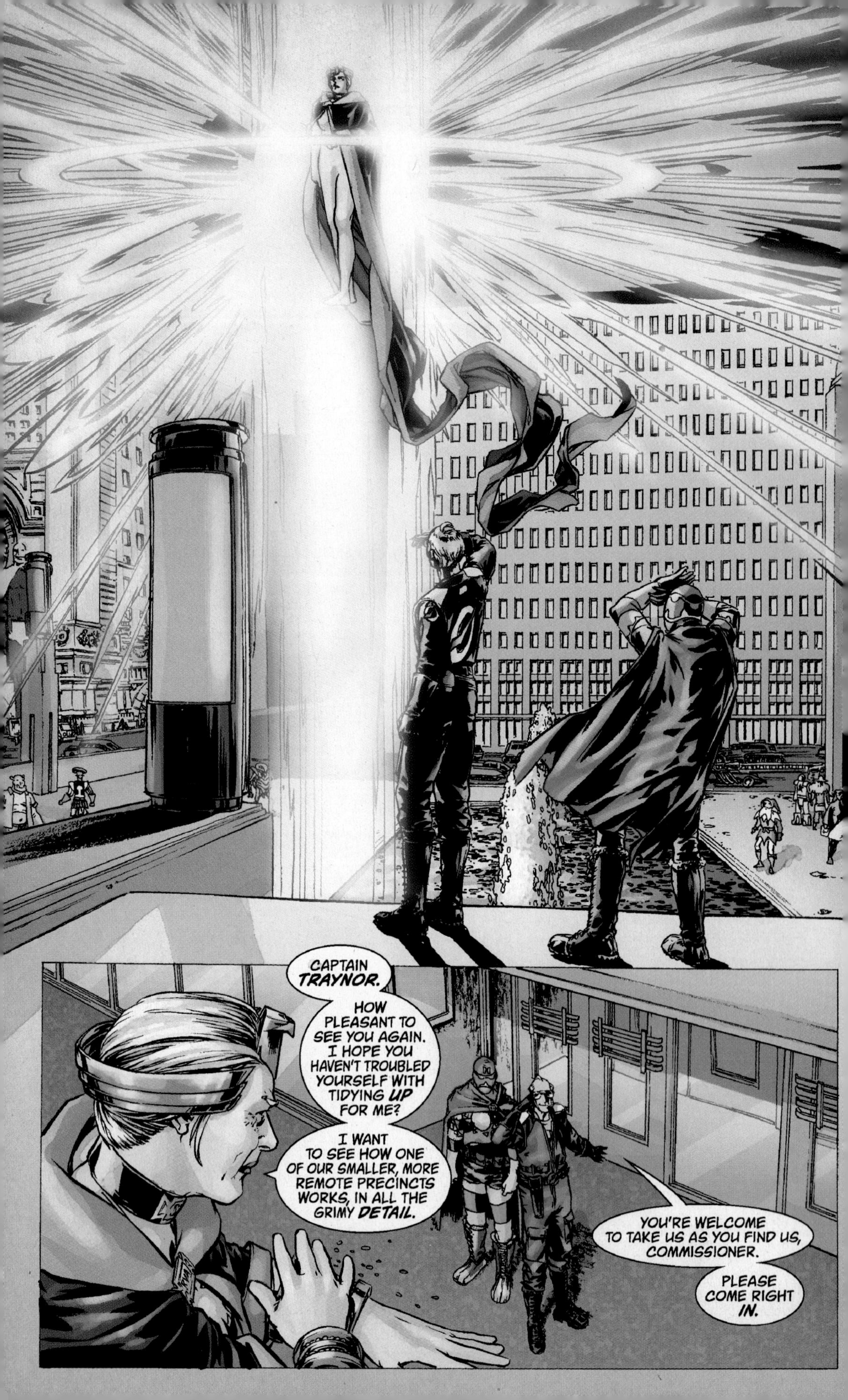
CAPTAIN TRAYNOR.
HOW PLEASANT TO SEE YOU AGAIN. I HOPE YOU HAVEN'T TROUBLED YOURSELF WITH TIDYING UP FOR ME?
I WANT TO SEE HOW ONE OF OUR SMALLER, MORE REMOTE PRECINCTS WORKS, IN ALL THE GRIMY DETAIL.
YOU'RE WELCOME TO TAKE US AS YOU FIND US, COMMISSIONER.
PLEASE COME RIGHT IN.

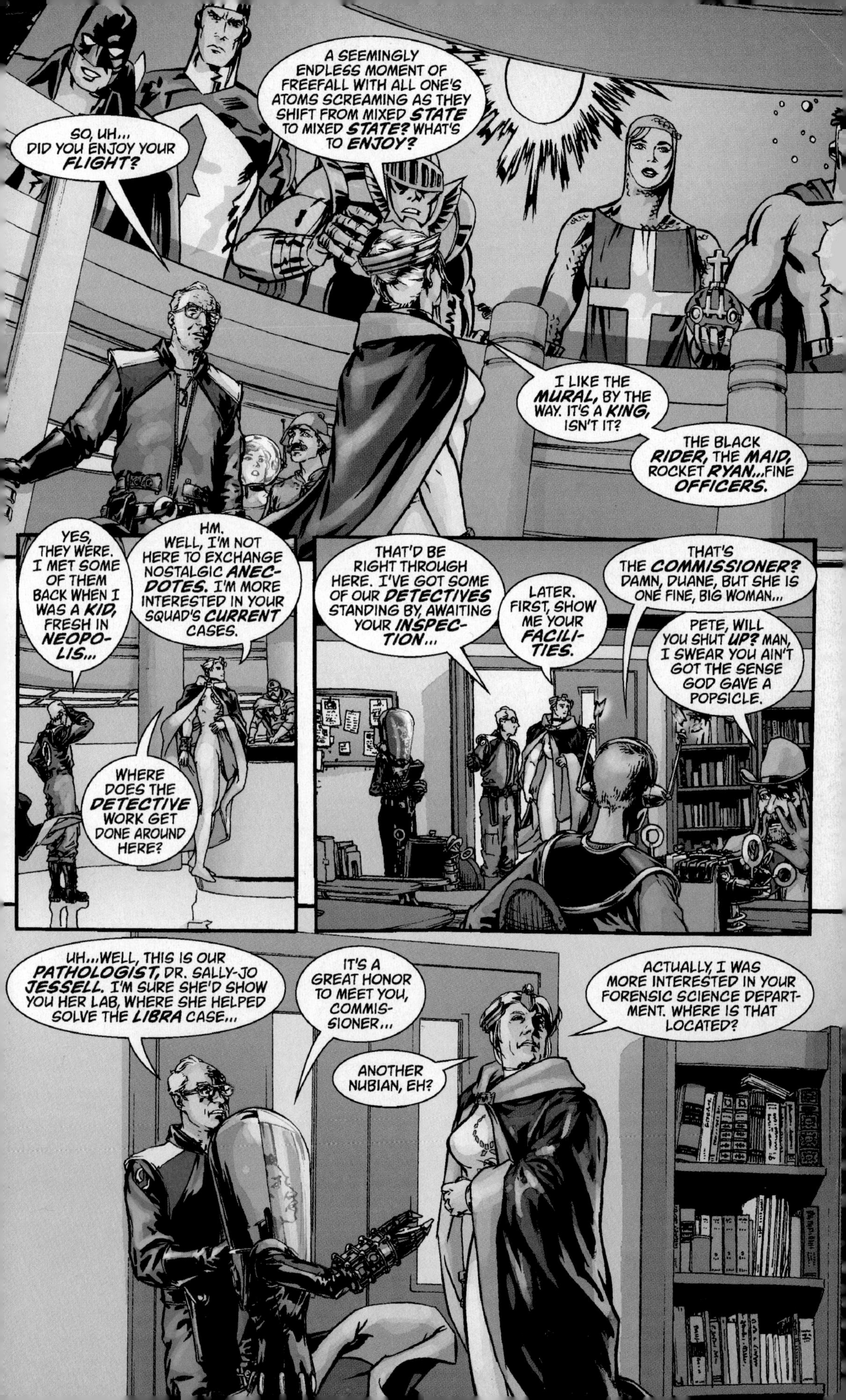
SO, UH... DID YOU ENJOY YOUR FLIGHT?
A SEEMINGLY ENDLESS MOMENT OF FREEFALL WITH ALL ONE'S ATOMS SCREAMING AS THEY SHIFT FROM MIXED STATE TO MIXED STATE? WHAT'S TO ENJOY?
I LIKE THE MURAL, BY THE WAY. IT'S A KING, ISN'T IT?
THE BLACK RIDER, THE MAID, ROCKET RYAN...FINE OFFICERS.
YES, THEY WERE. I MET SOME OF THEM BACK WHEN I WAS A KID, FRESH IN NEOPOLIS...
HM. WELL, I'M NOT HERE TO EXCHANGE NOSTALGIC ANECDOTES. I'M MORE INTERESTED IN YOUR SQUAD'S CURRENT CASES.
WHERE DOES THE DETECTIVE WORK GET DONE AROUND HERE?
THAT'D BE RIGHT THROUGH HERE. I'VE GOT SOME OF OUR DETECTIVES STANDING BY, AWAITING YOUR INSPECTION...
LATER. FIRST, SHOW ME YOUR FACILITIES.
THAT'S THE COMMISSIONER? DAMN, DUANE, BUT SHE IS ONE FINE, BIG WOMAN...
PETE, WILL YOU SHUT UP? MAN, I SWEAR YOU AIN'T GOT THE SENSE GOD GAVE A POPSICLE.
UH...WELL, THIS IS OUR PATHOLOGIST, DR. SALLY-JO JESSELL. I'M SURE SHE'D SHOW YOU HER LAB, WHERE SHE HELPED SOLVE THE LIBRA CASE...
IT'S A GREAT HONOR TO MEET YOU, COMMISSIONER...
ANOTHER NUBIAN, EH?
ACTUALLY, I WAS MORE INTERESTED IN YOUR FORENSIC SCIENCE DEPARTMENT. WHERE IS THAT LOCATED?

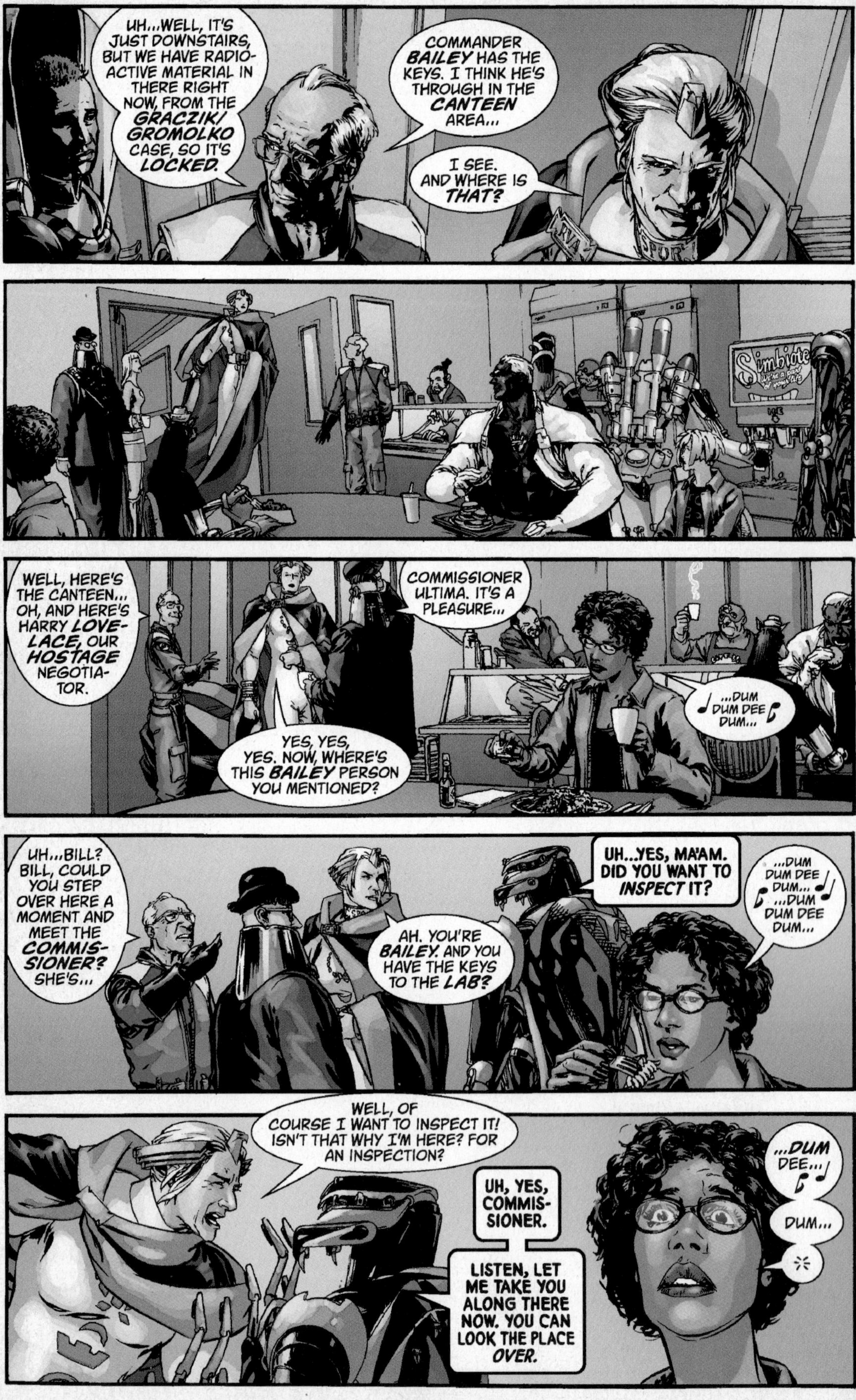
UH...WELL, IT'S JUST DOWNSTAIRS, BUT WE HAVE RADIO-ACTIVE MATERIAL IN THERE RIGHT NOW, FROM THE GRACZIK/ GROMOLKO CASE, SO IT'S LOCKED.
COMMANDER BAILEY HAS THE KEYS. I THINK HE'S THROUGH IN THE CANTEEN AREA...
I SEE. AND WHERE IS THAT?
Simbiote
WELL, HERE'S THE CANTEEN... OH, AND HERE'S HARRY LOVE-LACE, OUR HOSTAGE NEGOTIA-TOR.
COMMISSIONER ULTIMA. IT'S A PLEASURE...
YES, YES, YES. NOW, WHERE'S THIS BAILEY PERSON YOU MENTIONED?
...DUM DUM DEE DUM...
UH...BILL? BILL, COULD YOU STEP OVER HERE A MOMENT AND MEET THE COMMIS-SIONER? SHE'S...
AH. YOU'RE BAILEY. AND YOU HAVE THE KEYS TO THE LAB?
UH...YES, MA'AM. DID YOU WANT TO INSPECT IT?
...DUM DUM DEE DUM... ...DUM DUM DEE DUM...
WELL, OF COURSE I WANT TO INSPECT IT! ISN'T THAT WHY I'M HERE? FOR AN INSPECTION?
UH, YES, COMMIS-SIONER.
LISTEN, LET ME TAKE YOU ALONG THERE NOW. YOU CAN LOOK THE PLACE OVER.
...DUM DEE...
DUM...

WAIT!

UM...COMMISSIONER, I....I COULDN'T HELP NOTICING THAT *PERFUME* YOU'RE WEARING.

IT'S VERY *BEAUTIFUL.* WHAT'S IT *CALLED?*

HMMPH. WELL, I'M SURE IT'S NOTHING *YOU* COULD AFFORD.

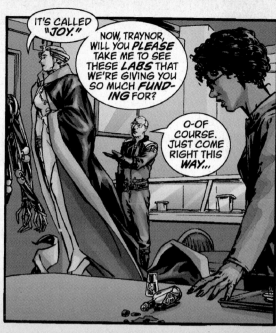

IT'S CALLED *"JOY."*

NOW, TRAYNOR, WILL YOU *PLEASE* TAKE ME TO SEE THESE *LABS* THAT WE'RE GIVING YOU SO MUCH *FUND-ING* FOR?

O-OF COURSE. JUST COME RIGHT THIS *WAY...*

COMMISSIONER ULTIMA, I... OH JESUS.

COMMISSIONER ULTIMA. I'M PLACING YOU UNDER ARREST FOR THE MURDER OF STEFAN *GRACZIK.*

D-DETECTIVE *JACKSON?* YOU'RE OUT OF LINE. I WANT YOU TO GO STRAIGHT TO MY OFFICE, AND...

SIR, NO SIR. IT WAS HER *PERFUME* I SMELLED ON GRACZIK'S BODY, BUT I TRANSLATED IT INTO *MUSIC.*

SHE WAS GRACZIK'S OFF-WORLD *DRUG* CUSTOMER.

SYN...SYN, LOOK, WHAT YOU'RE SAYING, THIS IS...

CAPTAIN, THAT RAID ON *GROMOLKO'S,* THEY KNEW WE WERE *COMING!* SOMEBODY TIPPED THEM *OFF!* SHE...

OH £$%&. CAPTAIN, LOOK *OUT!* SHE'S PACKING....

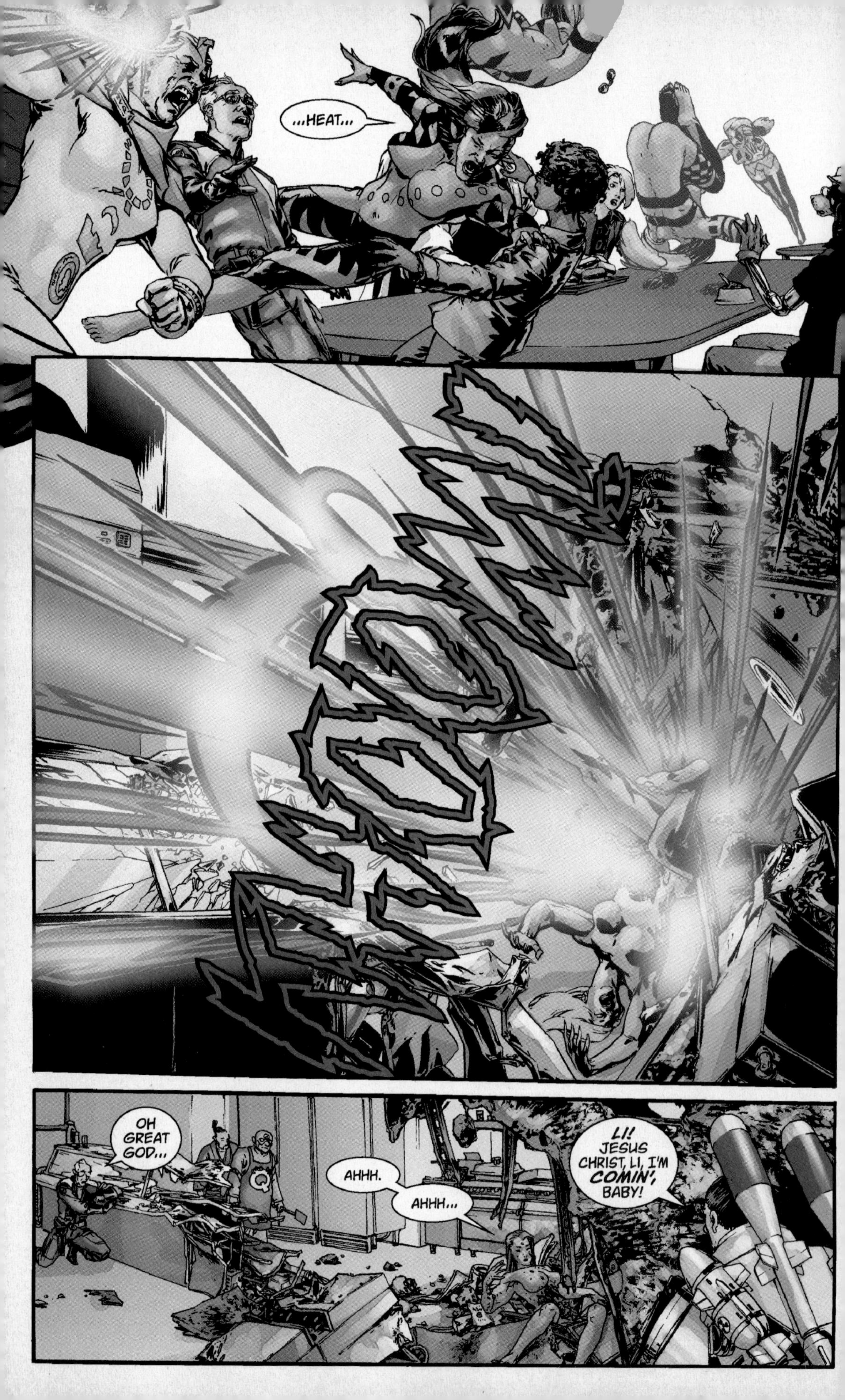
...HEAT...
OH GREAT GOD...
AHHH.
AHHH...
LI! JESUS CHRIST, LI, I'M COMIN', BABY!

STUPID. ALL STUPID. YOU COULD SEE HOW TENSE I WAS. YOU COULD HAVE JUST GIVEN ME THE XENITE, BUT NO...
TH-THIS IS THE FRIGGING COMMISSIONER! WHAT DO WE DO?
HIT HER, BILL. EVERYTHING YOU'VE GOT.
POOM! POOM! BADDADOOM!
LI? AW, LI. IT... IT DOESN'T LOOK TOO BAD. YOU'RE GONNA BE OKAY...
UH...
URH...
IRMA, SHE'S GOING. I'M SORRY. LI'S GOING. SHE...
URHM...
NO! NO, NO, NO!
£&$%& THIS! THIS IS WRONG! THAT BITCH, SHE'S £$%&ING DEAD!
OFFICER WORNOW...?
KTIK
I DON'T CARE WHO SHE IS! I DON'T £$%&ING CARE!
IRMA? WHAT ARE YOU...?
OH GOD.
OFFICER WORNOW, DISARM YOUR NUCLEAR WEAPON AND BACK OFF! NOW, IRMA!
£$%& YOU, HARRY! £$%& YOU! DON'T MAKE ME DO THIS, HARRY...
FOR GOD'S SAKE, SOMEBODY GET ME SOME BACKUP!
IRMA, I'M SORRY. PLEASE, JUST DO IT.
PDOOM! PDOOM! PDOOM!

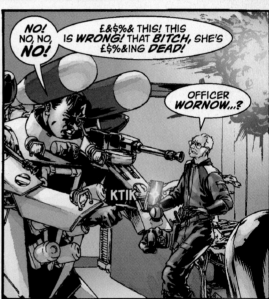

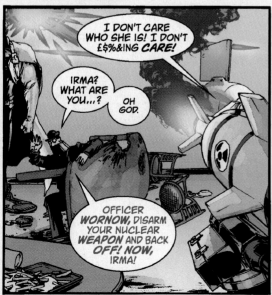

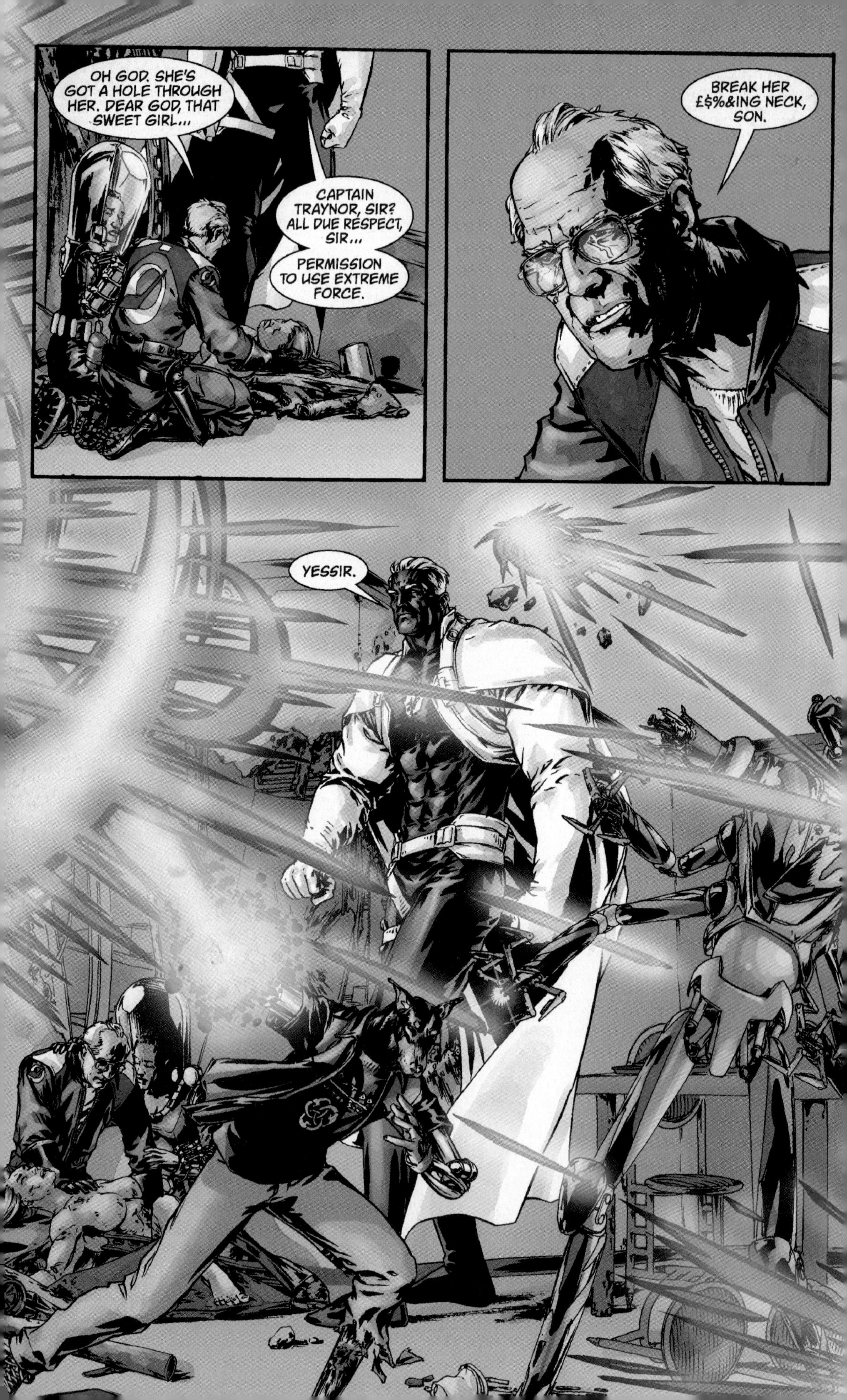
OH GOD. SHE'S GOT A HOLE THROUGH HER. DEAR GOD, THAT SWEET GIRL...
CAPTAIN TRAYNOR, SIR? ALL DUE RESPECT, SIR...
PERMISSION TO USE EXTREME FORCE.
BREAK HER £$%&ING NECK, SON.
YESSIR.

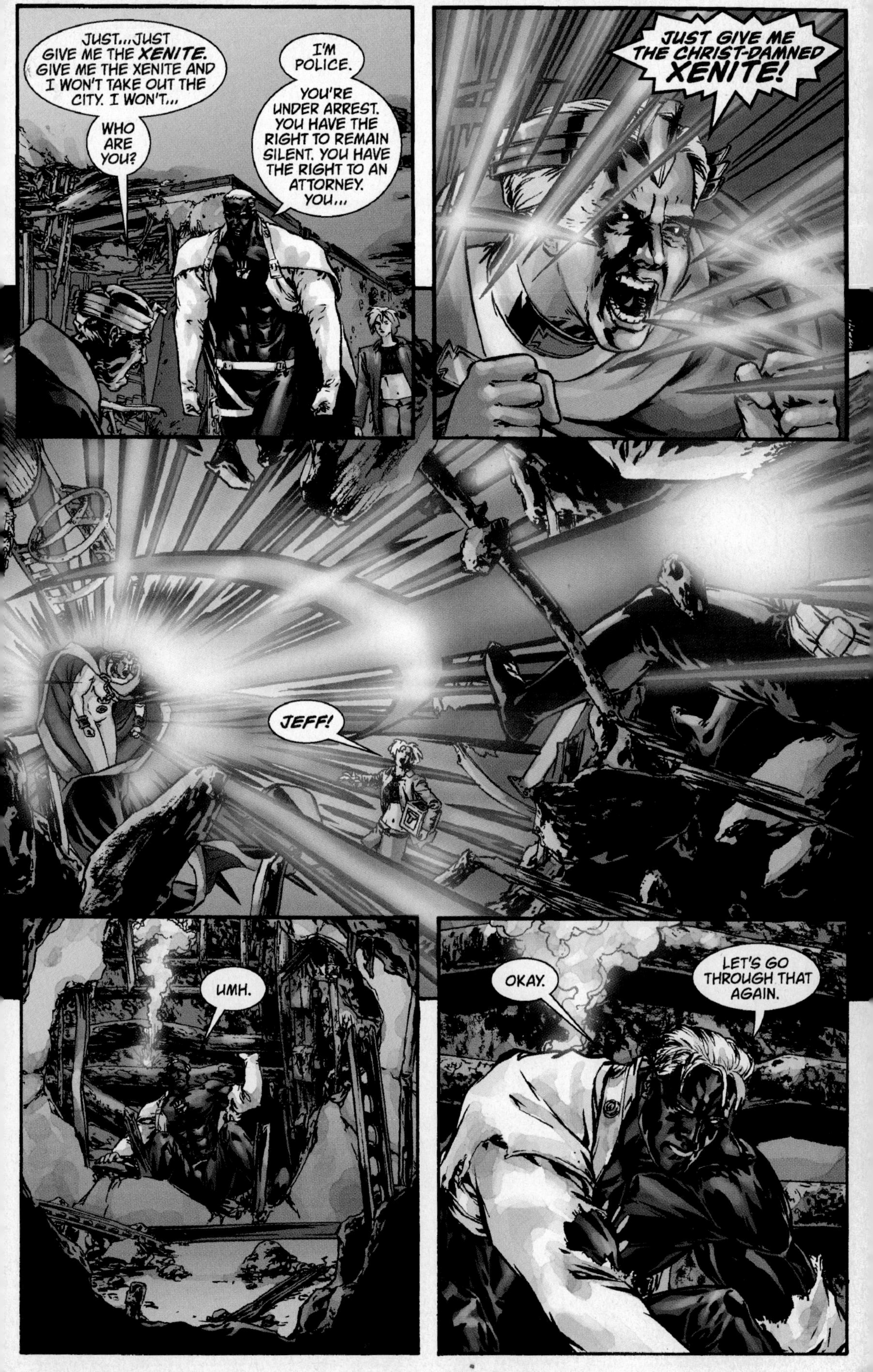
JUST...JUST GIVE ME THE XENITE. GIVE ME THE XENITE AND I WON'T TAKE OUT THE CITY. I WON'T...
WHO ARE YOU?
I'M POLICE.
YOU'RE UNDER ARREST. YOU HAVE THE RIGHT TO REMAIN SILENT. YOU HAVE THE RIGHT TO AN ATTORNEY. YOU...
JUST GIVE ME THE CHRIST-DAMNED XENITE!
JEFF!
UMH.
OKAY.
LET'S GO THROUGH THAT AGAIN.

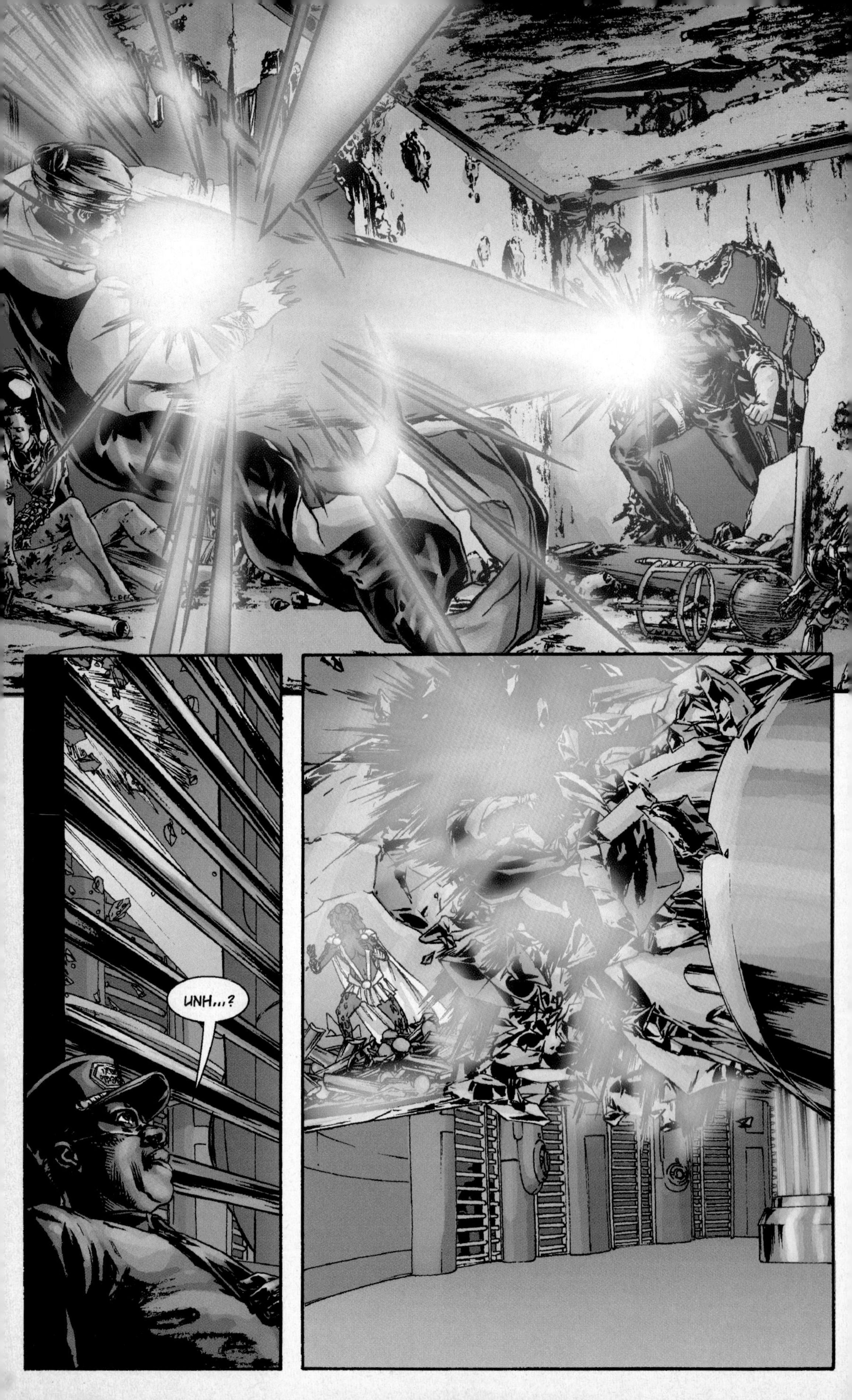
UNH...?

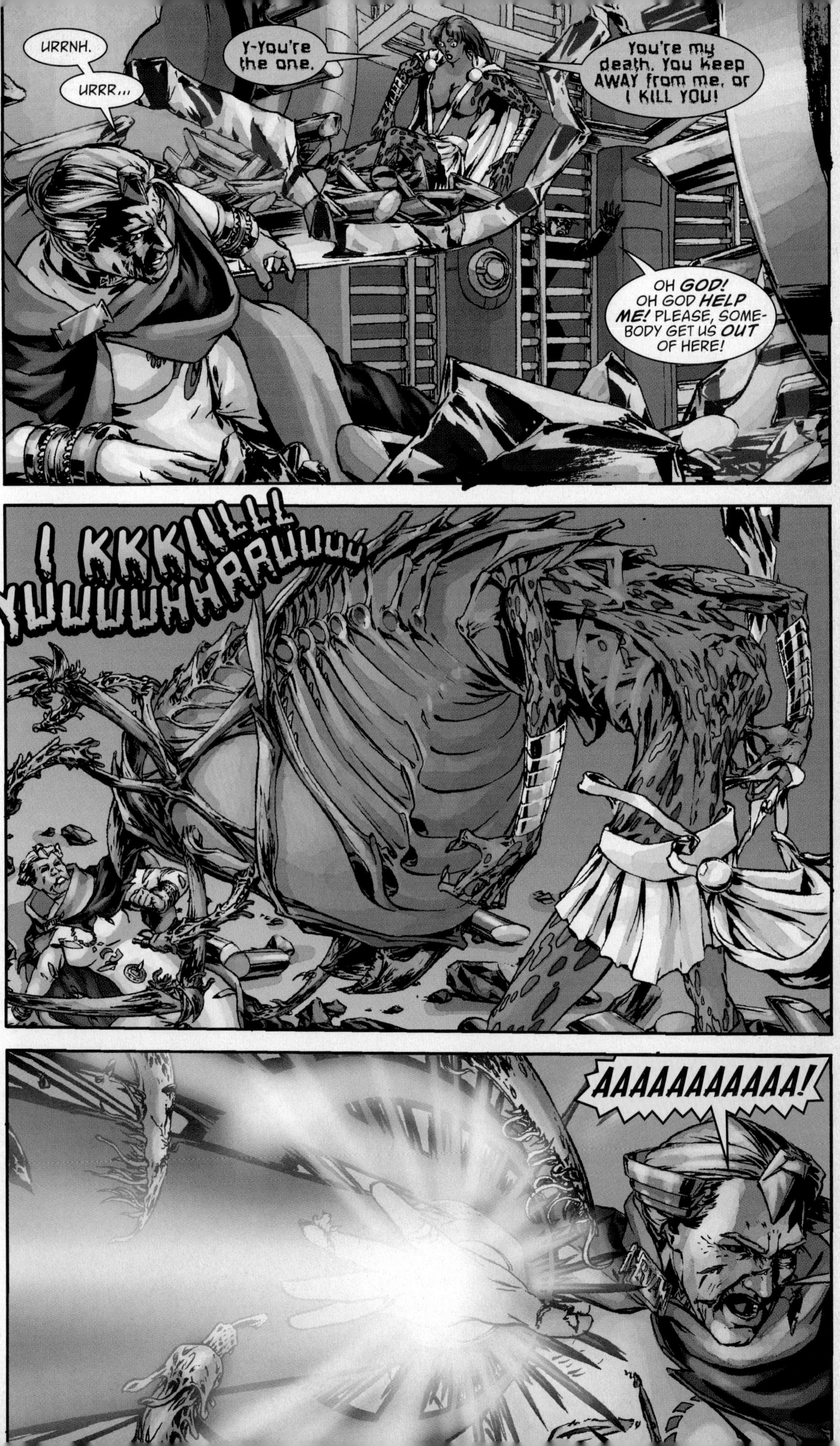
URRNH.
URRR...
Y-You're the one.
You're my death. You keep AWAY from me, or I KILL YOU!
OH GOD! OH GOD HELP ME! PLEASE, SOMEBODY GET US OUT OF HERE!
I KKKIILLL YUUUUUHRRUuuuu
AAAAAAAAAAA!

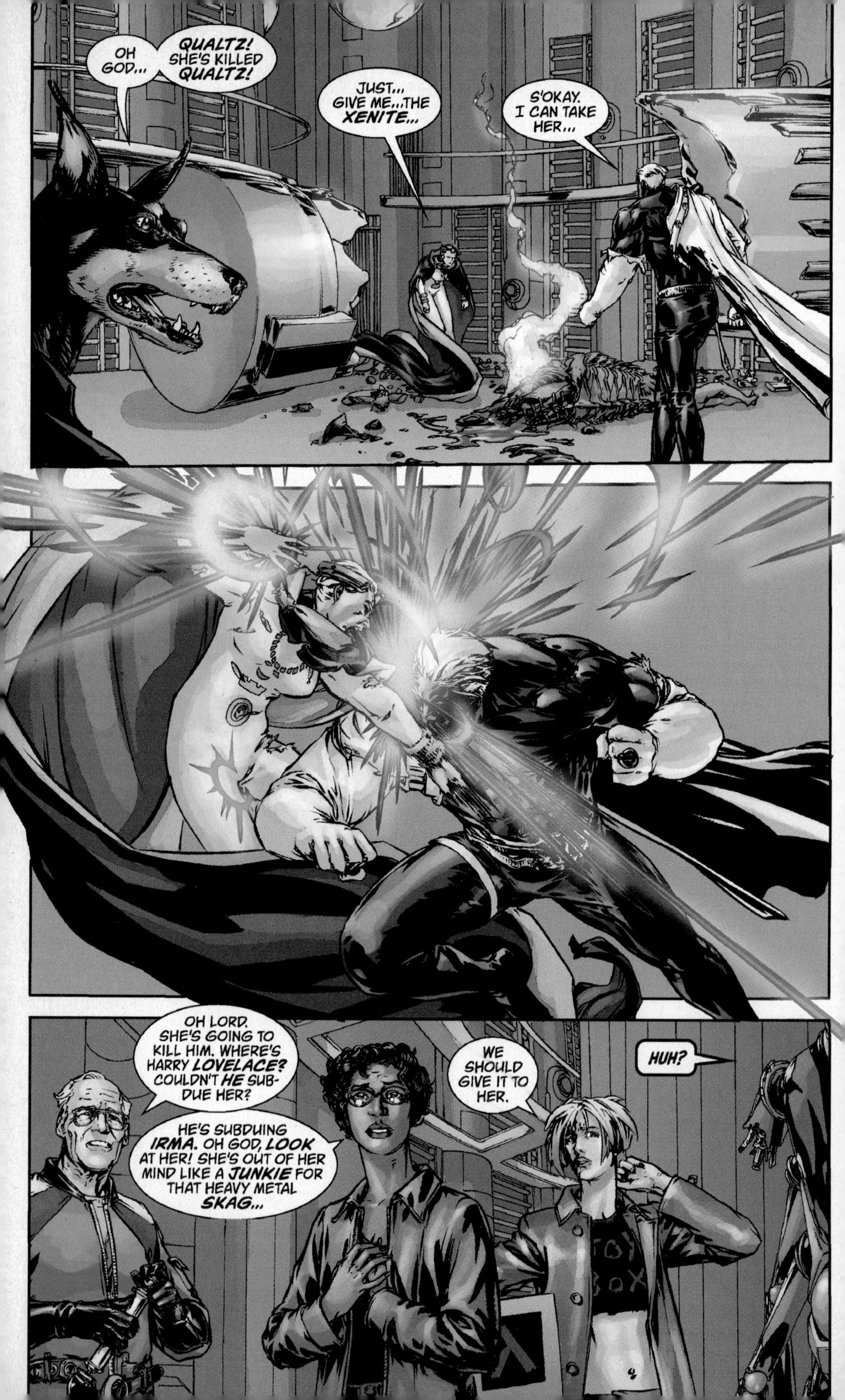
OH GOD...
QUALTZ! SHE'S KILLED QUALTZ!
JUST... GIVE ME... THE XENITE...
S'OKAY. I CAN TAKE HER...
OH LORD. SHE'S GOING TO KILL HIM. WHERE'S HARRY LOVELACE? COULDN'T HE SUBDUE HER?
HE'S SUBDUING IRMA. OH GOD, LOOK AT HER! SHE'S OUT OF HER MIND LIKE A JUNKIE FOR THAT HEAVY METAL SKAG...
WE SHOULD GIVE IT TO HER.
HUH?

EXPLAIN YOURSELF, OFFICER SLINGER...

I MEAN SHE'S *ADDICTED* TO THIS STUFF. WE *GIVE* IT TO HER, MAYBE SHE'LL CALM *DOWN* OR NOD *OFF* OR SOMETHING...

MAYBE SHE'LL *O.D.*

ROBYN'S IDEA SMELLS GOOD TO ME, CAPTAIN...

IF YOU COULD LOAD IT INTO A *SYRINGE* OF SOME SORT, MY GUYS COULD *DELIVER* IT...

OKAY. OKAY, I DON'T HAVE ANY *BETTER* IDEAS. BILL...?

WAY AHEAD OF YOU, CAPTAIN.

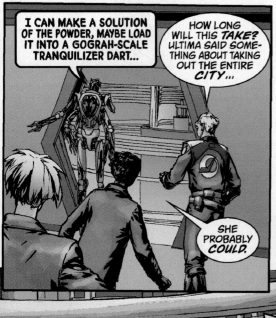

I CAN MAKE A SOLUTION OF THE POWDER, MAYBE LOAD IT INTO A GOGRAH-SCALE TRANQUILIZER DART...

HOW LONG WILL THIS *TAKE?* ULTIMA SAID SOMETHING ABOUT TAKING OUT THE ENTIRE *CITY*...

SHE PROBABLY *COULD.*

I MEAN, FACE IT, IF SHE WANTS TO STOP THIS GETTING BACK TO *GRAND CENTRAL,* SHE'LL HAVE TO TAKE OUT NEOPOLIS...

I'M NEARLY THERE. COUPLE OF MINUTES...

GOD. GOD, I HOPE JEFF CAN HOLD *OUT*...

HHRRRRAAAAAGH!!

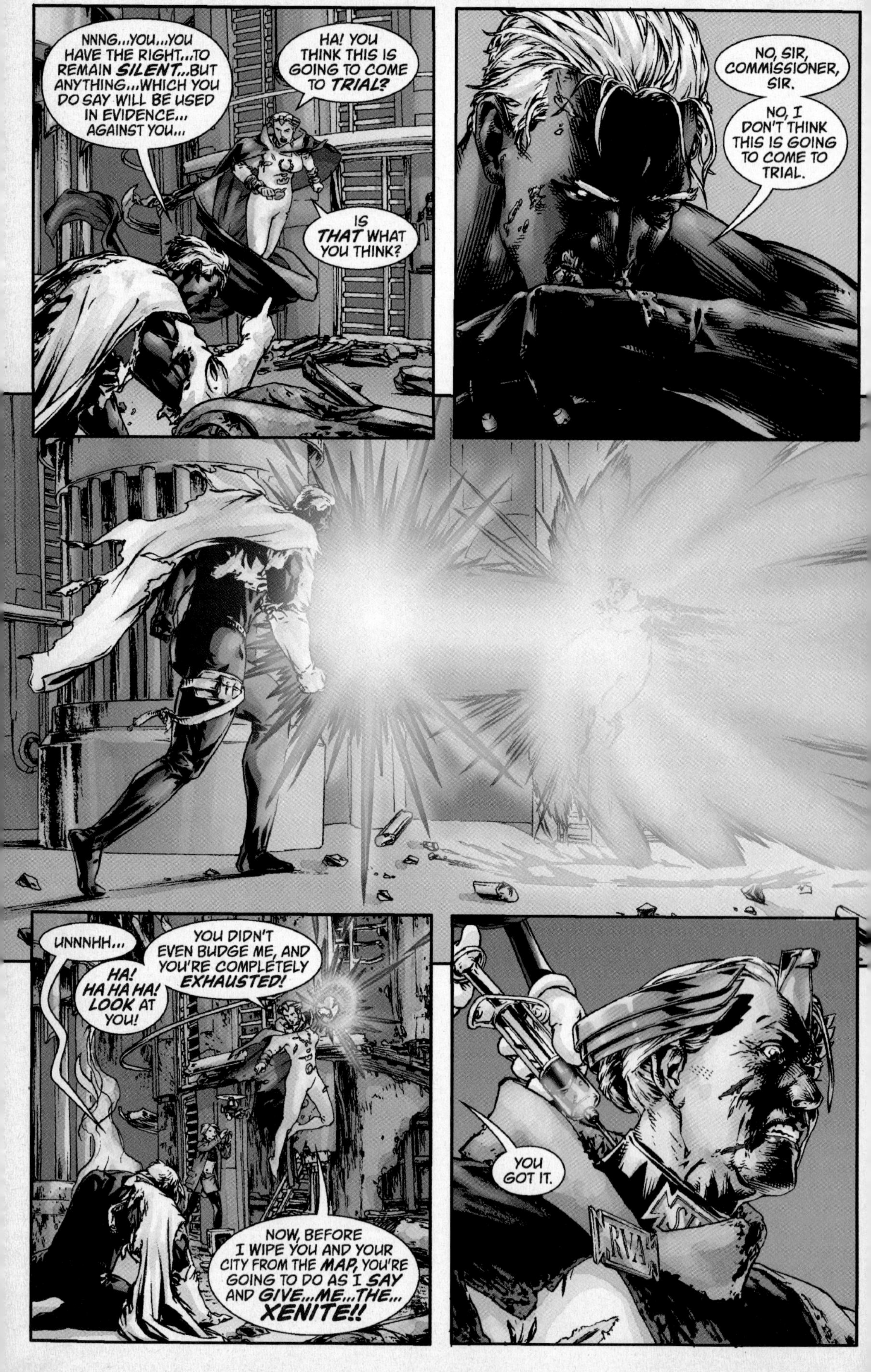
NNNG...YOU...YOU HAVE THE RIGHT...TO REMAIN SILENT...BUT ANYTHING...WHICH YOU DO SAY WILL BE USED IN EVIDENCE... AGAINST YOU...
HA! YOU THINK THIS IS GOING TO COME TO TRIAL?
IS THAT WHAT YOU THINK?
NO, SIR, COMMISSIONER, SIR.
NO, I DON'T THINK THIS IS GOING TO COME TO TRIAL.
UNNNHH...
YOU DIDN'T EVEN BUDGE ME, AND YOU'RE COMPLETELY EXHAUSTED!
HA! HA HA HA! LOOK AT YOU!
NOW, BEFORE I WIPE YOU AND YOUR CITY FROM THE MAP, YOU'RE GOING TO DO AS I SAY AND GIVE...ME...THE... XENITE!!
YOU GOT IT.
RVA

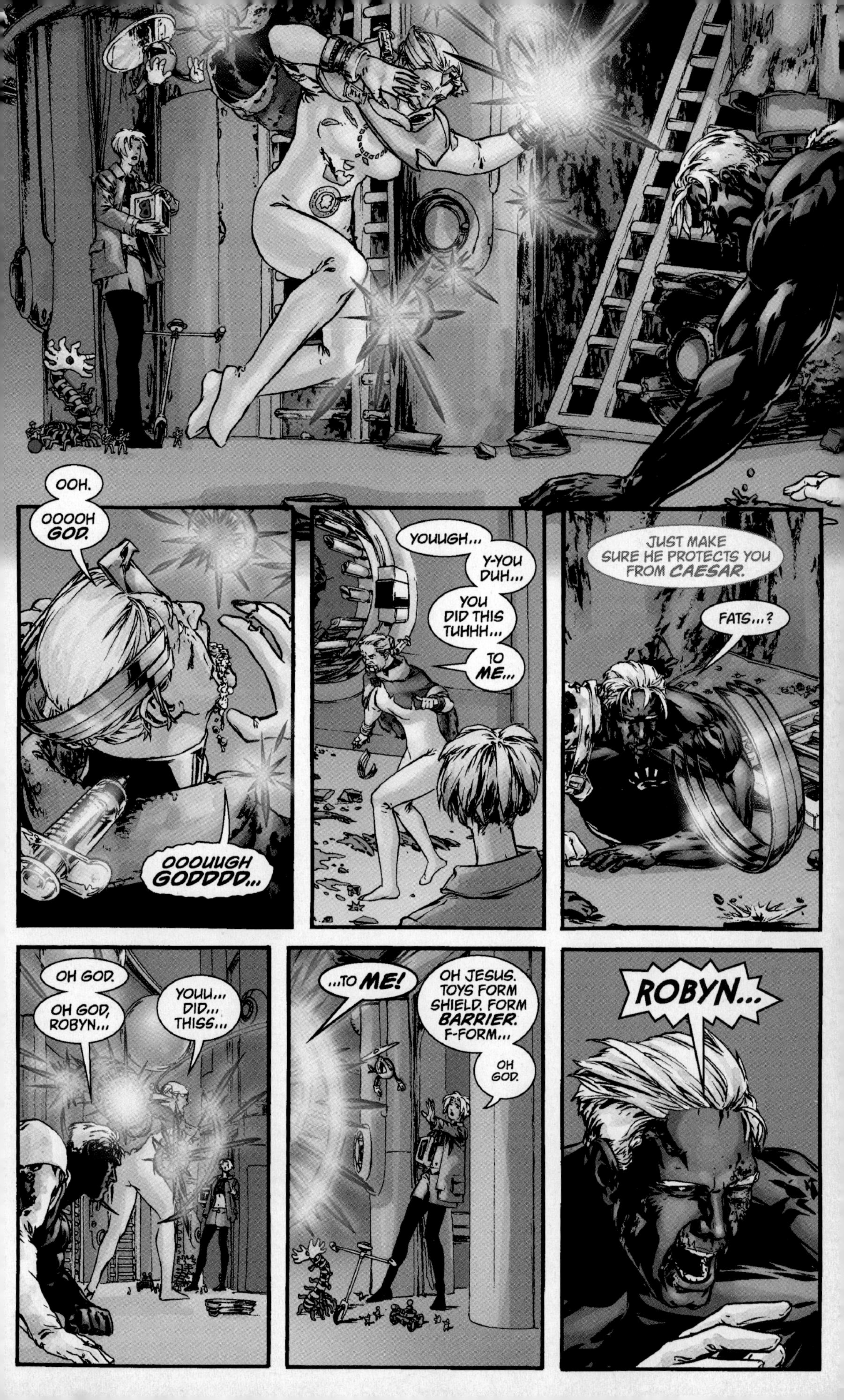
OOH.
OOOOH GOD.
OOOUUGH GODDDD...
YOUUGH...
Y-YOU DUH...
YOU DID THIS TUHHH...
TO ME...
JUST MAKE SURE HE PROTECTS YOU FROM CAESAR.
FATS...?
OH GOD.
OH GOD, ROBYN...
YOUU... DID... THISS...
...TO ME!
OH JESUS. TOYS FORM SHIELD. FORM BARRIER. F-FORM...
OH GOD.
ROBYN...

I'M GONNA *KILL* YOU!

I'M GONNA *KILL* YOU, YOU PIECE OF CRAP JUNKIE SKELL BITCH COP-KILLING...

JEFF, BABY, SHE'S *DEAD.* COME ON. LEAVE IT.

BILL, WE HAVE TO SHIFT THIS *RUBBLE.* SLINGER WAS RIGHT *UNDER* IT...

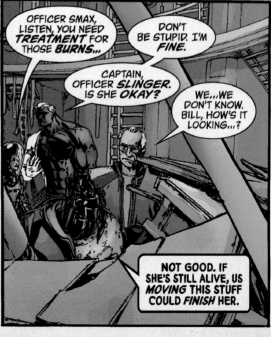

OFFICER SMAX, LISTEN, YOU NEED *TREATMENT* FOR THOSE *BURNS*...

DON'T BE STUPID. I'M *FINE.*

CAPTAIN, OFFICER *SLINGER.* IS SHE *OKAY?*

WE...WE DON'T KNOW. BILL, HOW'S IT LOOKING...?

NOT GOOD. IF SHE'S STILL ALIVE, US *MOVING* THIS STUFF COULD *FINISH* HER.

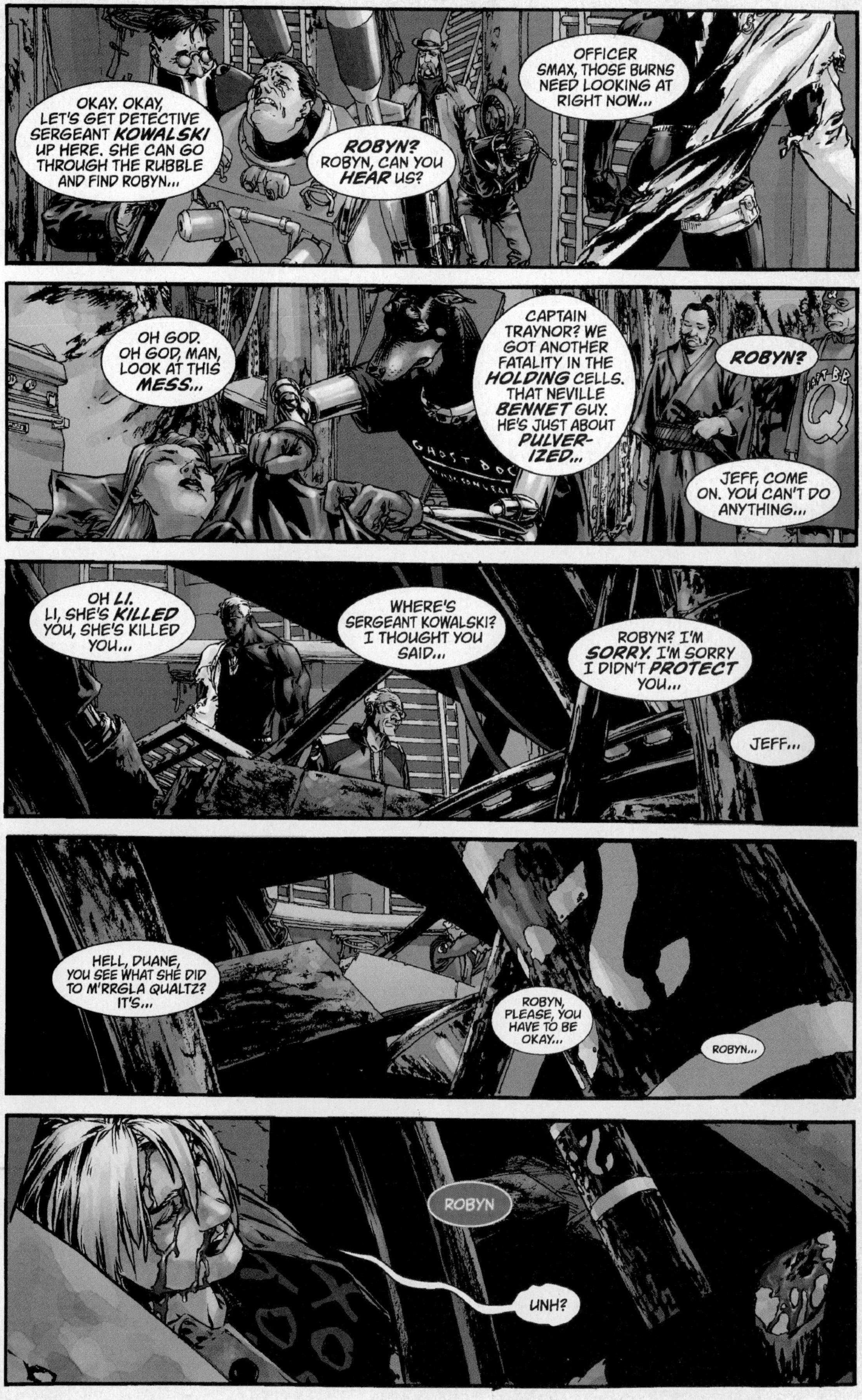
OKAY. OKAY, LET'S GET DETECTIVE SERGEANT KOWALSKI UP HERE. SHE CAN GO THROUGH THE RUBBLE AND FIND ROBYN...
ROBYN? ROBYN, CAN YOU HEAR US?
OFFICER SMAX, THOSE BURNS NEED LOOKING AT RIGHT NOW...
OH GOD. OH GOD, MAN, LOOK AT THIS MESS...
CAPTAIN TRAYNOR? WE GOT ANOTHER FATALITY IN THE HOLDING CELLS. THAT NEVILLE BENNET GUY. HE'S JUST ABOUT PULVER-IZED...
ROBYN?
JEFF, COME ON. YOU CAN'T DO ANYTHING...
OH LI. LI, SHE'S KILLED YOU, SHE'S KILLED YOU...
WHERE'S SERGEANT KOWALSKI? I THOUGHT YOU SAID...
ROBYN? I'M SORRY. I'M SORRY I DIDN'T PROTECT YOU...
JEFF...
HELL, DUANE, YOU SEE WHAT SHE DID TO M'RRGLA QUALTZ? IT'S...
ROBYN, PLEASE, YOU HAVE TO BE OKAY...
ROBYN...
ROBYN
UNH?

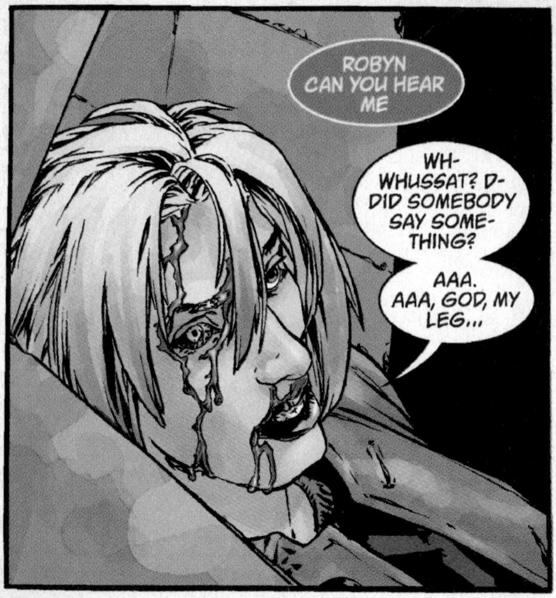
ROBYN CAN YOU HEAR ME
WH-WHUSSAT? D-DID SOMEBODY SAY SOME-THING?
AAA. AAA, GOD, MY LEG...

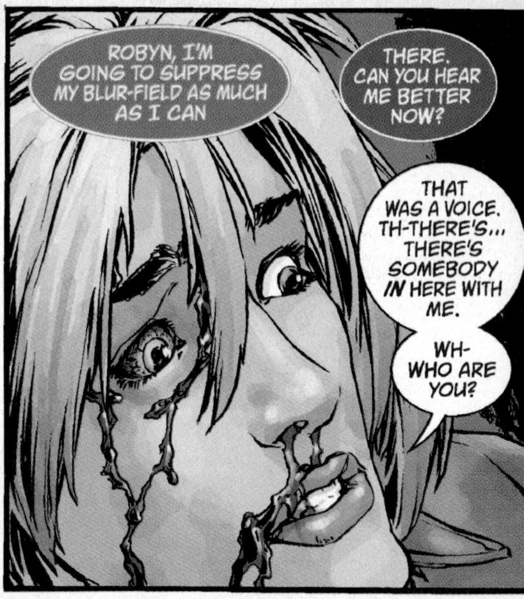
ROBYN, I'M GOING TO SUPPRESS MY BLUR-FIELD AS MUCH AS I CAN
THERE. CAN YOU HEAR ME BETTER NOW?
THAT WAS A VOICE. TH-THERE'S... THERE'S SOMEBODY *IN* HERE WITH ME.
WH-WHO ARE YOU?

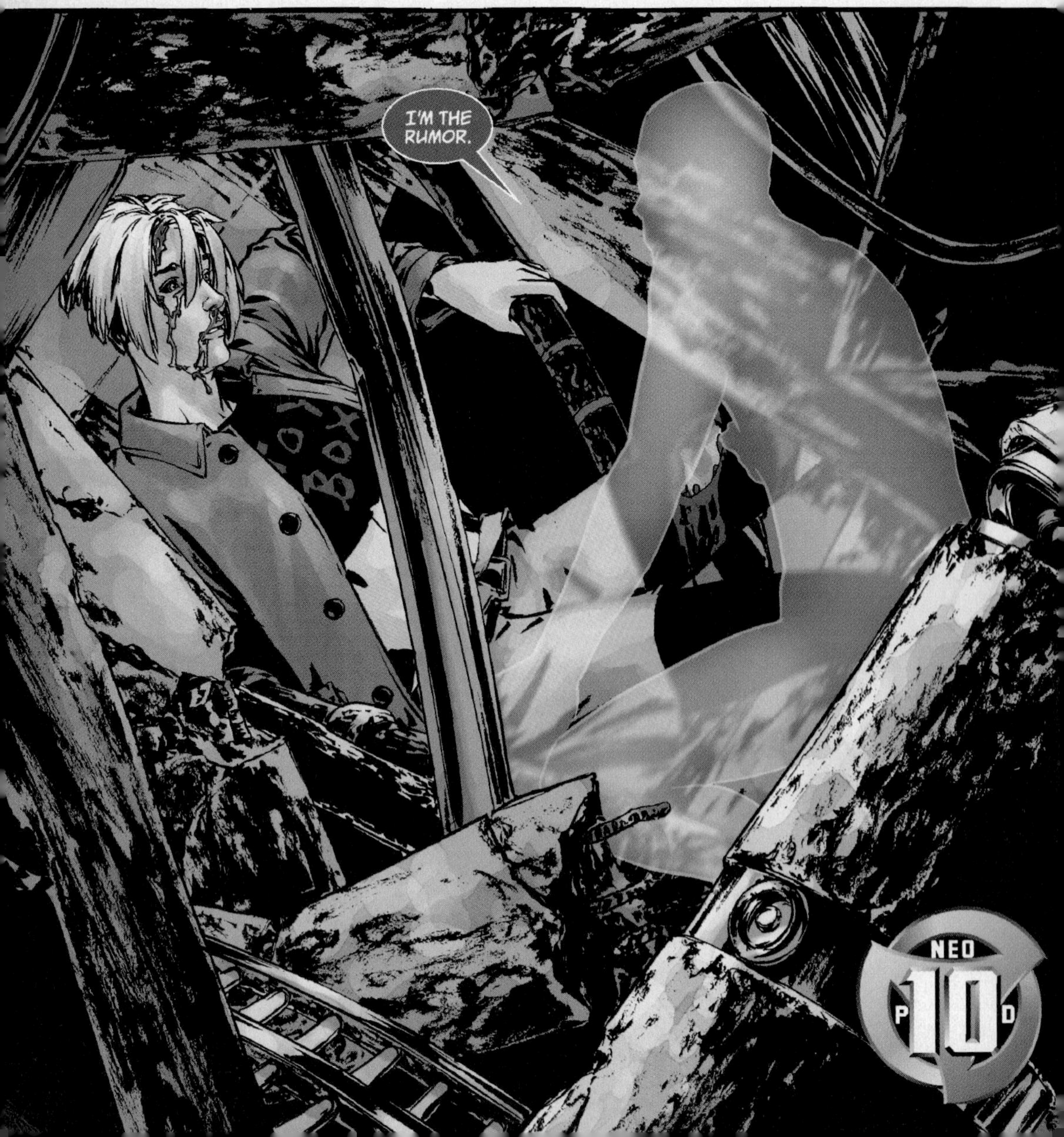
I'M THE RUMOR.

CHAPTER FOUR

ON THE DOCKET:
Officer Joe Pi gets a cold reception,
Shock-Headed Peter misses the joke,
and Irma Geddon brings work home.

Cover art:
Gene Ha and
Zander Cannon

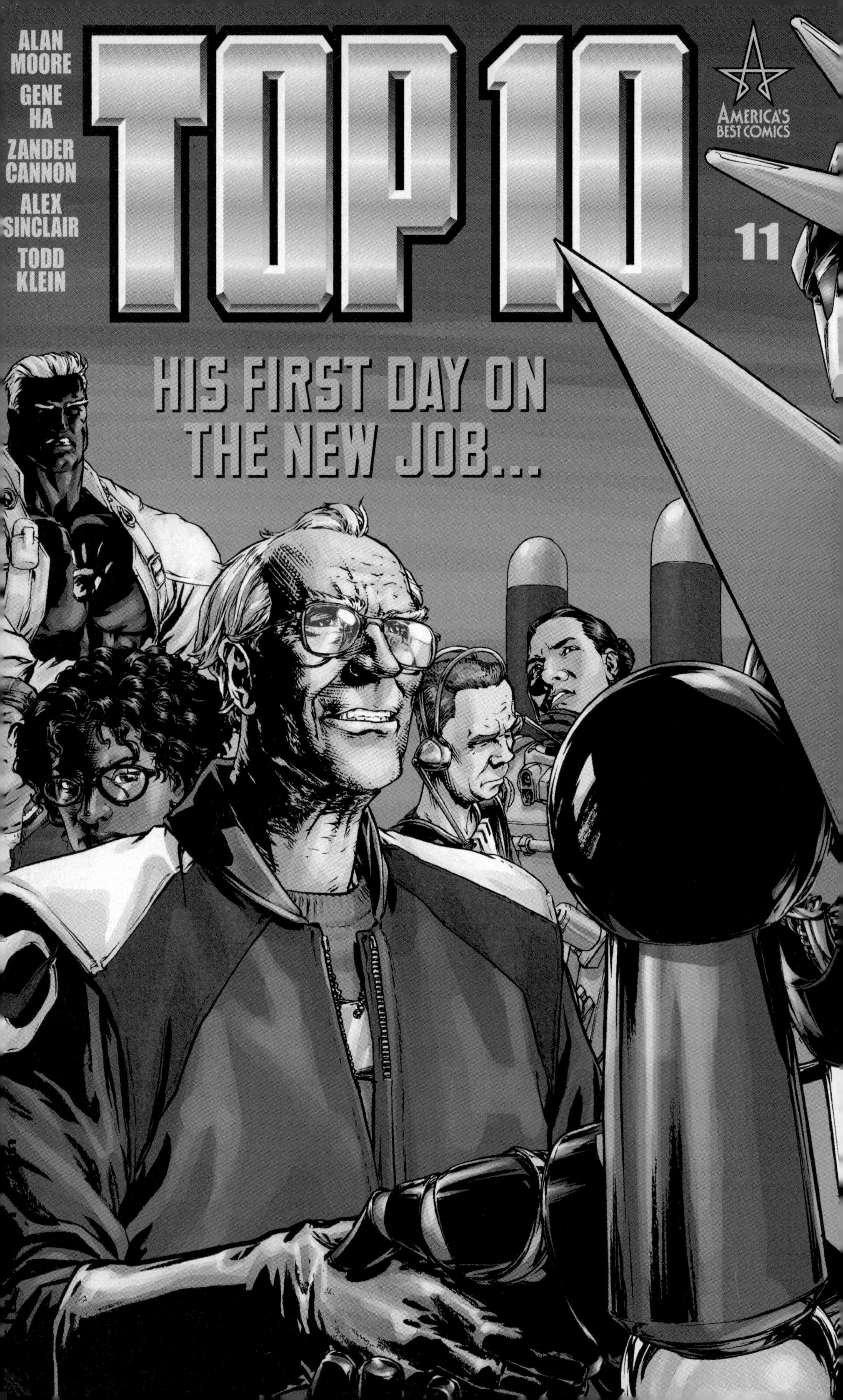
ALAN MOORE
GENE HA
ZANDER CANNON
ALEX SINCLAIR
TODD KLEIN
TOP 10
AMERICA'S BEST COMICS
11
HIS FIRST DAY ON THE NEW JOB...

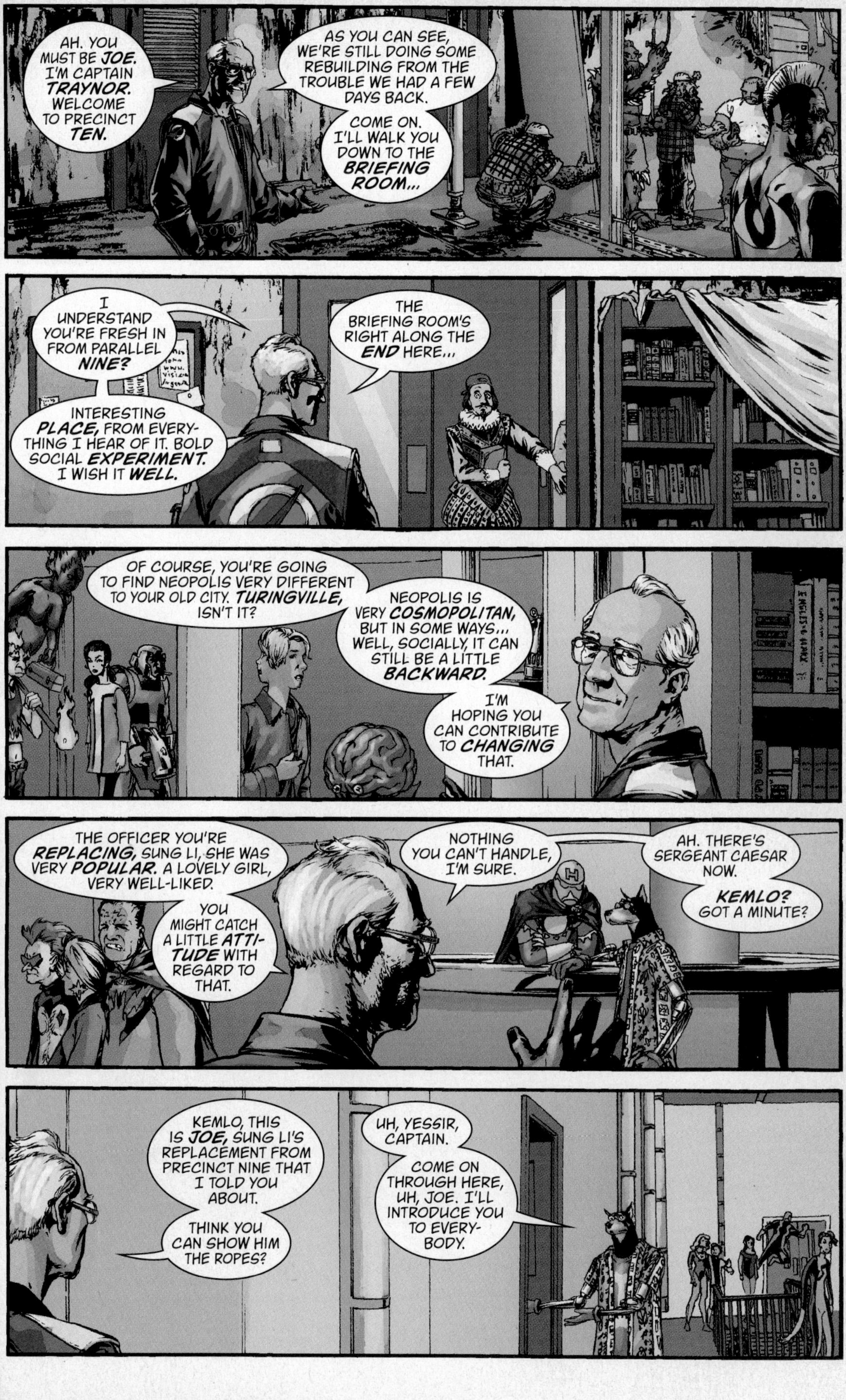
AH. YOU MUST BE JOE. I'M CAPTAIN TRAYNOR. WELCOME TO PRECINCT TEN.
AS YOU CAN SEE, WE'RE STILL DOING SOME REBUILDING FROM THE TROUBLE WE HAD A FEW DAYS BACK.
COME ON. I'LL WALK YOU DOWN TO THE BRIEFING ROOM...
I UNDERSTAND YOU'RE FRESH IN FROM PARALLEL NINE?
INTERESTING PLACE, FROM EVERYTHING I HEAR OF IT. BOLD SOCIAL EXPERIMENT. I WISH IT WELL.
THE BRIEFING ROOM'S RIGHT ALONG THE END HERE...
OF COURSE, YOU'RE GOING TO FIND NEOPOLIS VERY DIFFERENT TO YOUR OLD CITY. TURINGVILLE, ISN'T IT?
NEOPOLIS IS VERY COSMOPOLITAN, BUT IN SOME WAYS... WELL, SOCIALLY, IT CAN STILL BE A LITTLE BACKWARD.
I'M HOPING YOU CAN CONTRIBUTE TO CHANGING THAT.
THE OFFICER YOU'RE REPLACING, SUNG LI, SHE WAS VERY POPULAR. A LOVELY GIRL, VERY WELL-LIKED.
YOU MIGHT CATCH A LITTLE ATTITUDE WITH REGARD TO THAT.
NOTHING YOU CAN'T HANDLE, I'M SURE.
AH. THERE'S SERGEANT CAESAR NOW.
KEMLO? GOT A MINUTE?
KEMLO, THIS IS JOE, SUNG LI'S REPLACEMENT FROM PRECINCT NINE THAT I TOLD YOU ABOUT.
THINK YOU CAN SHOW HIM THE ROPES?
UH, YESSIR, CAPTAIN.
COME ON THROUGH HERE, UH, JOE. I'LL INTRODUCE YOU TO EVERYBODY.

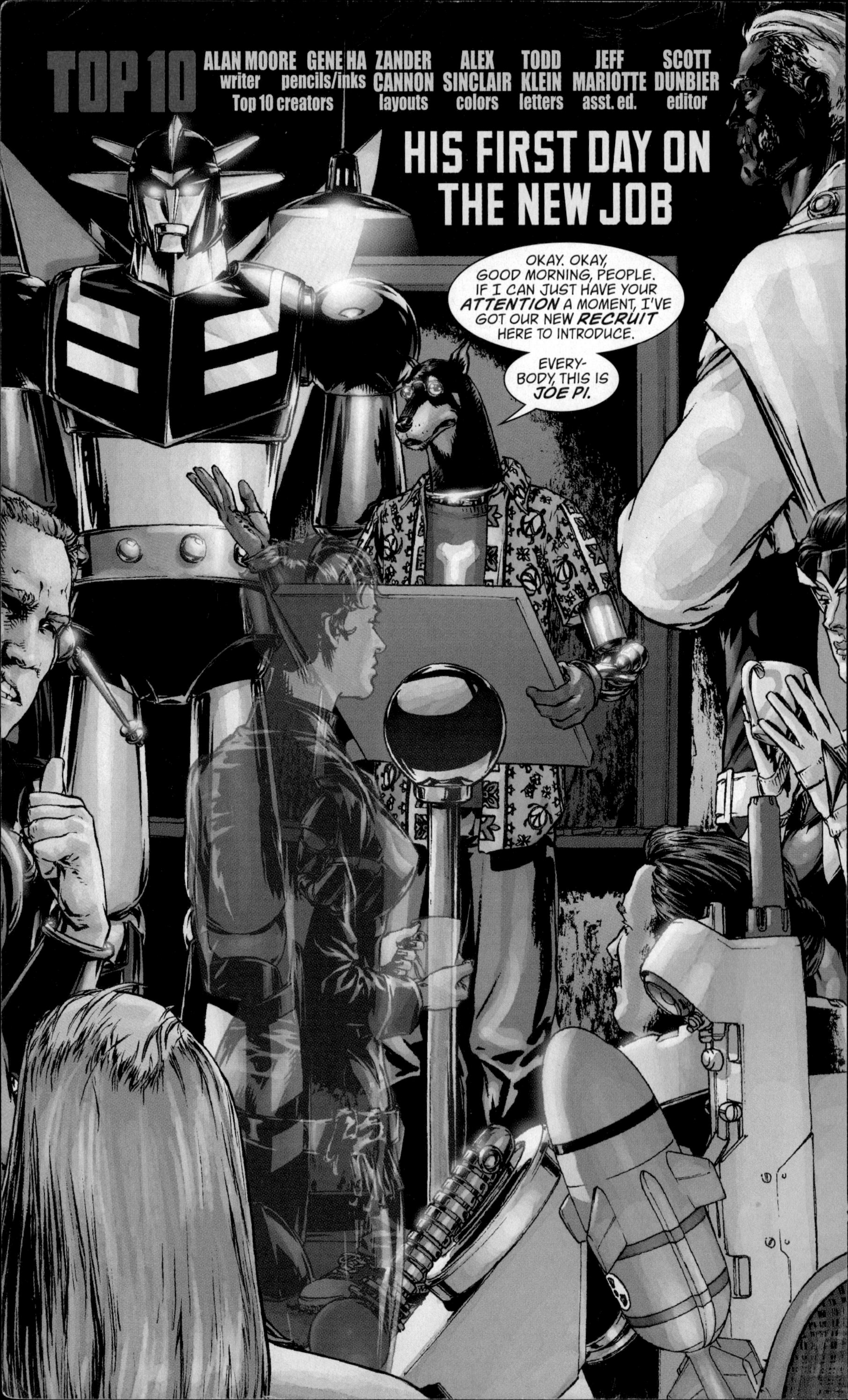
TOP 10
ALAN MOORE writer
GENE HA pencils/inks
Top 10 creators
ZANDER CANNON layouts
ALEX SINCLAIR colors
TODD KLEIN letters
JEFF MARIOTTE asst. ed.
SCOTT DUNBIER editor
HIS FIRST DAY ON THE NEW JOB
OKAY. OKAY, GOOD MORNING, PEOPLE. IF I CAN JUST HAVE YOUR ATTENTION A MOMENT, I'VE GOT OUR NEW RECRUIT HERE TO INTRODUCE.
EVERY-BODY, THIS IS JOE PI.

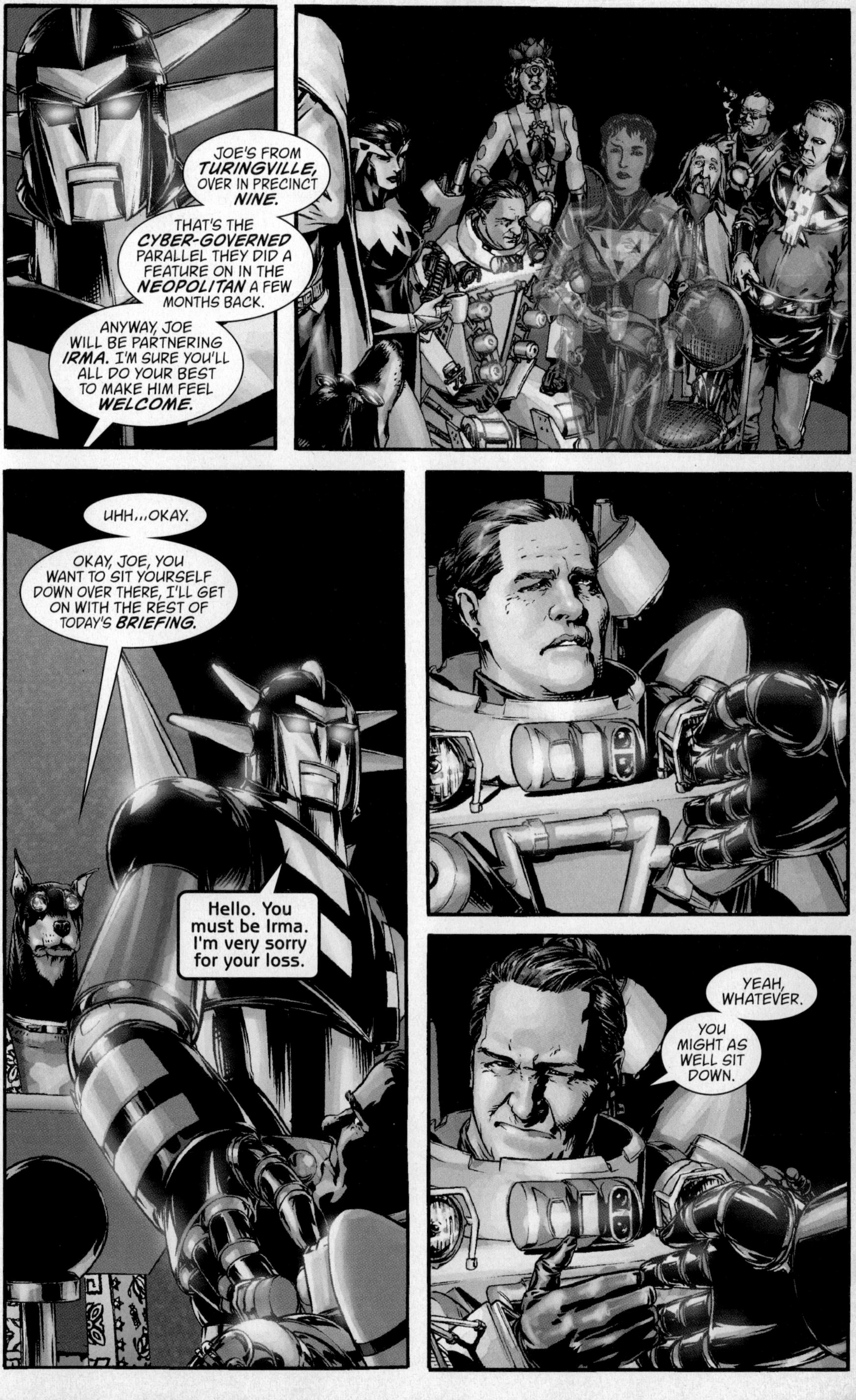
JOE'S FROM TURINGVILLE, OVER IN PRECINCT NINE.
THAT'S THE CYBER-GOVERNED PARALLEL THEY DID A FEATURE ON IN THE NEOPOLITAN A FEW MONTHS BACK.
ANYWAY, JOE WILL BE PARTNERING IRMA. I'M SURE YOU'LL ALL DO YOUR BEST TO MAKE HIM FEEL WELCOME.
UHH...OKAY.
OKAY, JOE, YOU WANT TO SIT YOURSELF DOWN OVER THERE, I'LL GET ON WITH THE REST OF TODAY'S BRIEFING.
Hello. You must be Irma. I'm very sorry for your loss.
YEAH, WHATEVER.
YOU MIGHT AS WELL SIT DOWN.

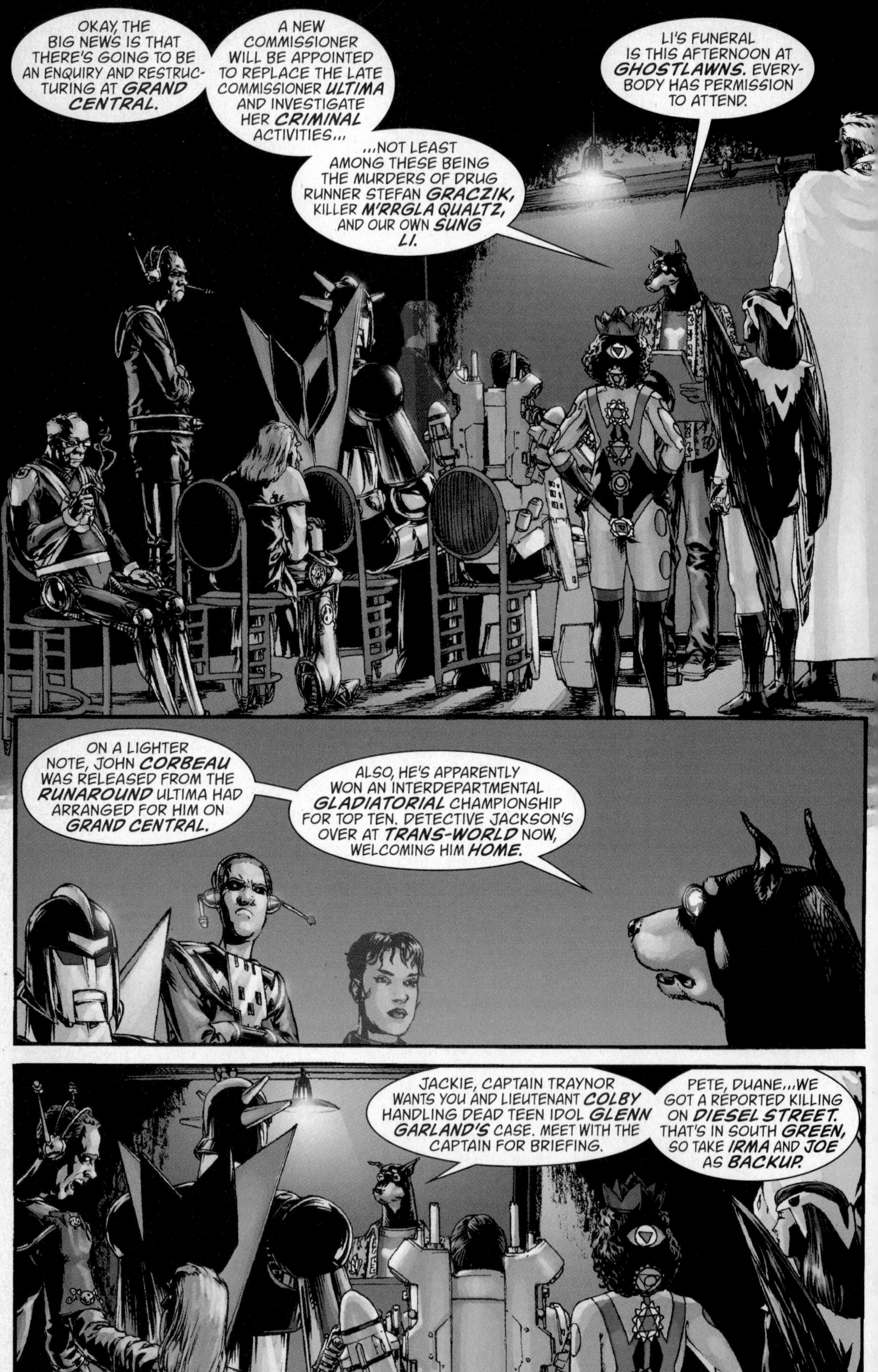
OKAY, THE BIG NEWS IS THAT THERE'S GOING TO BE AN ENQUIRY AND RESTRUCTURING AT GRAND CENTRAL.
A NEW COMMISSIONER WILL BE APPOINTED TO REPLACE THE LATE COMMISSIONER ULTIMA AND INVESTIGATE HER CRIMINAL ACTIVITIES...
...NOT LEAST AMONG THESE BEING THE MURDERS OF DRUG RUNNER STEFAN GRACZIK, KILLER M'RRGLA QUALTZ, AND OUR OWN SUNG LI.
LI'S FUNERAL IS THIS AFTERNOON AT GHOSTLAWNS. EVERYBODY HAS PERMISSION TO ATTEND.
ON A LIGHTER NOTE, JOHN CORBEAU WAS RELEASED FROM THE RUNAROUND ULTIMA HAD ARRANGED FOR HIM ON GRAND CENTRAL.
ALSO, HE'S APPARENTLY WON AN INTERDEPARTMENTAL GLADIATORIAL CHAMPIONSHIP FOR TOP TEN. DETECTIVE JACKSON'S OVER AT TRANS-WORLD NOW, WELCOMING HIM HOME.
JACKIE, CAPTAIN TRAYNOR WANTS YOU AND LIEUTENANT COLBY HANDLING DEAD TEEN IDOL GLENN GARLAND'S CASE. MEET WITH THE CAPTAIN FOR BRIEFING.
PETE, DUANE...WE GOT A REPORTED KILLING ON DIESEL STREET. THAT'S IN SOUTH GREEN, SO TAKE IRMA AND JOE AS BACKUP.

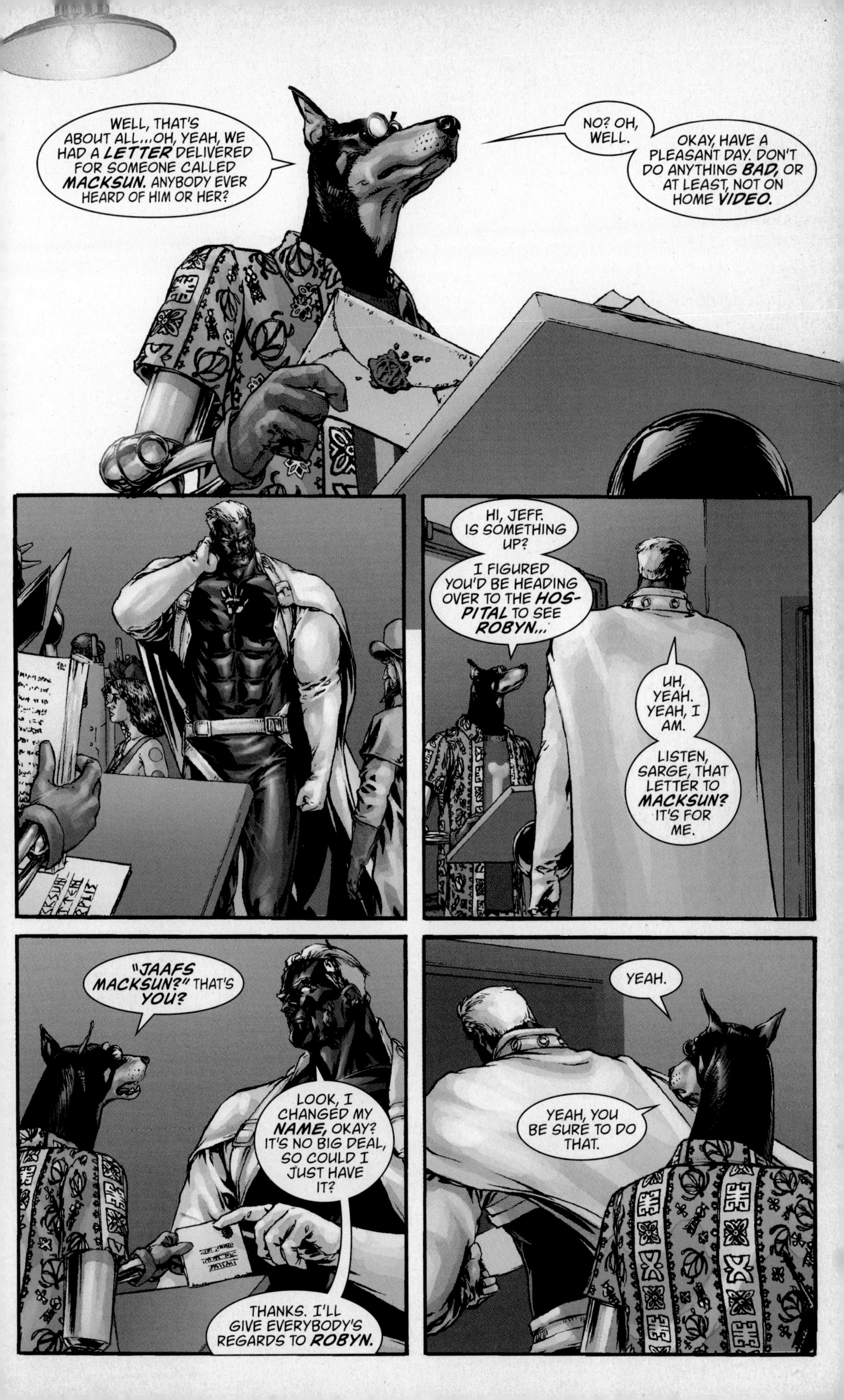

WELL, THAT'S ABOUT ALL...OH, YEAH, WE HAD A LETTER DELIVERED FOR SOMEONE CALLED MACKSUN. ANYBODY EVER HEARD OF HIM OR HER?
NO? OH, WELL.
OKAY, HAVE A PLEASANT DAY. DON'T DO ANYTHING BAD, OR AT LEAST, NOT ON HOME VIDEO.
HI, JEFF. IS SOMETHING UP?
I FIGURED YOU'D BE HEADING OVER TO THE HOSPITAL TO SEE ROBYN...
UH, YEAH. YEAH, I AM.
LISTEN, SARGE, THAT LETTER TO MACKSUN? IT'S FOR ME.
"JAAFS MACKSUN?" THAT'S YOU?
LOOK, I CHANGED MY NAME, OKAY? IT'S NO BIG DEAL, SO COULD I JUST HAVE IT?
THANKS. I'LL GIVE EVERYBODY'S REGARDS TO ROBYN.
YEAH.
YEAH, YOU BE SURE TO DO THAT.

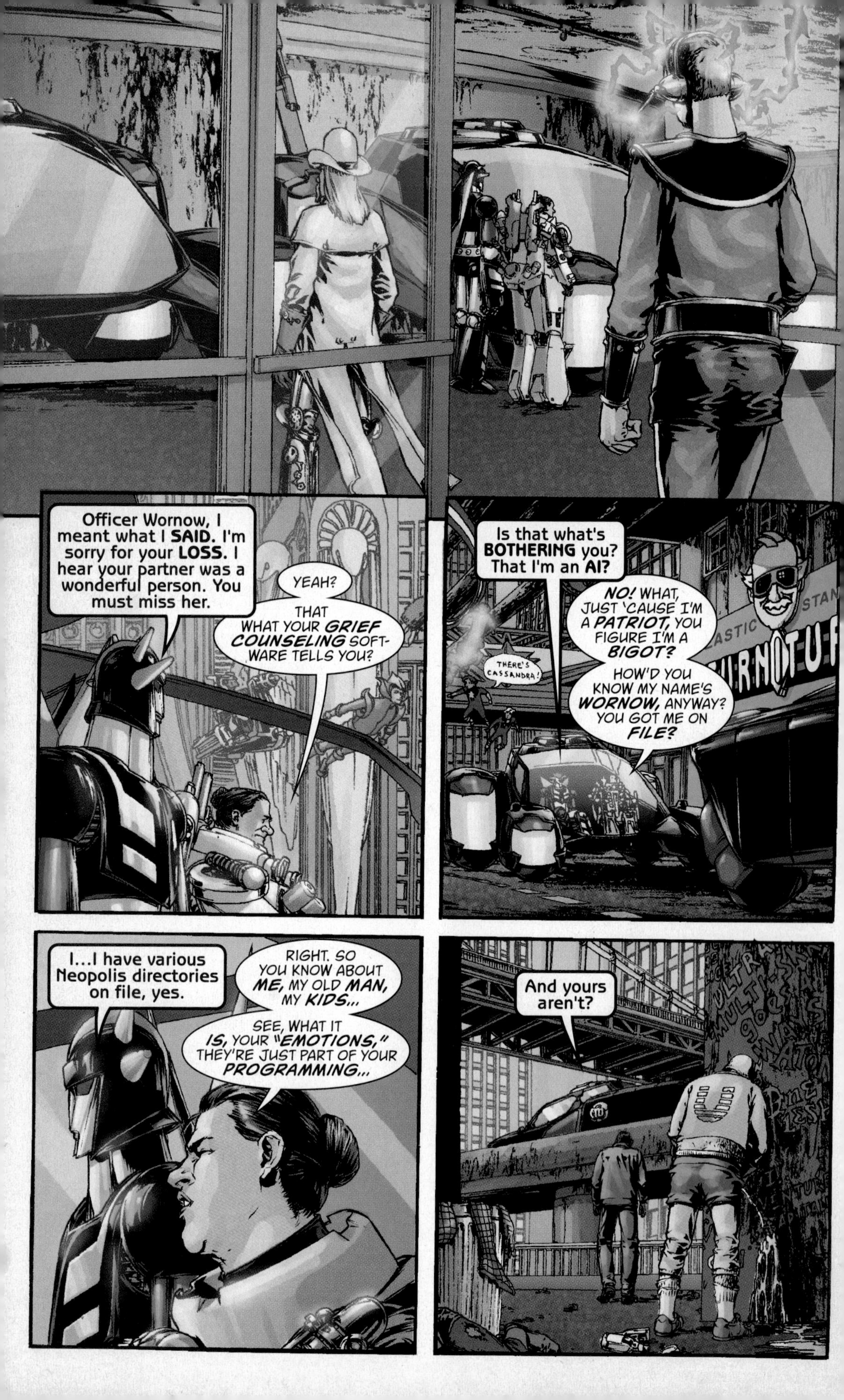

Officer Wornow, I meant what I SAID. I'm sorry for your LOSS. I hear your partner was a wonderful person. You must miss her.
YEAH?
THAT WHAT YOUR GRIEF COUNSELING SOFT-WARE TELLS YOU?
Is that what's BOTHERING you? That I'm an AI?
NO! WHAT, JUST 'CAUSE I'M A PATRIOT, YOU FIGURE I'M A BIGOT?
HOW'D YOU KNOW MY NAME'S WORNOW, ANYWAY? YOU GOT ME ON FILE?
THERE'S CASSANDRA!
I...I have various Neopolis directories on file, yes.
RIGHT. SO YOU KNOW ABOUT ME, MY OLD MAN, MY KIDS...
SEE, WHAT IT IS, YOUR "EMOTIONS," THEY'RE JUST PART OF YOUR PROGRAMMING...
And yours aren't?

LISTEN, YOU DON'T KNOW WHAT I FEEL LIKE. THERE AIN'T *BINARY CODE* FOR WHAT I FEEL LIKE, OKAY?

NOW JUST LET ME DRIVE. THIS IS SOUTH GREEN COMIN' UP HERE...

YES. I'M TOLD THIS IS GANG TERRITORY.

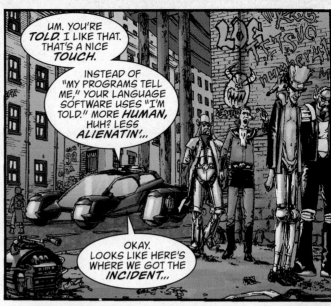

UM. YOU'RE *TOLD*. I LIKE THAT. THAT'S A NICE *TOUCH*.

INSTEAD OF "MY PROGRAMS TELL ME," YOUR LANGUAGE SOFTWARE USES "I'M TOLD." MORE *HUMAN*, HUH? LESS *ALIENATIN'*...

OKAY. LOOKS LIKE HERE'S WHERE WE GOT THE *INCIDENT*...

HI, GUYS. HOW'S IT LOOK?

HEY, IRMA, HEY JOE...

HUH. "HEY, JOE, WHERE YA GOIN' WITH THAT BATTERY UP YER BUTT?"

HI, IRMA. I GUESS OUR *D.O.A.* IS THIS MESS ON THE *SIDEWALK*...

I MEAN, IT'S SOME *BUBBLEGUM BOY* OR OTHER, MAYBE GOT DONE IN BY *GANG-BANGERS*. WE BETTER RADIO *JANUS* FOR AN *ID* CHECK...

It's okay, Officer Cheney, I've got that. This is Trent Edison Teller. His apartment's here on Diesel Street.

YEAH? WELL OFFICER *PIE-TIN*, TELL YOU WHAT, MAYBE I'LL CHECK THAT WITH JANUS *ANYWAY*, HUH?

PETE, SHUT THE £$%& UP. WHY'D YOU WANNA CALL *JANUS*? SHE'S JUST GONNA CHECK IT AGAINST THE SAME PROGRAM *HE'S* GOT...

Look! They got a SPAMBO!

HEY! SPAMBO! They let you use the SHAVER SOCKET in their WASHROOM?

Sure.

Incidentally, that DAT you're stored on?

It will gradually lose its information. Me, I'm on a Trillion-byte Cube.

HEY! WHAT ARE YOU DOING, HANDLING THE BODY LIKE THAT?

Wha'd he say?

I dunno. >ZZT< Some Trilobite Cube @#&$. >ZZT<

With respect, why shouldn't I? I don't leave contaminating fingerprints.

Plus, I can suction up particles for immediate micro-analysis.

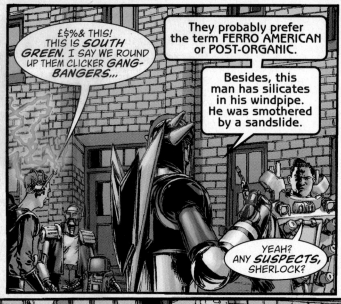

£$%& THIS! THIS IS SOUTH GREEN. I SAY WE ROUND UP THEM CLICKER GANG-BANGERS...

They probably prefer the term FERRO AMERICAN or POST-ORGANIC.

Besides, this man has silicates in his windpipe. He was smothered by a sandslide.

YEAH? ANY SUSPECTS, SHERLOCK?

Listen, I'll be right out.

And I don't mean to step on any toes here. It's just that I'm told how to handle situations like this.

HUH? SITUATIONS LIKE WHAT? WHERE'S IT GOIN'?

PETE, BUDDY, YOU ARE RILIN' ME.

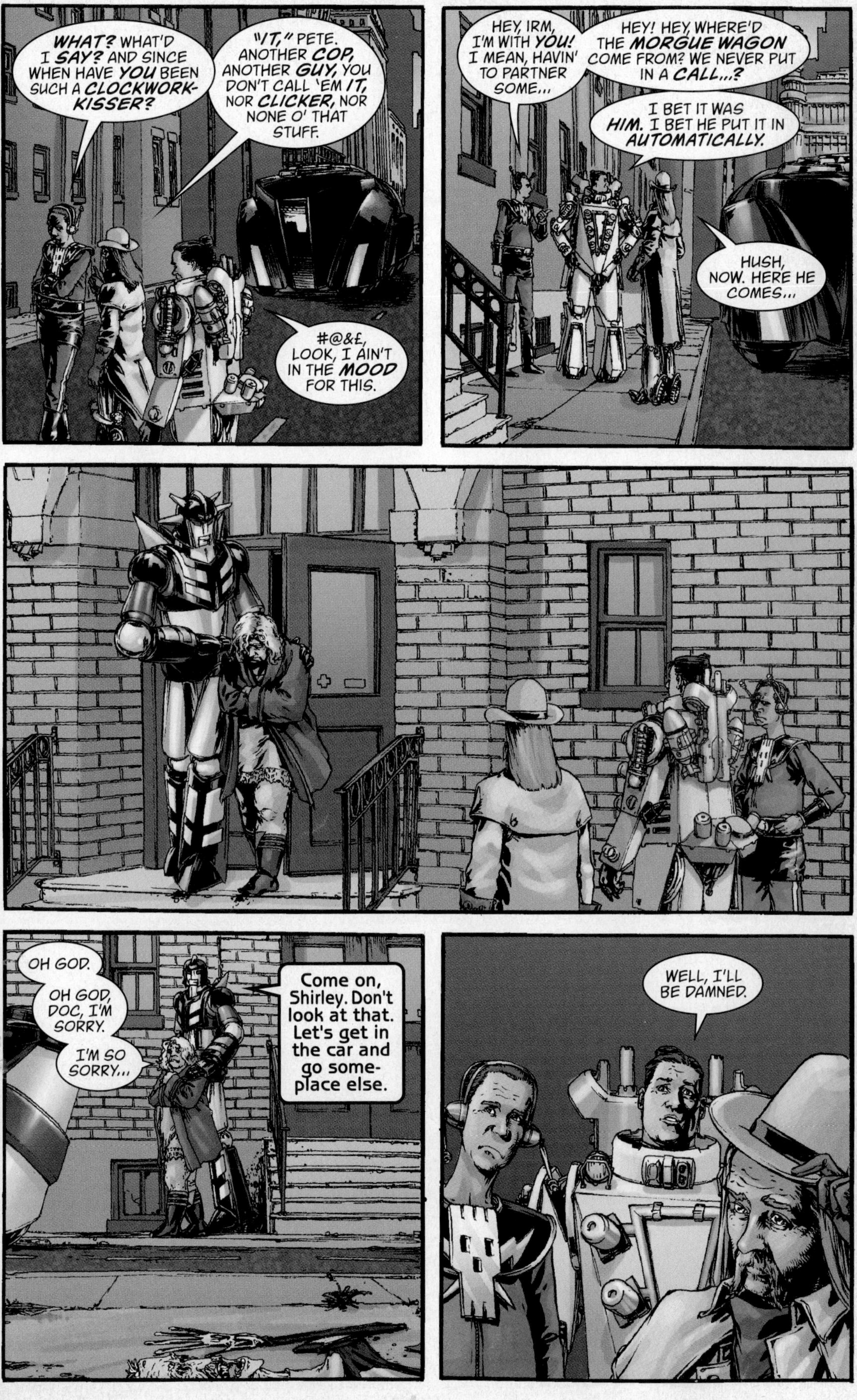
WHAT? WHAT'D I SAY? AND SINCE WHEN HAVE YOU BEEN SUCH A CLOCKWORK-KISSER?
"IT," PETE. ANOTHER COP, ANOTHER GUY, YOU DON'T CALL 'EM IT, NOR CLICKER, NOR NONE O' THAT STUFF.
#@&£, LOOK, I AIN'T IN THE MOOD FOR THIS.
HEY, IRM, I'M WITH YOU! I MEAN, HAVIN' TO PARTNER SOME...
HEY! HEY, WHERE'D THE MORGUE WAGON COME FROM? WE NEVER PUT IN A CALL...?
I BET IT WAS HIM. I BET HE PUT IT IN AUTOMATICALLY.
HUSH, NOW. HERE HE COMES...
OH GOD.
OH GOD, DOC, I'M SORRY.
I'M SO SORRY...
Come on, Shirley. Don't look at that. Let's get in the car and go some-place else.
WELL, I'LL BE DAMNED.

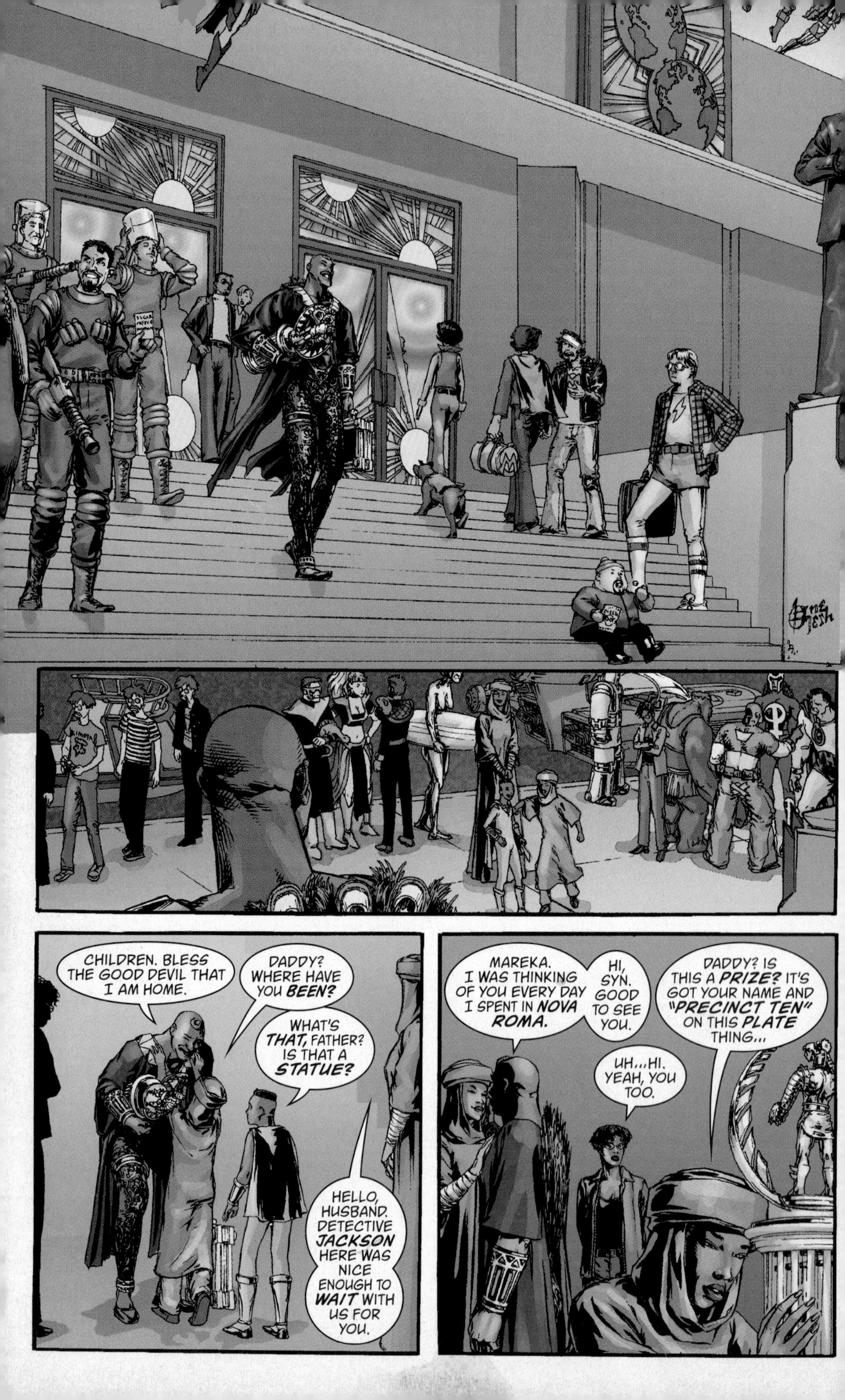
SUGAR COFFEE
CHILDREN. BLESS THE GOOD DEVIL THAT I AM HOME.
DADDY? WHERE HAVE YOU BEEN?
WHAT'S THAT, FATHER? IS THAT A STATUE?
HELLO, HUSBAND. DETECTIVE JACKSON HERE WAS NICE ENOUGH TO WAIT WITH US FOR YOU.
MAREKA. I WAS THINKING OF YOU EVERY DAY I SPENT IN NOVA ROMA.
HI, SYN. GOOD TO SEE YOU.
UH...HI. YEAH, YOU TOO.
DADDY? IS THIS A PRIZE? IT'S GOT YOUR NAME AND "PRECINCT TEN" ON THIS PLATE THING...

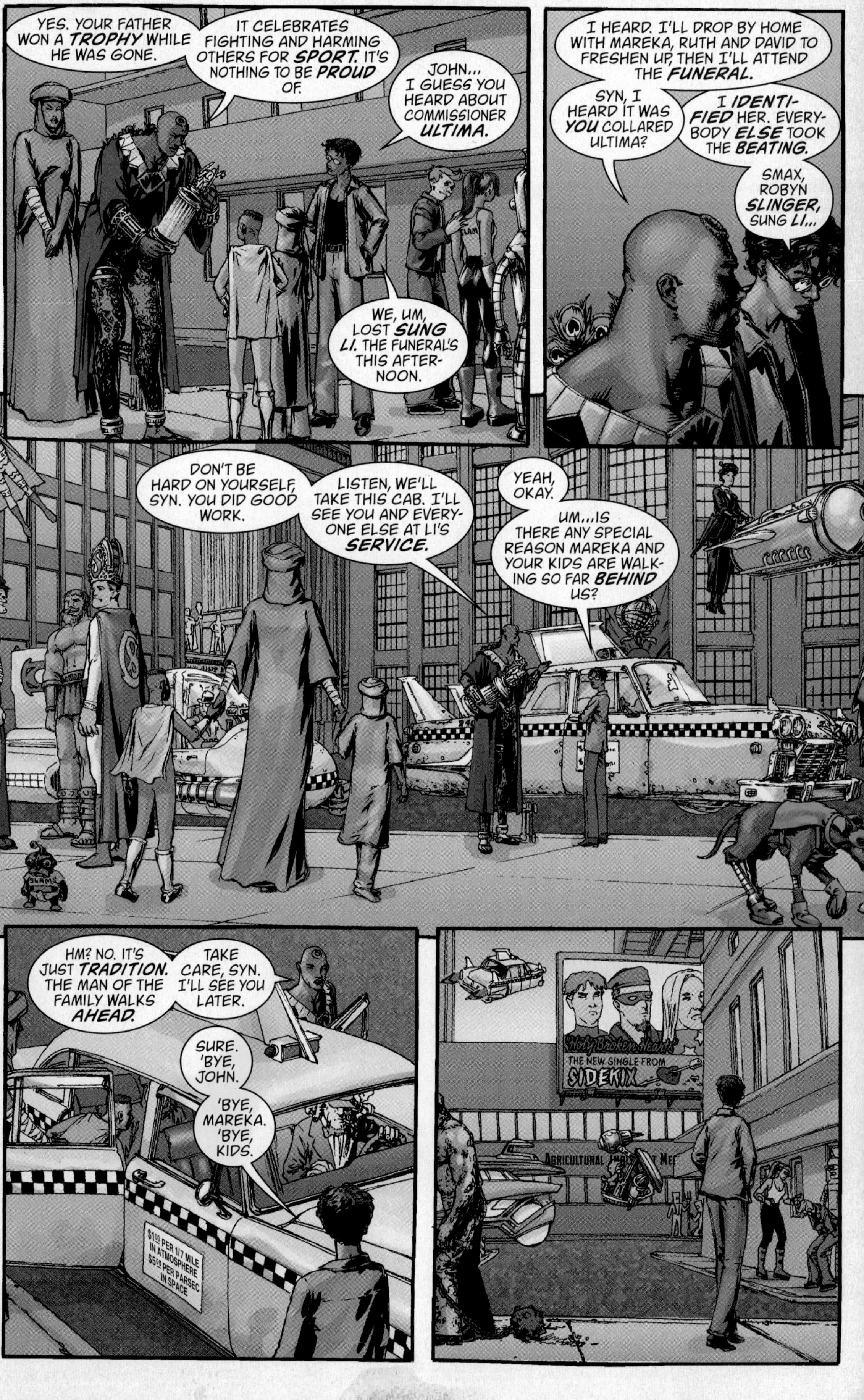
YES. YOUR FATHER WON A TROPHY WHILE HE WAS GONE.
IT CELEBRATES FIGHTING AND HARMING OTHERS FOR SPORT. IT'S NOTHING TO BE PROUD OF.
JOHN... I GUESS YOU HEARD ABOUT COMMISSIONER ULTIMA.
WE, UM, LOST SUNG LI. THE FUNERAL'S THIS AFTERNOON.
I HEARD. I'LL DROP BY HOME WITH MAREKA, RUTH AND DAVID TO FRESHEN UP, THEN I'LL ATTEND THE FUNERAL.
SYN, I HEARD IT WAS YOU COLLARED ULTIMA?
I IDENTIFIED HER. EVERYBODY ELSE TOOK THE BEATING.
SMAX, ROBYN SLINGER, SUNG LI...
DON'T BE HARD ON YOURSELF, SYN. YOU DID GOOD WORK.
LISTEN, WE'LL TAKE THIS CAB. I'LL SEE YOU AND EVERYONE ELSE AT LI'S SERVICE.
YEAH, OKAY.
UM...IS THERE ANY SPECIAL REASON MAREKA AND YOUR KIDS ARE WALKING SO FAR BEHIND US?
HM? NO. IT'S JUST TRADITION. THE MAN OF THE FAMILY WALKS AHEAD.
TAKE CARE, SYN. I'LL SEE YOU LATER.
SURE. 'BYE, JOHN.
'BYE, MAREKA. 'BYE, KIDS.
$1.99 PER 1/7 MILE IN ATMOSPHERE
$5.99 PER PARSEC IN SPACE
'Holy Broken Hearts'
THE NEW SINGLE FROM
SIDEKIX

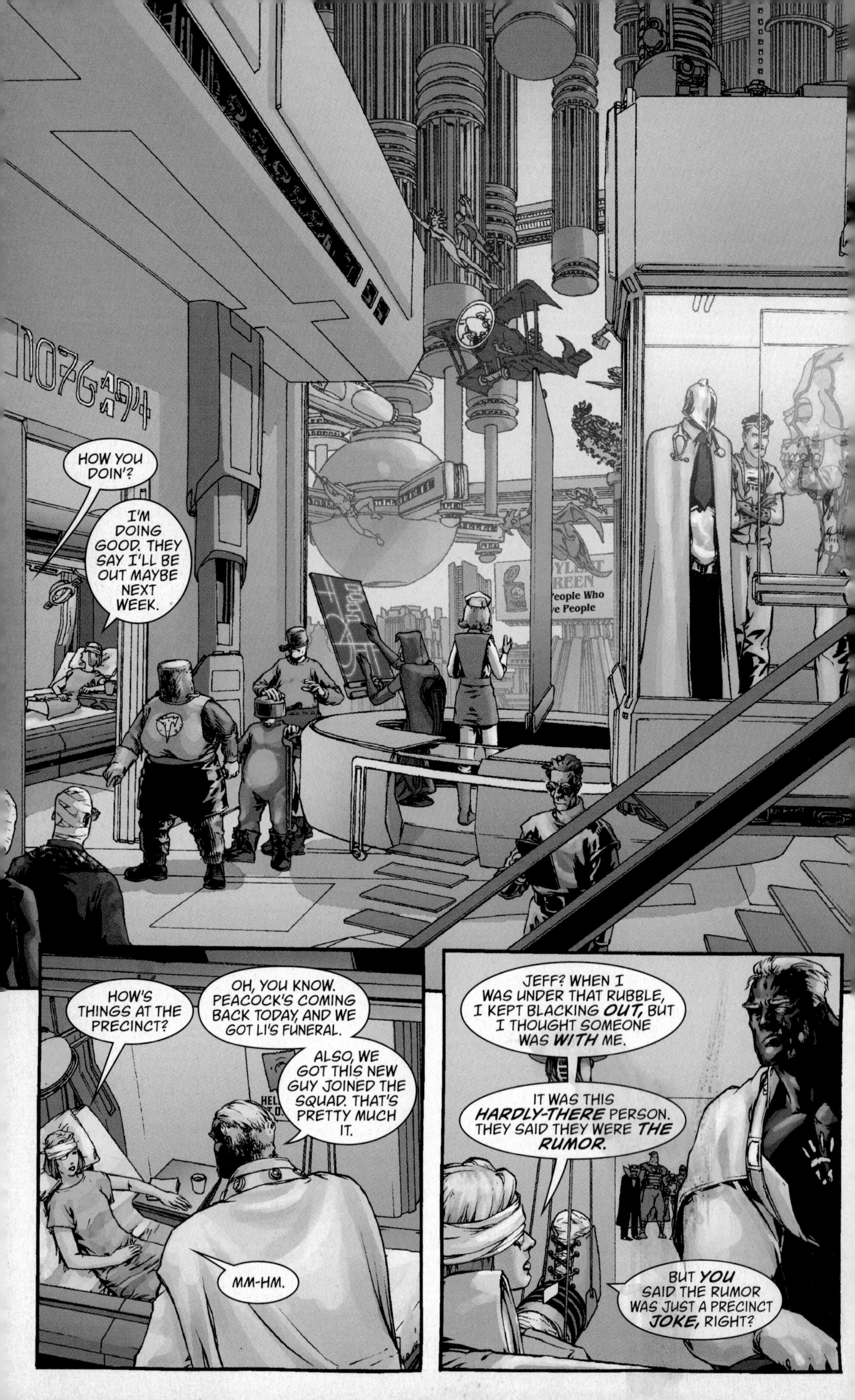
HOW YOU DOIN'?
I'M DOING GOOD. THEY SAY I'LL BE OUT MAYBE NEXT WEEK.
HOW'S THINGS AT THE PRECINCT?
OH, YOU KNOW. PEACOCK'S COMING BACK TODAY, AND WE GOT LI'S FUNERAL.
ALSO, WE GOT THIS NEW GUY JOINED THE SQUAD. THAT'S PRETTY MUCH IT.
MM-HM.
JEFF? WHEN I WAS UNDER THAT RUBBLE, I KEPT BLACKING ***OUT,*** BUT I THOUGHT SOMEONE WAS ***WITH*** ME.
IT WAS THIS ***HARDLY-THERE*** PERSON. THEY SAID THEY WERE ***THE RUMOR.***
BUT ***YOU*** SAID THE RUMOR WAS JUST A PRECINCT ***JOKE,*** RIGHT?

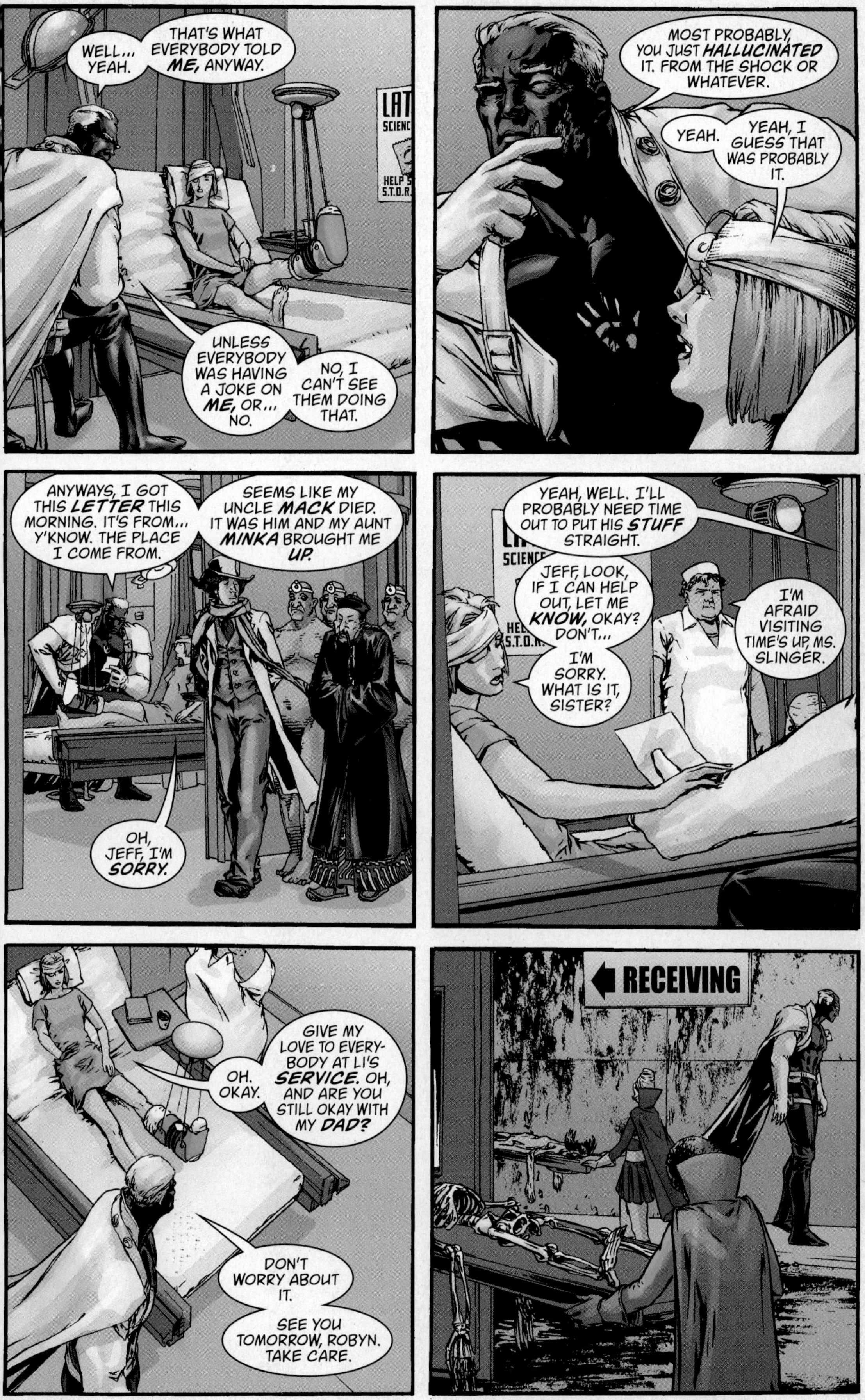
WELL... YEAH.
THAT'S WHAT EVERYBODY TOLD ME, ANYWAY.
UNLESS EVERYBODY WAS HAVING A JOKE ON ME, OR... NO.
NO, I CAN'T SEE THEM DOING THAT.
MOST PROBABLY, YOU JUST HALLUCINATED IT. FROM THE SHOCK OR WHATEVER.
YEAH.
YEAH, I GUESS THAT WAS PROBABLY IT.
ANYWAYS, I GOT THIS LETTER THIS MORNING. IT'S FROM... Y'KNOW. THE PLACE I COME FROM.
SEEMS LIKE MY UNCLE MACK DIED. IT WAS HIM AND MY AUNT MINKA BROUGHT ME UP.
OH, JEFF, I'M SORRY.
YEAH, WELL. I'LL PROBABLY NEED TIME OUT TO PUT HIS STUFF STRAIGHT.
JEFF, LOOK, IF I CAN HELP OUT, LET ME KNOW, OKAY? DON'T...
I'M AFRAID VISITING TIME'S UP, MS. SLINGER.
I'M SORRY. WHAT IS IT, SISTER?
OH. OKAY.
GIVE MY LOVE TO EVERY-BODY AT LI'S SERVICE. OH, AND ARE YOU STILL OKAY WITH MY DAD?
DON'T WORRY ABOUT IT.
SEE YOU TOMORROW, ROBYN. TAKE CARE.
RECEIVING

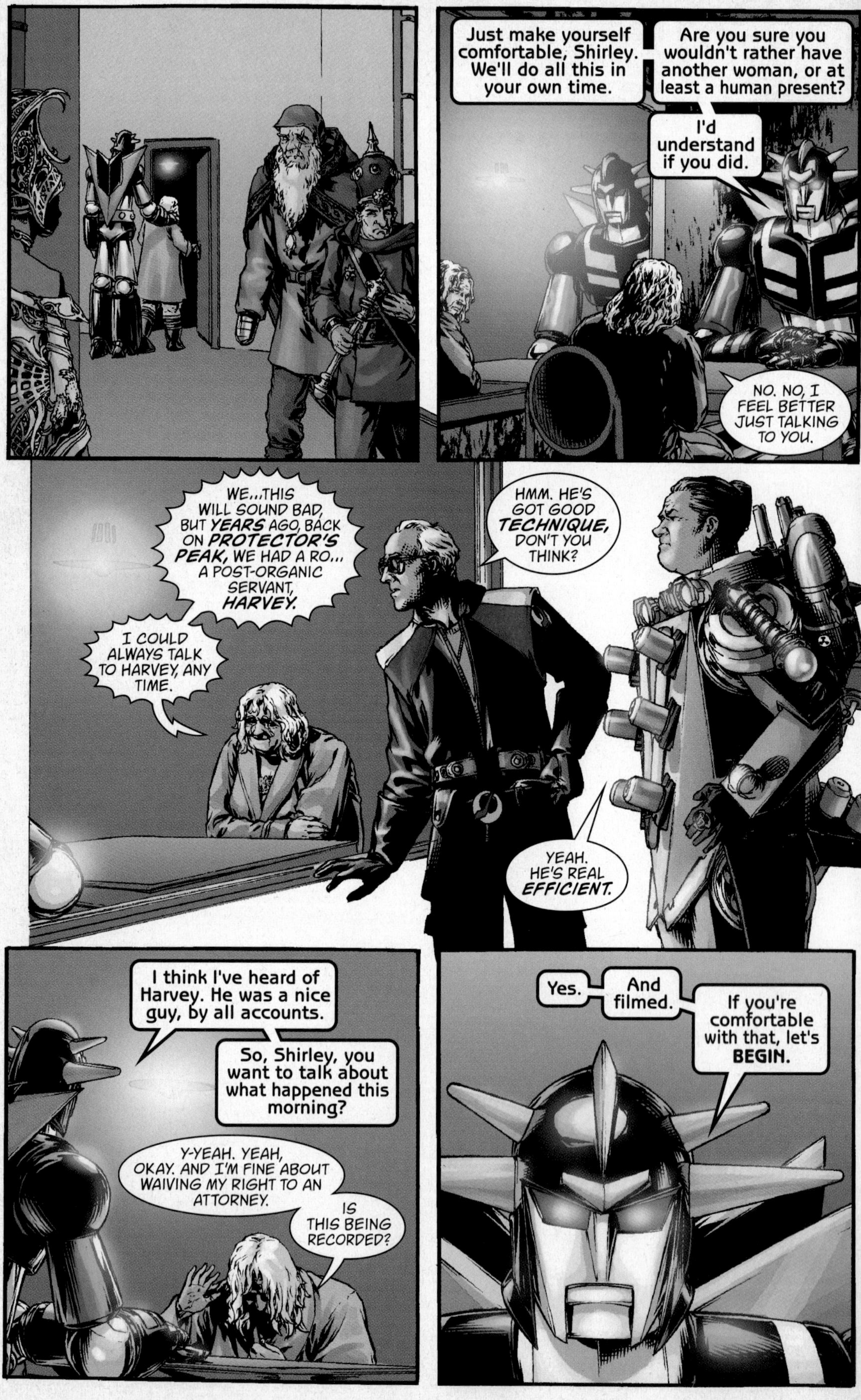
Just make yourself comfortable, Shirley. We'll do all this in your own time.
Are you sure you wouldn't rather have another woman, or at least a human present?
I'd understand if you did.
NO. NO, I FEEL BETTER JUST TALKING TO YOU.
WE...THIS WILL SOUND BAD, BUT YEARS AGO, BACK ON PROTECTOR'S PEAK, WE HAD A RO... A POST-ORGANIC SERVANT, HARVEY.
I COULD ALWAYS TALK TO HARVEY, ANY TIME.
HMM. HE'S GOT GOOD TECHNIQUE, DON'T YOU THINK?
YEAH. HE'S REAL EFFICIENT.
I think I've heard of Harvey. He was a nice guy, by all accounts.
So, Shirley, you want to talk about what happened this morning?
Y-YEAH. YEAH, OKAY. AND I'M FINE ABOUT WAIVING MY RIGHT TO AN ATTORNEY.
IS THIS BEING RECORDED?
Yes.
And filmed.
If you're comfortable with that, let's BEGIN.

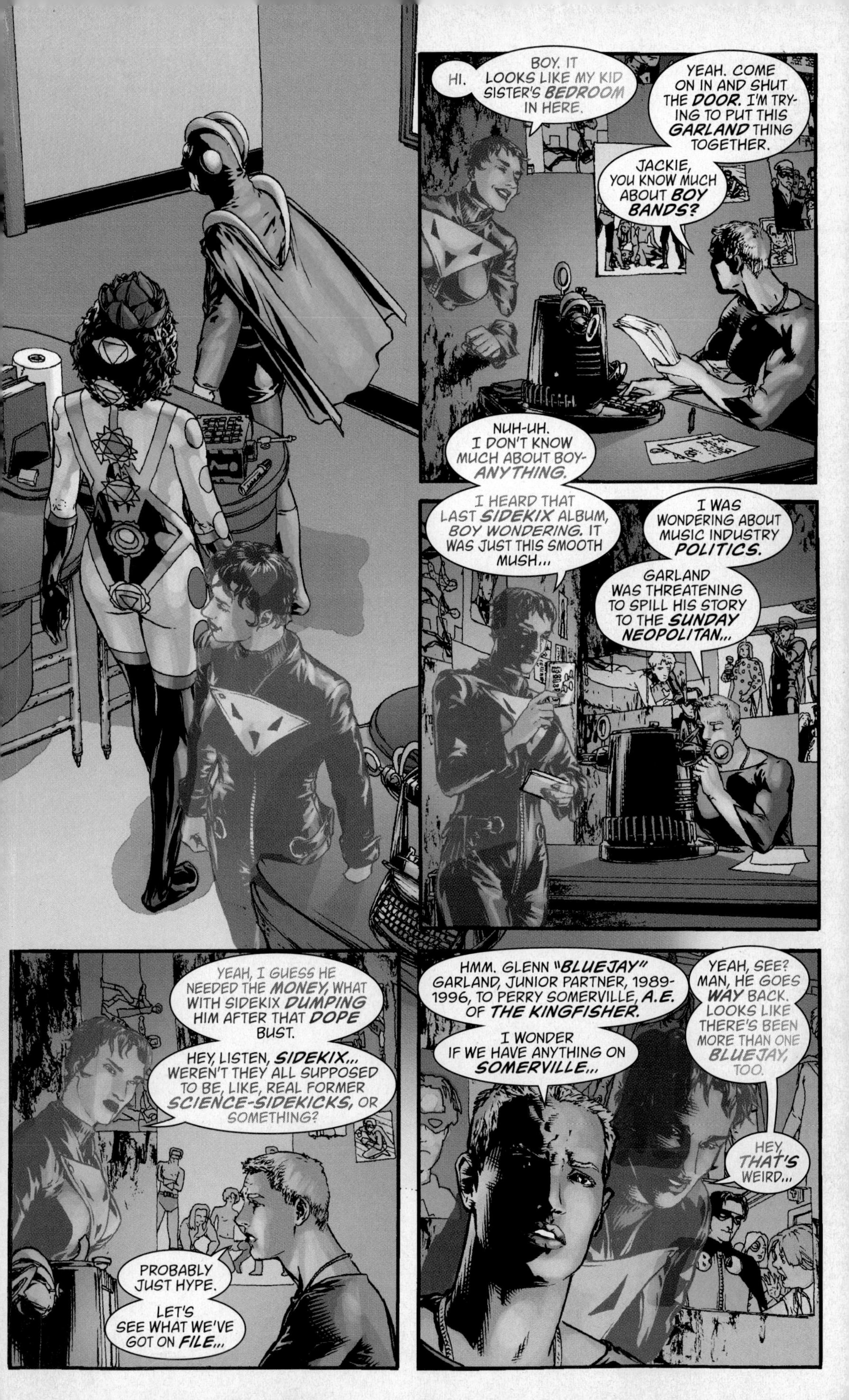

HI.
BOY. IT LOOKS LIKE MY KID SISTER'S BEDROOM IN HERE.
YEAH. COME ON IN AND SHUT THE DOOR. I'M TRYING TO PUT THIS GARLAND THING TOGETHER.
JACKIE, YOU KNOW MUCH ABOUT BOY BANDS?
NUH-UH. I DON'T KNOW MUCH ABOUT BOY-ANYTHING.
I HEARD THAT LAST SIDEKIX ALBUM, BOY WONDERING. IT WAS JUST THIS SMOOTH MUSH...
I WAS WONDERING ABOUT MUSIC INDUSTRY POLITICS.
GARLAND WAS THREATENING TO SPILL HIS STORY TO THE SUNDAY NEOPOLITAN...
YEAH, I GUESS HE NEEDED THE MONEY, WHAT WITH SIDEKIX DUMPING HIM AFTER THAT DOPE BUST.
HEY, LISTEN, SIDEKIX... WEREN'T THEY ALL SUPPOSED TO BE, LIKE, REAL FORMER SCIENCE-SIDEKICKS, OR SOMETHING?
PROBABLY JUST HYPE.
LET'S SEE WHAT WE'VE GOT ON FILE...
HMM. GLENN "BLUEJAY" GARLAND, JUNIOR PARTNER, 1989-1996, TO PERRY SOMERVILLE, A.E. OF THE KINGFISHER.
I WONDER IF WE HAVE ANYTHING ON SOMERVILLE...
YEAH, SEE? MAN, HE GOES WAY BACK. LOOKS LIKE THERE'S BEEN MORE THAN ONE BLUEJAY, TOO.
HEY, THAT'S WEIRD...

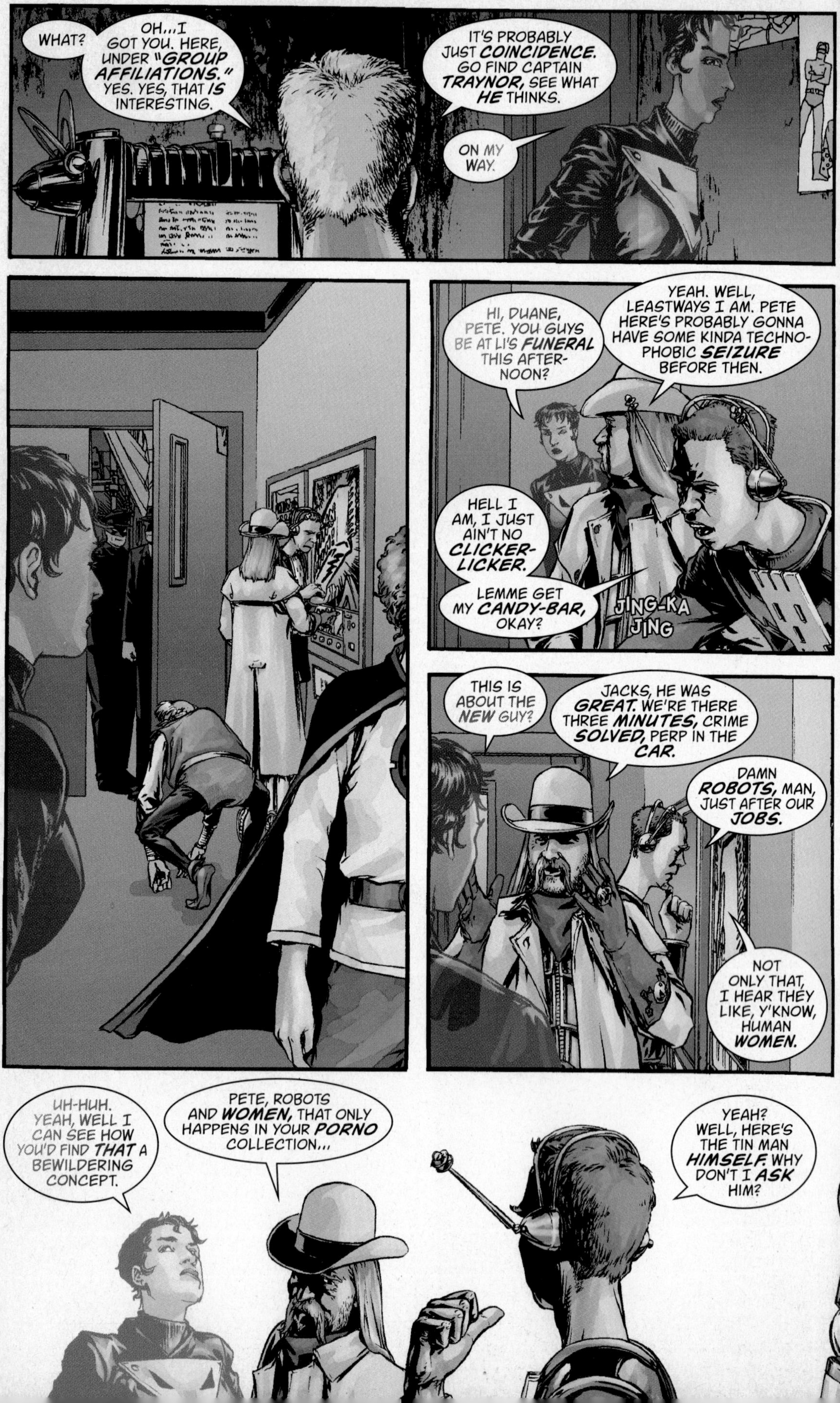
WHAT?
OH...I GOT YOU. HERE, UNDER "GROUP AFFILIATIONS." YES. YES, THAT IS INTERESTING.
IT'S PROBABLY JUST COINCIDENCE. GO FIND CAPTAIN TRAYNOR, SEE WHAT HE THINKS.
ON MY WAY.
HI, DUANE, PETE. YOU GUYS BE AT LI'S FUNERAL THIS AFTER-NOON?
YEAH. WELL, LEASTWAYS I AM. PETE HERE'S PROBABLY GONNA HAVE SOME KINDA TECHNO-PHOBIC SEIZURE BEFORE THEN.
HELL I AM, I JUST AIN'T NO CLICKER-LICKER.
LEMME GET MY CANDY-BAR, OKAY?
JING-KA JING
THIS IS ABOUT THE NEW GUY?
JACKS, HE WAS GREAT. WE'RE THERE THREE MINUTES, CRIME SOLVED, PERP IN THE CAR.
DAMN ROBOTS, MAN, JUST AFTER OUR JOBS.
NOT ONLY THAT, I HEAR THEY LIKE, Y'KNOW, HUMAN WOMEN.
UH-HUH. YEAH, WELL I CAN SEE HOW YOU'D FIND THAT A BEWILDERING CONCEPT.
PETE, ROBOTS AND WOMEN, THAT ONLY HAPPENS IN YOUR PORNO COLLECTION...
YEAH? WELL, HERE'S THE TIN MAN HIMSELF. WHY DON'T I ASK HIM?

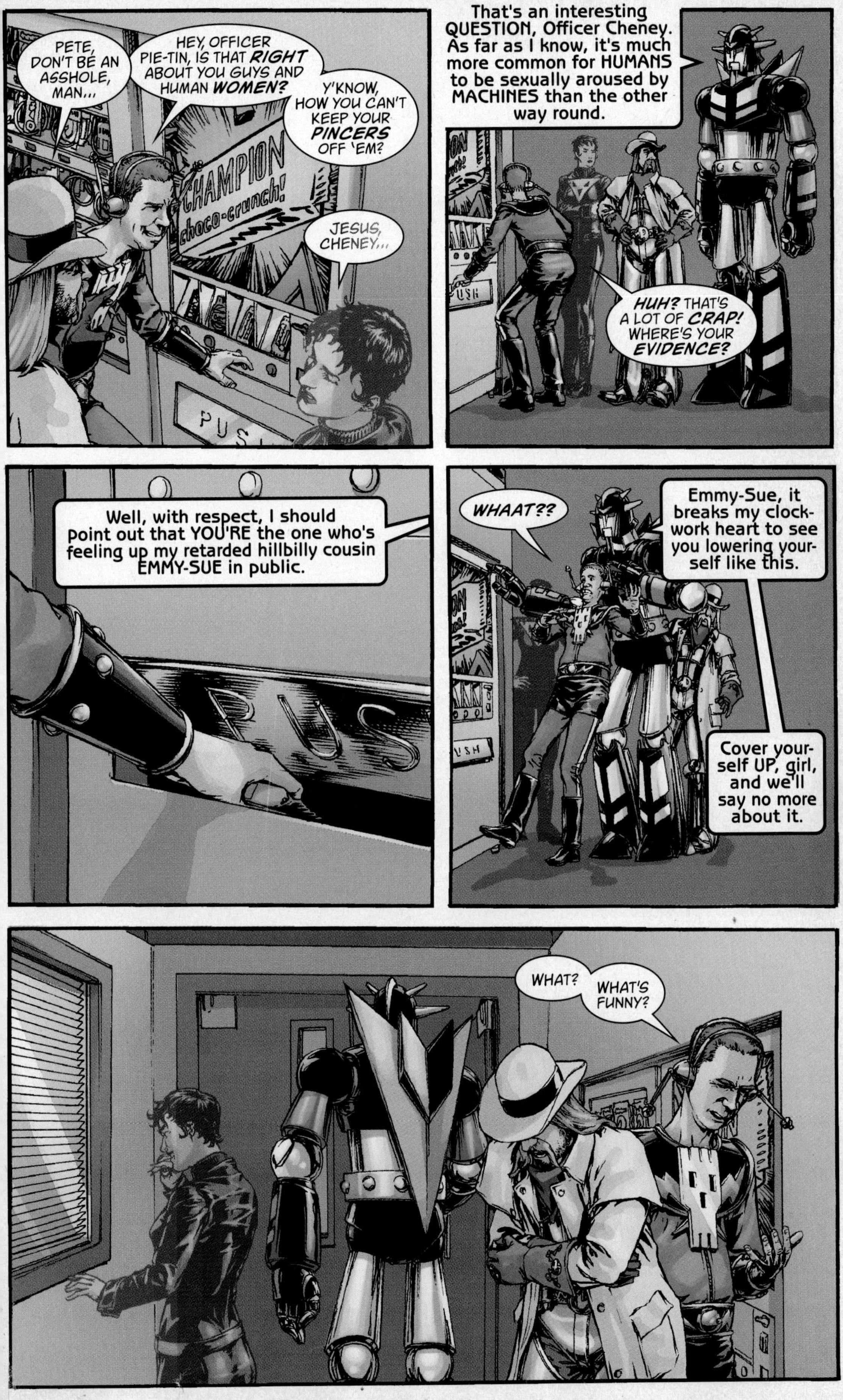
PETE, DON'T BE AN ASSHOLE, MAN...
HEY, OFFICER PIE-TIN, IS THAT **RIGHT** ABOUT YOU GUYS AND HUMAN **WOMEN?**
Y'KNOW, HOW YOU CAN'T KEEP YOUR **PINCERS** OFF 'EM?
CHAMPION choco-crunch!
JESUS, CHENEY...
PUSH
That's an interesting QUESTION, Officer Cheney. As far as I know, it's much more common for HUMANS to be sexually aroused by MACHINES than the other way round.
HUH? THAT'S A LOT OF **CRAP!** WHERE'S YOUR **EVIDENCE?**
Well, with respect, I should point out that YOU'RE the one who's feeling up my retarded hillbilly cousin EMMY-SUE in public.
WHAAT??
Emmy-Sue, it breaks my clock-work heart to see you lowering your-self like this.
Cover your-self UP, girl, and we'll say no more about it.
WHAT?
WHAT'S FUNNY?

HEY, SCREW *YOU*, BODINE! THINK THIS IS SO GODDAMN FUNNY, LAUGHIN' LIKE A LITTLE *IDIOT* KID!

DAMN, I GOTTA GO WASH MY *HAND*!

CAPTAIN *TRAYNOR*, SIR? SORRY TO BUST IN ON YOU. DO YOU HAVE A MINUTE?

UHH...S-SURE, SERGEANT KOWALSKI. COME RIGHT IN.

WHAT CAN I DO FOR YOU?

WELL, SERGEANT CAESAR SAID CATHY AND I SHOULD LIASE WITH YOU ON THIS *GARLAND* CASE, AND SOMETHING *INTERESTING* CAME UP.

I DUNNO. MAYBE IT'S NOTHING...

NO, NO, TELL ME ABOUT IT. HERE, TAKE A SEAT...

THANKS.

SEE, WHAT IT IS, WE CHECKED TO SEE IF GARLAND WAS EVER A REAL *BOY SIDEKICK*.

TURNS OUT HE *WAS*. HE PARTNERED A PERRY *SOMERVILLE*, A.E. OF *THE KINGFISHER*.

VAGUELY HEARD OF HIM. GO ON.

WELL, WHEN WE CHECKED SOMERVILLE, UNDER *GROUP AFFILIATIONS*, IT SAID HE WAS IN THE *SEVEN SENTINELS*.

I MEAN, IT'S PROBABLY A *COINCIDENCE*...

HMM. M'RRGLA QUALTZ WAS A *SENTINEL*.

SHE SAID SOMETHING *ODD* JUST BEFORE SHE *DIED*...

SHE...SHE SPOKE TO ME PRIVATELY. SHE WAS WORRIED HER FELLOW *SENTINELS* MIGHT BE PLANNING TO *KILL* HER.

SHE SAID MAYBE THEY DIDN'T WANT HER TO STAND *TRIAL*.

AND SHE SAID SOMETHING *ELSE*...

SHE SAID IF ANYTHING *HAPPENED* TO HER, I SHOULD CHECK HER *SHOWREEL*...

...OR THAT I SHOULD ASK THE "*CHICKEN-SOUPERS*."

THAT'S CHICKEN-*SUPERS*, SIR. IT'S NEOPOLIS PEDOPHILE SLANG FOR SEXUALLY AVAILABLE JUNIOR *SCIENCE-SIDEKICKS*.

IT *IS*?

SAY, M'RRGLA QUALTZ, SHE WORKED IN THE *SEX* INDUSTRY. COULD THE SEVEN SENTINELS BE...I DON'T KNOW...

...MIXED UP IN SOME *PEDOPHILE* OPERATION?

WELL, GARLAND *WAS* TAKING HIS STORY TO THE SUNDAY *NEOPOLITAN*...

HMM. WELL, THERE'S A MOTIVE FOR SOME BIG-NAME ABUSER TO WHACK HIM RIGHT THERE.

JACKIE, I'M STARTING TO *LIKE* THIS. IF *WALLACE* AND *LOMAX* AND THE REST WERE INVOLVED...

YEAH. BE *NICE*, WOULDN'T IT?

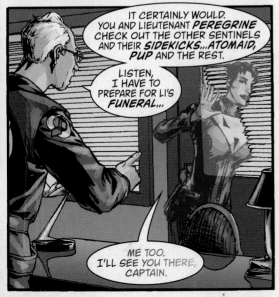

IT CERTAINLY WOULD. YOU AND LIEUTENANT *PEREGRINE* CHECK OUT THE OTHER SENTINELS AND THEIR *SIDEKICKS*...ATOMAID, PUP AND THE REST.

LISTEN, I HAVE TO PREPARE FOR LI'S *FUNERAL*...

ME TOO. I'LL SEE YOU THERE, CAPTAIN.

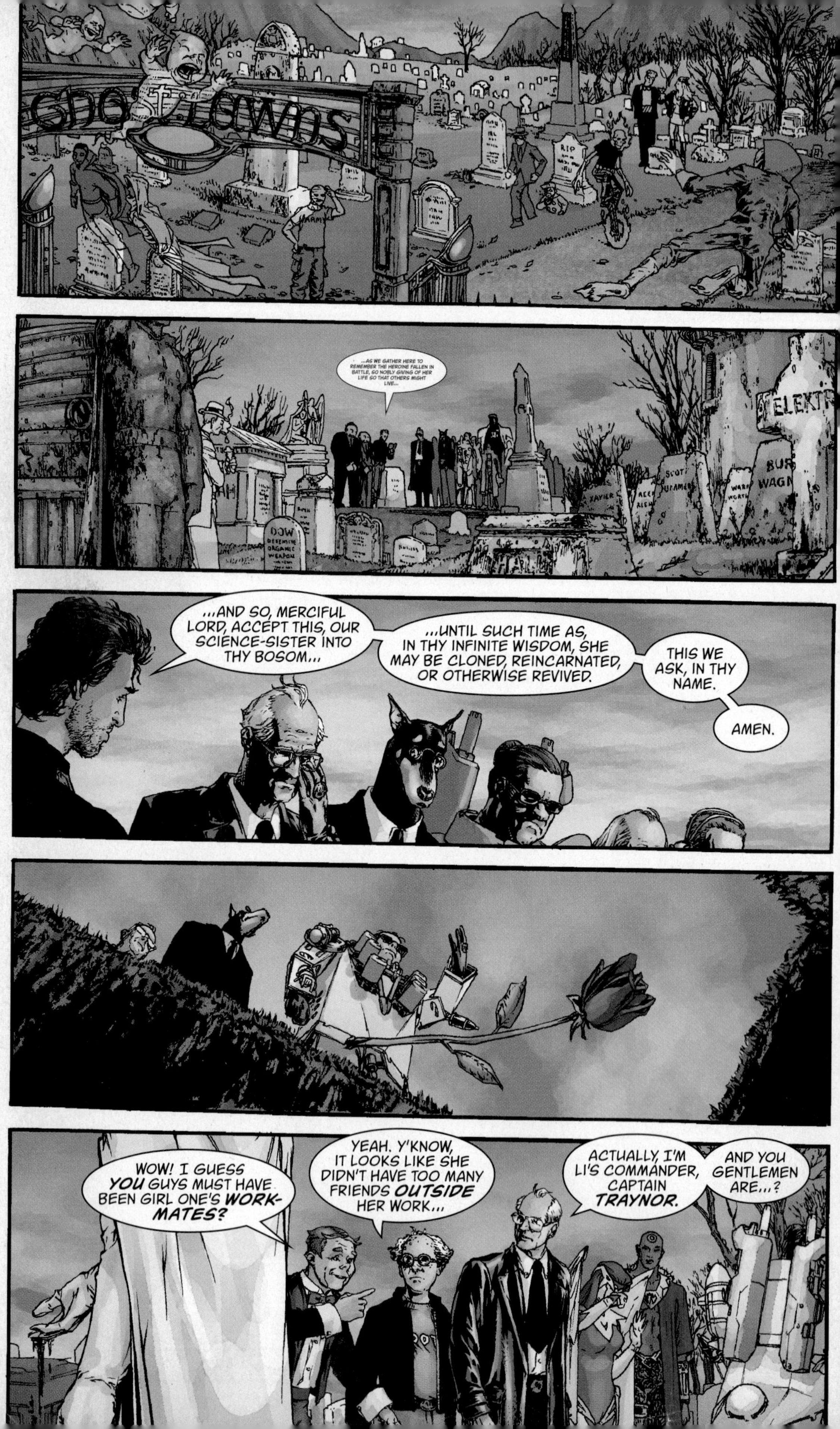
...AS WE GATHER HERE TO REMEMBER THE HEROINE FALLEN IN BATTLE, SO NOBLY GIVING OF HER LIFE SO THAT OTHERS MIGHT LIVE...
...AND SO, MERCIFUL LORD, ACCEPT THIS, OUR SCIENCE-SISTER INTO THY BOSOM...
...UNTIL SUCH TIME AS, IN THY INFINITE WISDOM, SHE MAY BE CLONED, REINCARNATED, OR OTHERWISE REVIVED.
THIS WE ASK, IN THY NAME.
AMEN.
WOW! I GUESS *YOU* GUYS MUST HAVE BEEN GIRL ONE'S *WORK-MATES?*
YEAH. Y'KNOW, IT LOOKS LIKE SHE DIDN'T HAVE TOO MANY FRIENDS *OUTSIDE* HER WORK...
ACTUALLY, I'M LI'S COMMANDER, CAPTAIN *TRAYNOR.*
AND YOU GENTLEMEN ARE...?

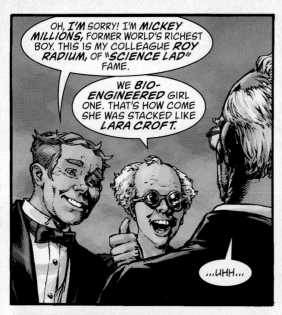

OH, *I'M* SORRY! I'M *MICKEY MILLIONS,* FORMER WORLD'S *RICHEST BOY.* THIS IS MY *COLLEAGUE ROY RADIUM,* OF *"SCIENCE LAD"* FAME.

WE *BIO-ENGINEERED* GIRL ONE. THAT'S HOW COME SHE WAS *STACKED* LIKE *LARA CROFT.*

...UHH...

WELL, ROY, NOT *EXACTLY* LIKE LARA CROFT.

CAPTAIN, BE *HONEST:* HOW DID SHE *PERFORM?* SHOULD HER *LEGS* HAVE BEEN LONGER?

LOOK, I HAVE TO JOIN MY MEN...

NO, BUT *SERIOUSLY,* HER *BOOBS.* TOO *BIG?* TOO *LITTLE?*

WILDE

OH. RIGHT.

YOU DIDN'T *RESPECT* HER ENOUGH TO GO TO HER *FUNERAL,* HUH?

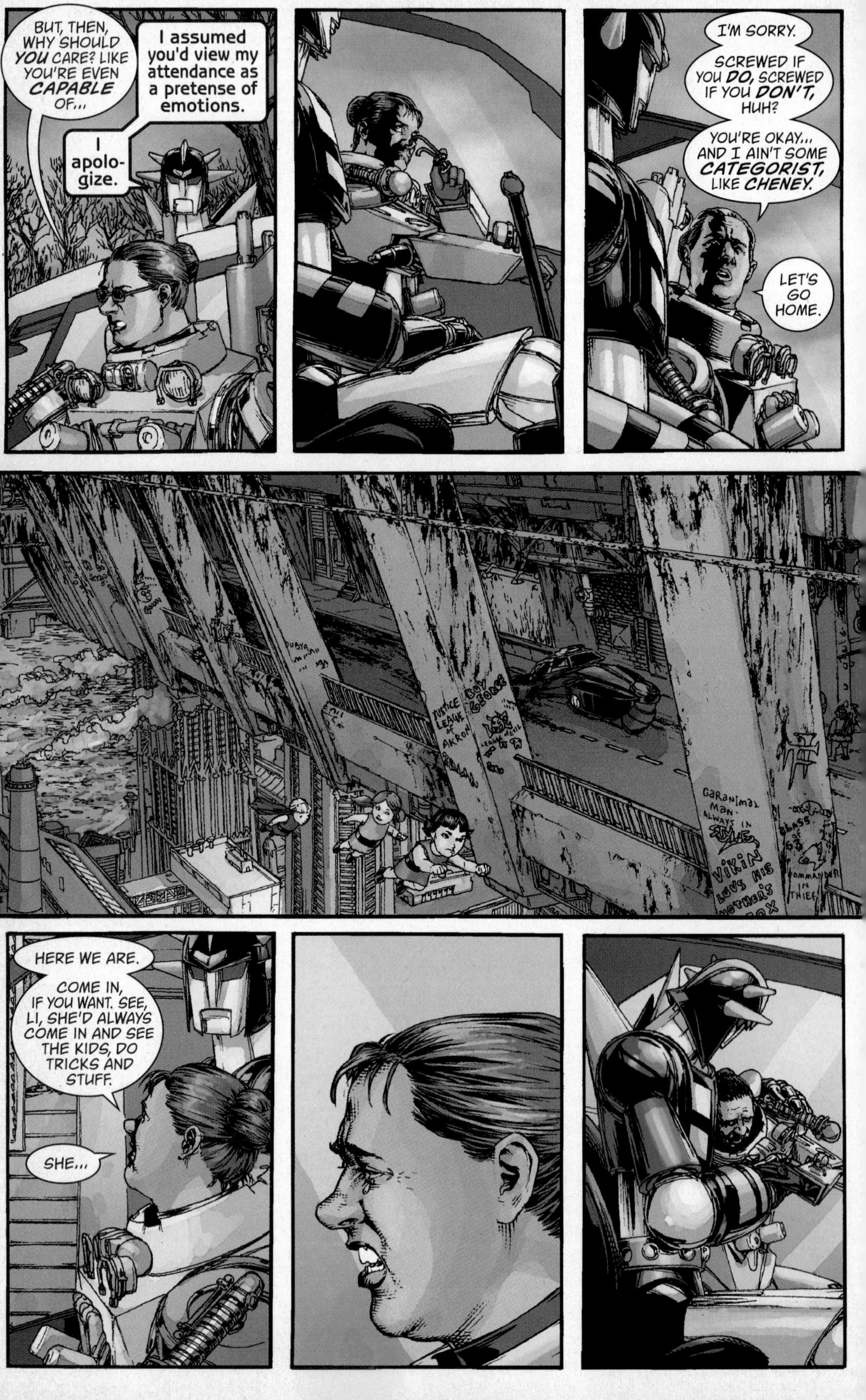
BUT, THEN, WHY SHOULD YOU CARE? LIKE YOU'RE EVEN CAPABLE OF...
I assumed you'd view my attendance as a pretense of emotions.
I apologize.
I'M SORRY.
SCREWED IF YOU DO, SCREWED IF YOU DON'T, HUH?
YOU'RE OKAY... AND I AIN'T SOME CATEGORIST, LIKE CHENEY.
LET'S GO HOME.
DUBYA
JUSTICE LEAGUE OF AKRON
BOY GEORGE
GARANIMAL MAN ALWAYS IN STYLE
CLASS of 63
COMMANDER IN THIEF
HERE WE ARE.
COME IN, IF YOU WANT. SEE, LI, SHE'D ALWAYS COME IN AND SEE THE KIDS, DO TRICKS AND STUFF.
SHE...

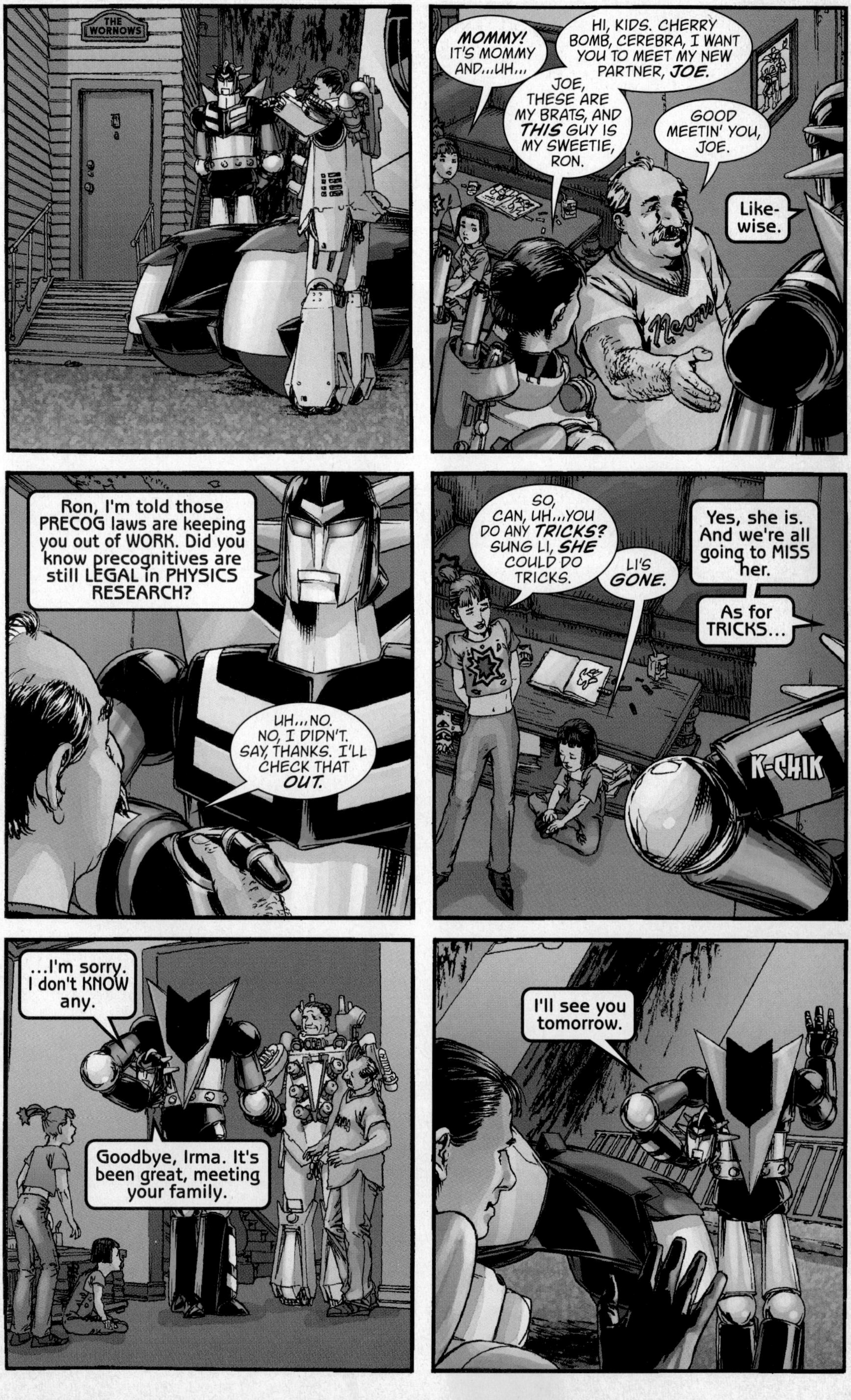
THE WORNOWS
MOMMY! IT'S MOMMY AND...UH...
HI, KIDS. CHERRY BOMB, CEREBRA, I WANT YOU TO MEET MY NEW PARTNER, JOE.
JOE, THESE ARE MY BRATS, AND THIS GUY IS MY SWEETIE, RON.
GOOD MEETIN' YOU, JOE.
Like-wise.
Ron, I'm told those PRECOG laws are keeping you out of WORK. Did you know precognitives are still LEGAL in PHYSICS RESEARCH?
UH...NO. NO, I DIDN'T. SAY, THANKS. I'LL CHECK THAT OUT.
SO, CAN, UH...YOU DO ANY TRICKS? SUNG LI, SHE COULD DO TRICKS.
LI'S GONE.
Yes, she is. And we're all going to MISS her.
As for TRICKS...
K-CHIK
...I'm sorry. I don't KNOW any.
Goodbye, Irma. It's been great, meeting your family.
I'll see you tomorrow.

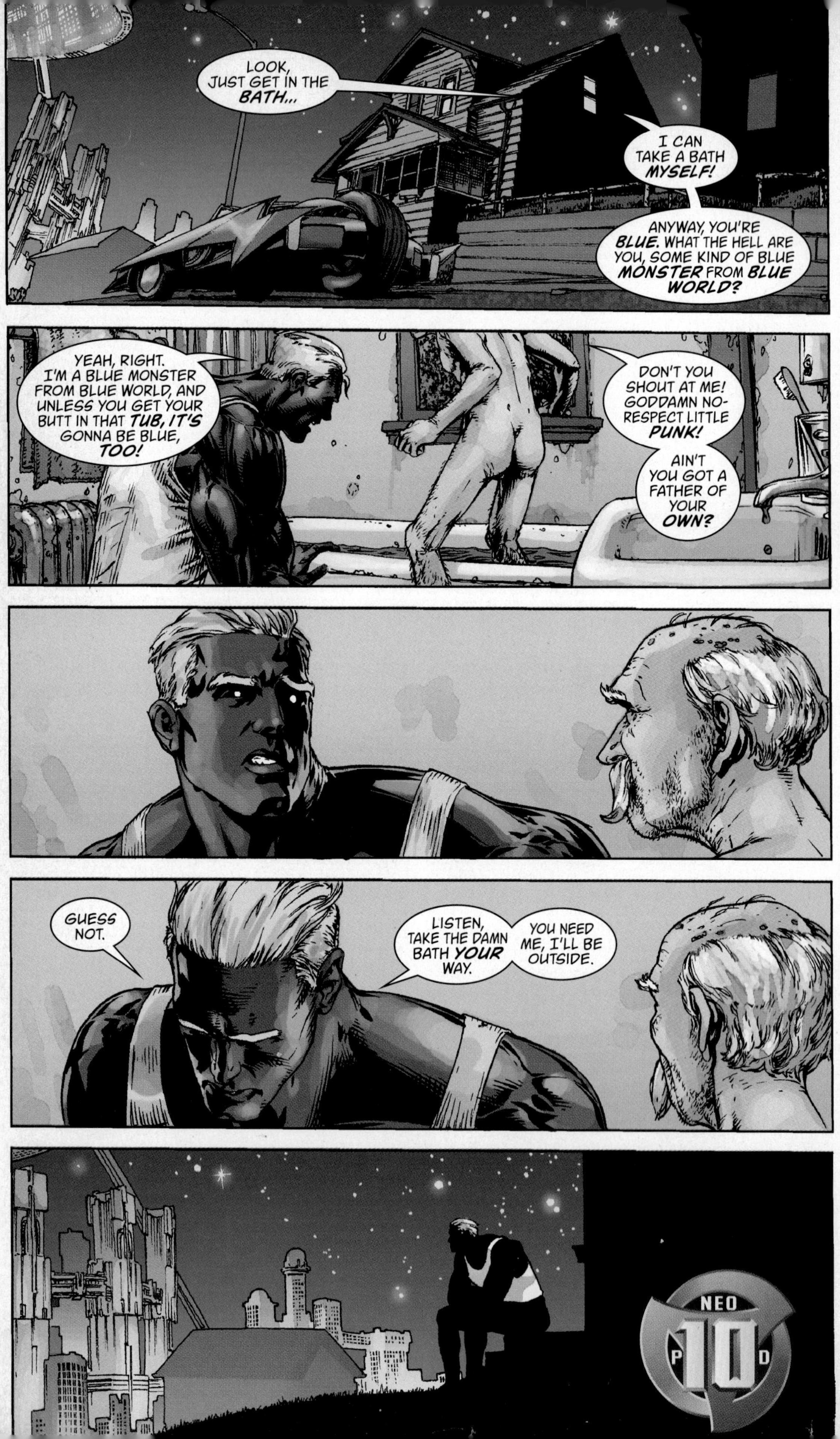

LOOK, JUST GET IN THE BATH...
I CAN TAKE A BATH MYSELF!
ANYWAY, YOU'RE BLUE. WHAT THE HELL ARE YOU, SOME KIND OF BLUE MONSTER FROM BLUE WORLD?
YEAH, RIGHT. I'M A BLUE MONSTER FROM BLUE WORLD, AND UNLESS YOU GET YOUR BUTT IN THAT TUB, IT'S GONNA BE BLUE, TOO!
DON'T YOU SHOUT AT ME! GODDAMN NO-RESPECT LITTLE PUNK!
AIN'T YOU GOT A FATHER OF YOUR OWN?
GUESS NOT.
LISTEN, TAKE THE DAMN BATH YOUR WAY.
YOU NEED ME, I'LL BE OUTSIDE.
NEO
P 10 D

CHAPTER FIVE

ON THE DOCKET:
Jack and Peregrine solve the big one,
the unusual suspects are rounded up,
and Captain Traynor calls it a day.

Cover art:
Gene Ha and
Zander Cannon

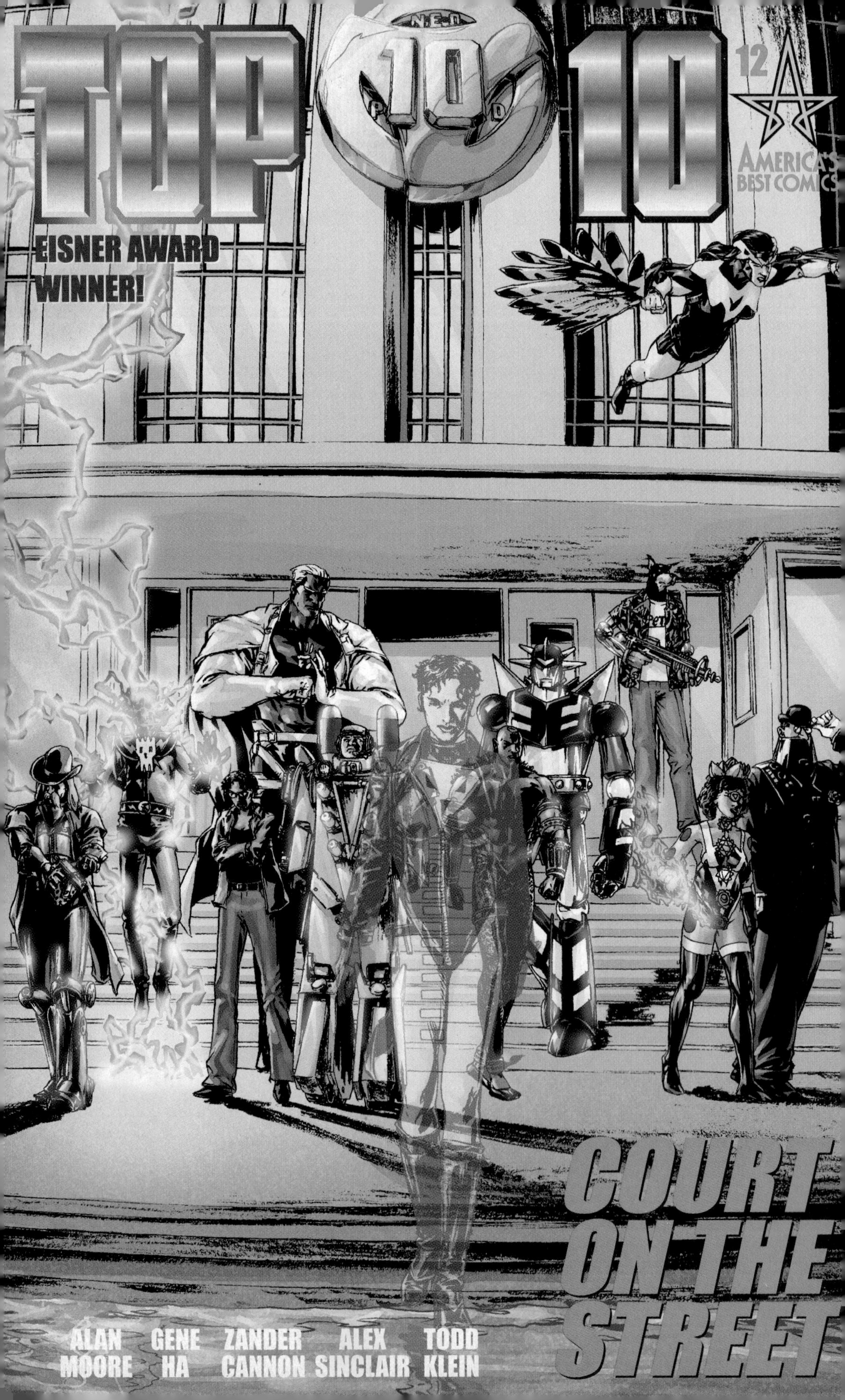

TOP 10
12
AMERICA'S BEST COMICS
EISNER AWARD WINNER!
COURT ON THE STREET
ALAN MOORE
GENE HA
ZANDER CANNON
ALEX SINCLAIR
TODD KLEIN

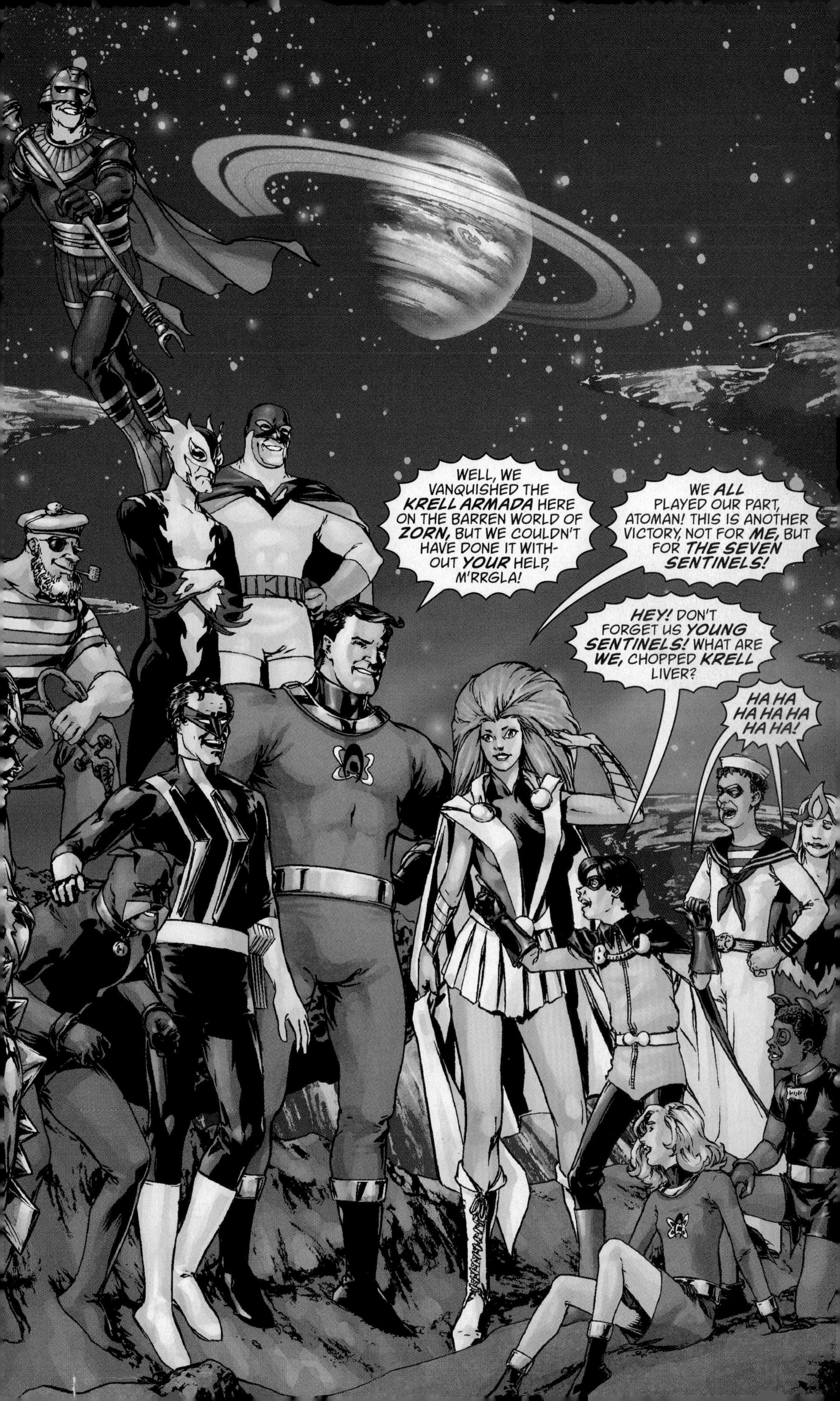
WELL, WE VANQUISHED THE KRELL ARMADA HERE ON THE BARREN WORLD OF ZORN, BUT WE COULDN'T HAVE DONE IT WITH-OUT YOUR HELP, M'RRGLA!
WE ALL PLAYED OUR PART, ATOMAN! THIS IS ANOTHER VICTORY, NOT FOR ME, BUT FOR THE SEVEN SENTINELS!
HEY! DON'T FORGET US YOUNG SENTINELS! WHAT ARE WE, CHOPPED KRELL LIVER?
HA HA HA HA HA HA HA!

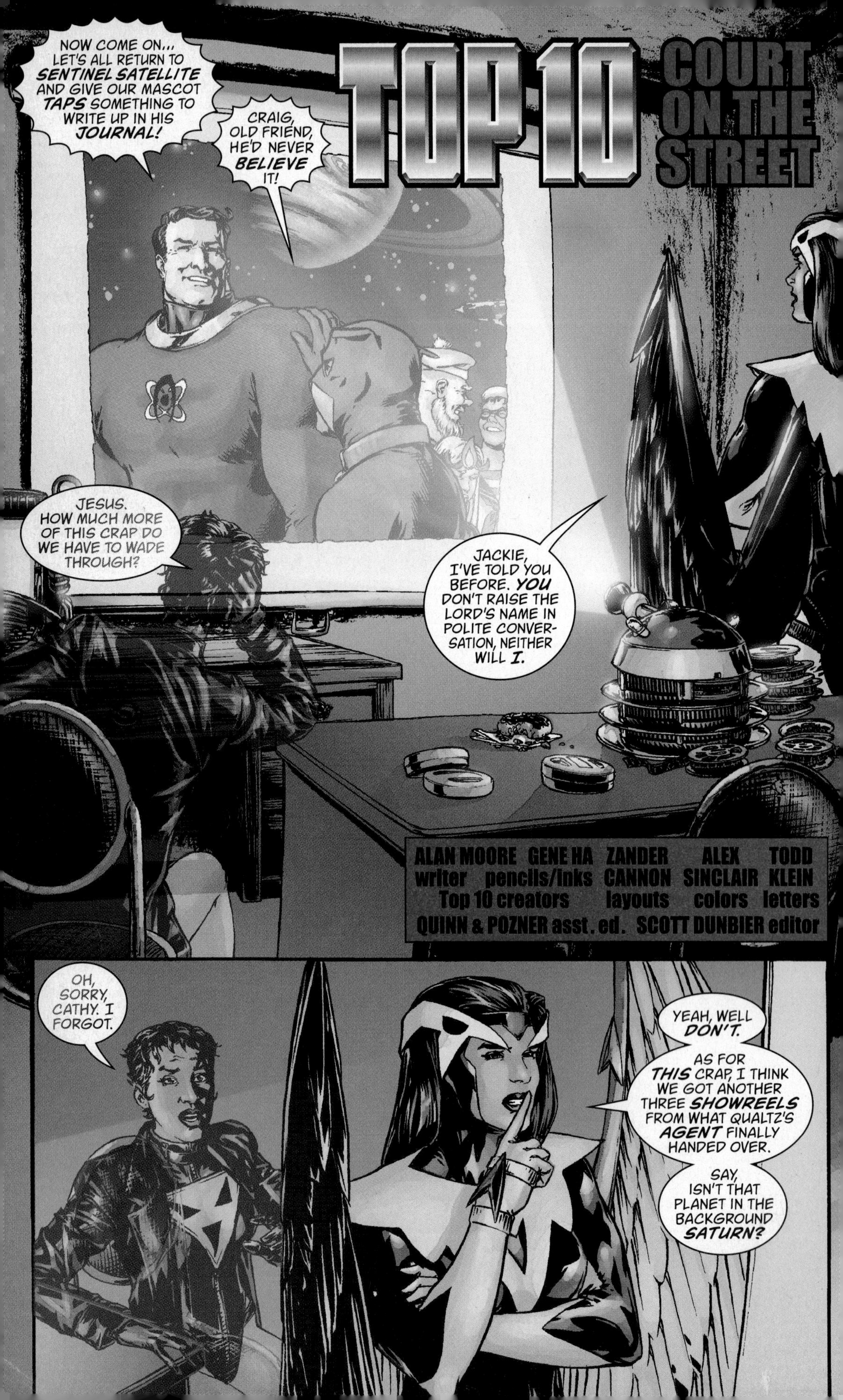
NOW COME ON... LET'S ALL RETURN TO SENTINEL SATELLITE AND GIVE OUR MASCOT TAPS SOMETHING TO WRITE UP IN HIS JOURNAL!
CRAIG, OLD FRIEND, HE'D NEVER BELIEVE IT!
TOP 10
COURT ON THE STREET
JESUS. HOW MUCH MORE OF THIS CRAP DO WE HAVE TO WADE THROUGH?
JACKIE, I'VE TOLD YOU BEFORE. YOU DON'T RAISE THE LORD'S NAME IN POLITE CONVERSATION, NEITHER WILL I.
ALAN MOORE writer
GENE HA pencils/inks
Top 10 creators
ZANDER CANNON layouts
ALEX SINCLAIR colors
TODD KLEIN letters
QUINN & POZNER asst. ed.
SCOTT DUNBIER editor
OH, SORRY, CATHY. I FORGOT.
YEAH, WELL DON'T.
AS FOR THIS CRAP, I THINK WE GOT ANOTHER THREE SHOWREELS FROM WHAT QUALTZ'S AGENT FINALLY HANDED OVER.
SAY, ISN'T THAT PLANET IN THE BACKGROUND SATURN?

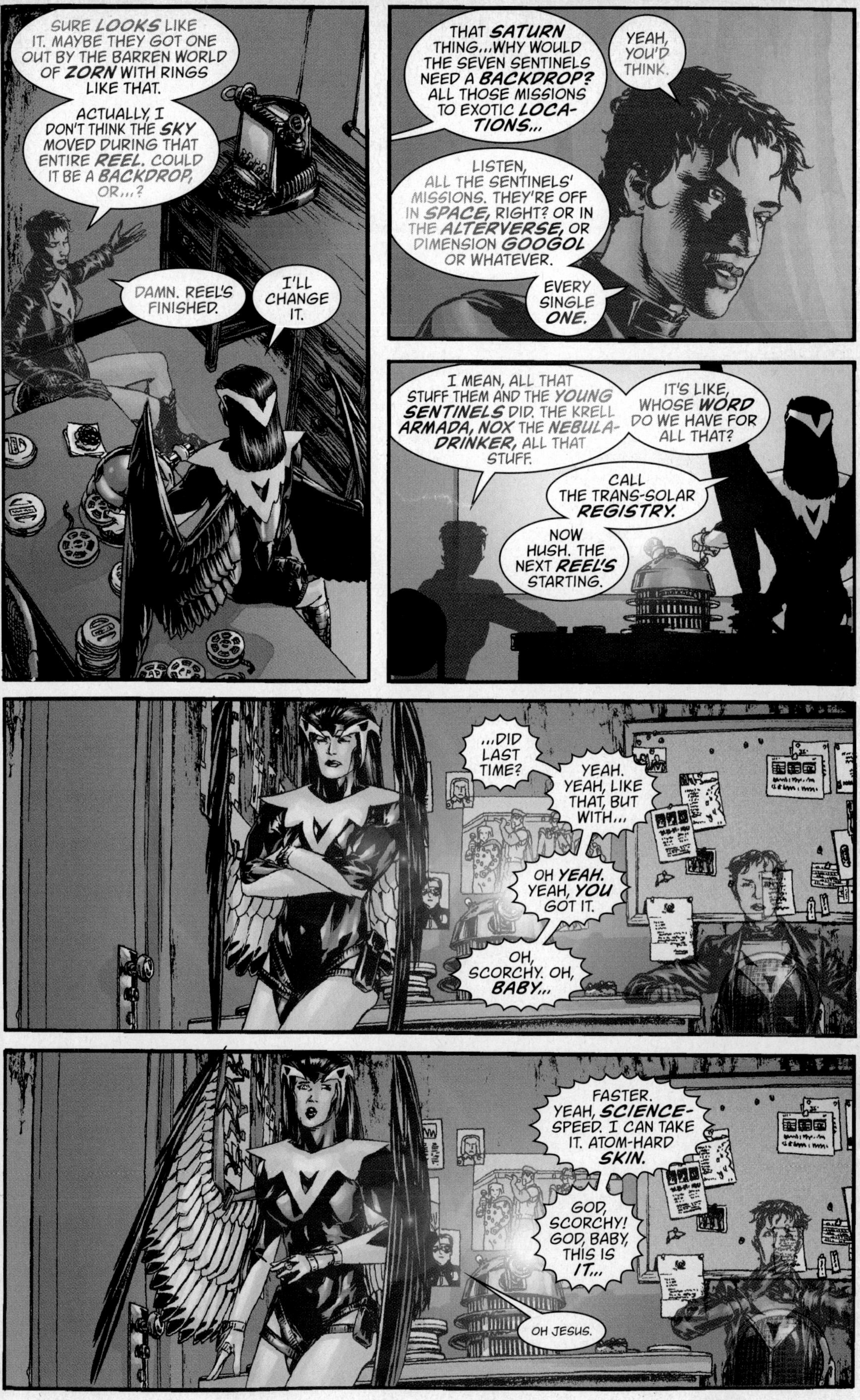
SURE LOOKS LIKE IT. MAYBE THEY GOT ONE OUT BY THE BARREN WORLD OF ZORN WITH RINGS LIKE THAT.
ACTUALLY, I DON'T THINK THE SKY MOVED DURING THAT ENTIRE REEL. COULD IT BE A BACKDROP, OR...?
DAMN. REEL'S FINISHED.
I'LL CHANGE IT.
THAT SATURN THING...WHY WOULD THE SEVEN SENTINELS NEED A BACKDROP? ALL THOSE MISSIONS TO EXOTIC LOCATIONS...
YEAH, YOU'D THINK.
LISTEN, ALL THE SENTINELS' MISSIONS. THEY'RE OFF IN SPACE, RIGHT? OR IN THE ALTERVERSE, OR DIMENSION GOOGOL OR WHATEVER.
EVERY SINGLE ONE.
I MEAN, ALL THAT STUFF THEM AND THE YOUNG SENTINELS DID. THE KRELL ARMADA, NOX THE NEBULA-DRINKER, ALL THAT STUFF.
IT'S LIKE, WHOSE WORD DO WE HAVE FOR ALL THAT?
CALL THE TRANS-SOLAR REGISTRY.
NOW HUSH. THE NEXT REEL'S STARTING.
...DID LAST TIME?
YEAH. YEAH, LIKE THAT, BUT WITH...
OH YEAH. YEAH, YOU GOT IT.
OH, SCORCHY. OH, BABY...
FASTER. YEAH, SCIENCE-SPEED. I CAN TAKE IT. ATOM-HARD SKIN.
GOD, SCORCHY! GOD, BABY, THIS IS IT...
OH JESUS.

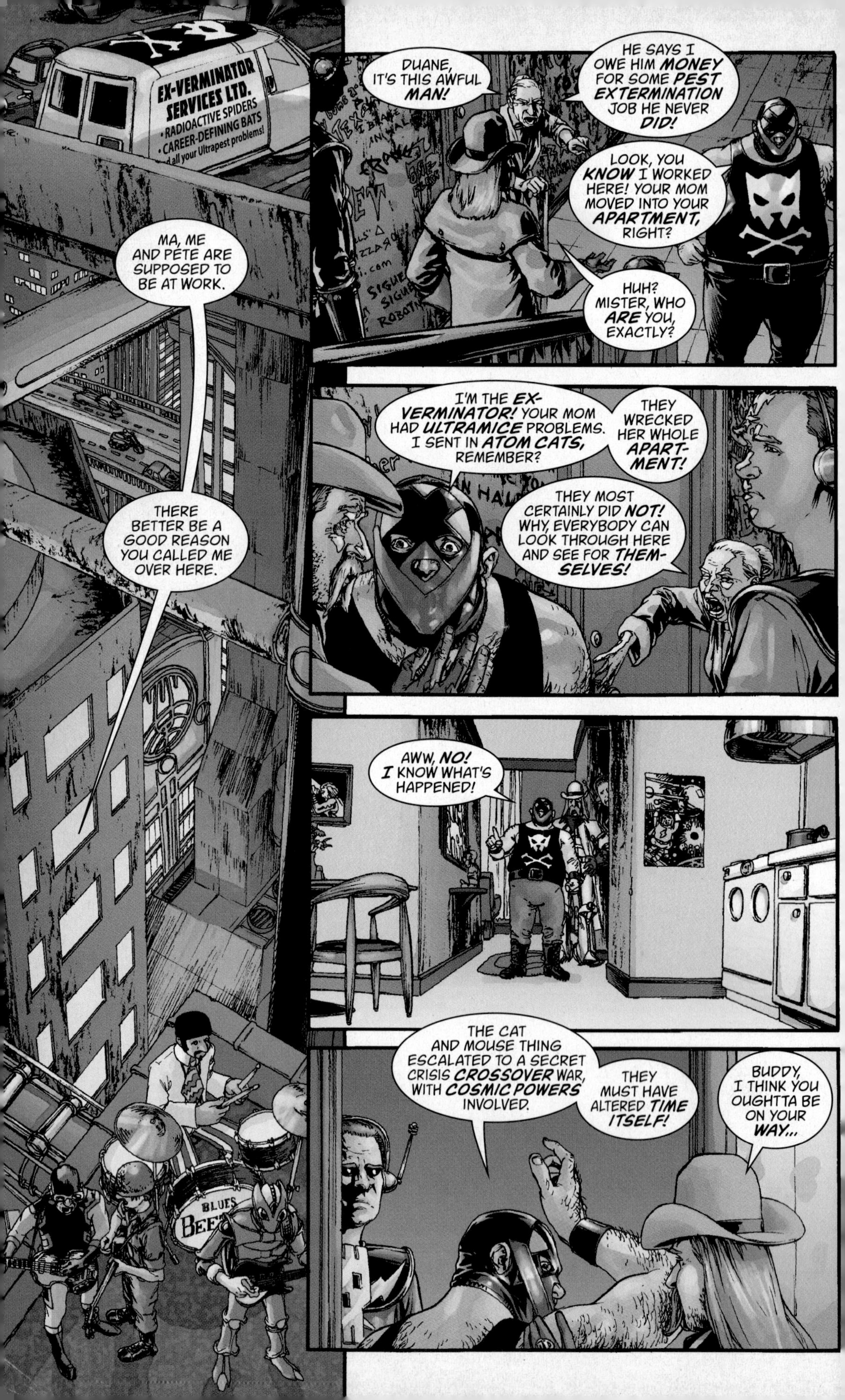
EX-VERMINATOR SERVICES LTD.
• RADIOACTIVE SPIDERS
• CAREER-DEFINING BATS
and all your Ultrapest problems!
MA, ME AND PETE ARE SUPPOSED TO BE AT WORK.
THERE BETTER BE A GOOD REASON YOU CALLED ME OVER HERE.
DUANE, IT'S THIS AWFUL MAN!
HE SAYS I OWE HIM MONEY FOR SOME PEST EXTERMINATION JOB HE NEVER DID!
LOOK, YOU KNOW I WORKED HERE! YOUR MOM MOVED INTO YOUR APARTMENT, RIGHT?
HUH? MISTER, WHO ARE YOU, EXACTLY?
I'M THE EX-VERMINATOR! YOUR MOM HAD ULTRAMICE PROBLEMS. I SENT IN ATOM CATS, REMEMBER?
THEY WRECKED HER WHOLE APARTMENT!
THEY MOST CERTAINLY DID NOT! WHY, EVERYBODY CAN LOOK THROUGH HERE AND SEE FOR THEMSELVES!
AWW, NO! I KNOW WHAT'S HAPPENED!
THE CAT AND MOUSE THING ESCALATED TO A SECRET CRISIS CROSSOVER WAR, WITH COSMIC POWERS INVOLVED.
THEY MUST HAVE ALTERED TIME ITSELF!
BUDDY, I THINK YOU OUGHTTA BE ON YOUR WAY...
BLUES BEE

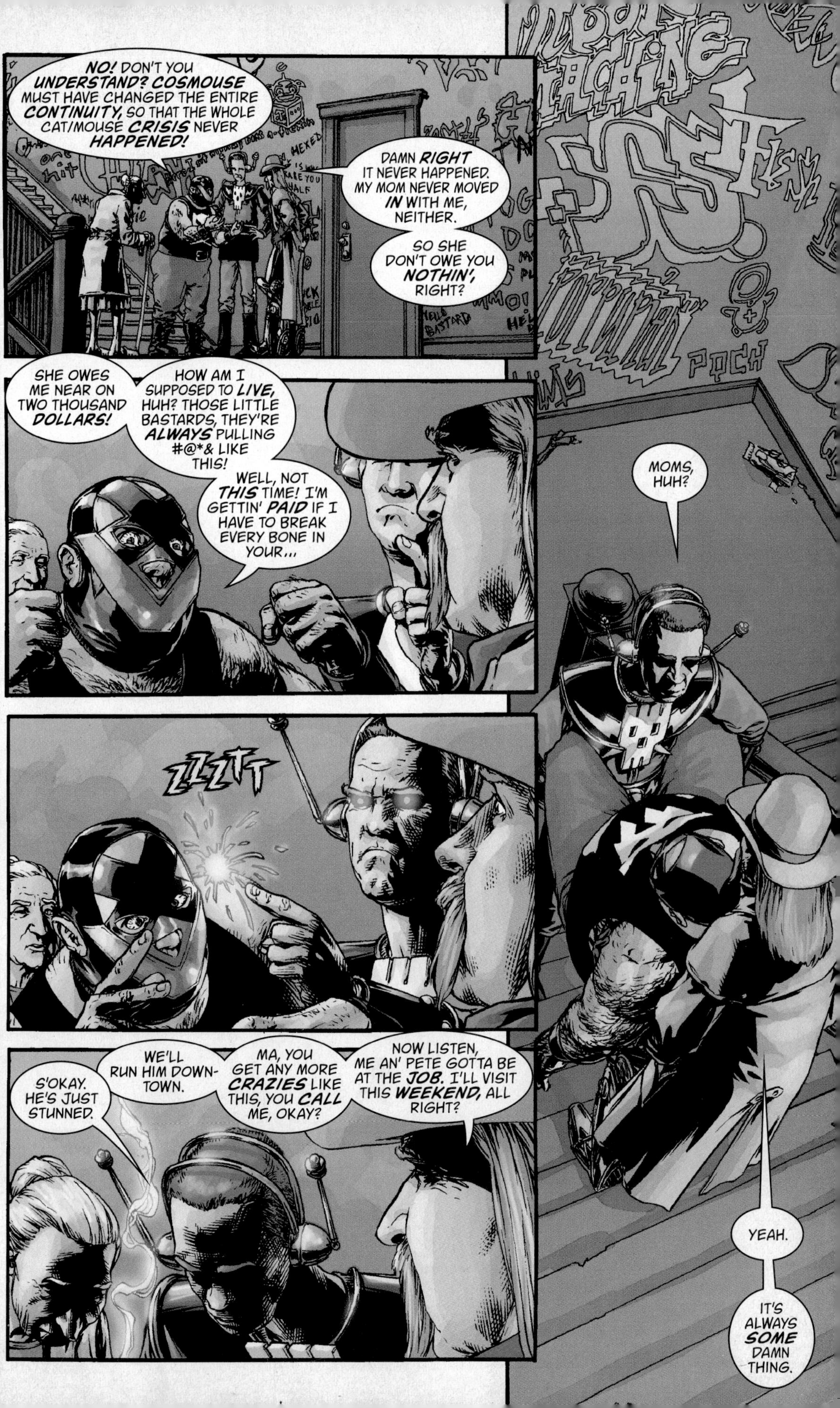
NO! DON'T YOU UNDERSTAND? COSMOUSE MUST HAVE CHANGED THE ENTIRE CONTINUITY, SO THAT THE WHOLE CAT/MOUSE CRISIS NEVER HAPPENED!
DAMN RIGHT IT NEVER HAPPENED. MY MOM NEVER MOVED IN WITH ME, NEITHER.
SO SHE DON'T OWE YOU NOTHIN', RIGHT?
SHE OWES ME NEAR ON TWO THOUSAND DOLLARS!
HOW AM I SUPPOSED TO LIVE, HUH? THOSE LITTLE BASTARDS, THEY'RE ALWAYS PULLING #@*& LIKE THIS!
WELL, NOT THIS TIME! I'M GETTIN' PAID IF I HAVE TO BREAK EVERY BONE IN YOUR...
MOMS, HUH?
S'OKAY. HE'S JUST STUNNED.
WE'LL RUN HIM DOWN-TOWN.
MA, YOU GET ANY MORE CRAZIES LIKE THIS, YOU CALL ME, OKAY?
NOW LISTEN, ME AN' PETE GOTTA BE AT THE JOB. I'LL VISIT THIS WEEKEND, ALL RIGHT?
YEAH.
IT'S ALWAYS SOME DAMN THING.

OHHH!

OOOHHH!

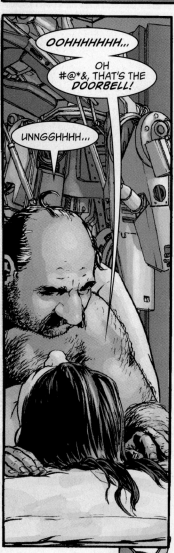

OOHHHHHHH...

OH #@*&, THAT'S THE *DOORBELL!*

UNNGGHHHH...

HI, JOE. MOM AND DAD AREN'T *UP* YET.

YOU WANNA COME IN AND WATCH SOME *CARTOONS* WITH ME AN' *CEREBRA?*

AW, JEEZ, JOE, UM...LOOK, YOU'RE GONNA HAVE TO GIVE ME A COUPLE *MINUTES* HERE.

WE'RE, UH, WE'RE LATE GETTING *UP.*

YEAH, BUT YOU'VE BEEN AWAKE FOR A WHILE.

WE COULD HEAR YOU MAKING ALL THOSE *NOISES.* WHAT WERE YOU *DOING?*

UM...

L-LOOK, KIDS, MOM'S GOTTA TAKE A SHOWER, OKAY?

SHE'S LATE FOR *WORK.* ASK ME *LATER.*

Oh dear. Irma, I hope you haven't been overdoing those strenuous POLICE EXERCISES they make us do every morning?

Sure, you want to be a better OFFICER and provide for your KIDS, but think of YOURSELF for once!

"POLICE EXERCISES?"

WHAT, *REALLY?*

OF COURSE. It's a hard job, and we have to keep FIT for it.

I mean, I'm a logical calculating MACHINE. It's not like I could just make stuff UP.

MORNIN', JOE. HEY, GUESS *WHAT?*

Hmm. Let me SEE. Those particle PHYSICS jobs I mentioned: you applied for one over the 'net, and you have an INTERVIEW?

UH... YEAH.

MOM? CAN *WE* DO POLICE EXERCISES?

WHEN YOU'RE OLDER. NOW *SCRAM.*

NO, SEE, JOE, WHAT IT *IS*, I ALREADY *KNOW* I'M GONNA GET THE JOB. I HAD A PRECOGNITIVE *FLASH.*

JOE? WILL YOU DO THAT *TRICK* AGAIN, WHERE YOUR HEAD COMES OFF?

HEY! LEAVE JOE *BE!*

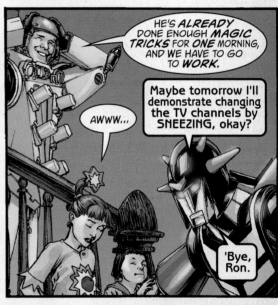

HE'S *ALREADY* DONE ENOUGH *MAGIC* TRICKS FOR *ONE* MORNING, AND WE HAVE TO GO TO *WORK.*

Maybe tomorrow I'll demonstrate changing the TV channels by SNEEZING, okay?

AWWW...

'Bye, Ron.

Y'KNOW, YOU'RE A PIECE O' *WORK*, COVERIN' FOR ME AND RON WITH THE *KIDS* LIKE THAT.

HOW COME YOU UNDERSTAND SO MUCH ABOUT *HUMAN* STUFF?

You were celebrating Ron's JOB interview. It's hardly ROCKET SCIENCE.

THE WORNOWS

HEH. YOU KNOW, YOU *AI*s ARE ALMOST *TOO* CUTE. HOW DO I *UNPLUG* YOU WHEN YOU TAKE OVER THE *WORLD?*

Ask me the purpose of EXISTENCE, and I EXPLODE.

Come on. Let's go to work.

OKAY, LISTEN *UP*, EVERYBODY. THIS ONE'S *SERIOUS*.

WE'VE HAD A BREAK ON THE *GARLAND* CASE. IT'S A *BIG* BREAK, AND IT GOES A LONG *WAY*.

ALL THE WAY TO OUR LATE, UNLAMENTED LIBRA KILLER *M'RRGLA QUALTZ*, AND *BEYOND*. LIEUTENANT *COLBY*?

THANKS, CAPTAIN...

FIRSTLY, GLENN GARLAND'S MURDER HAD NOTHING TO DO WITH HIS POP IDOL *BACKGROUND*.

IT HAD *EVERYTHING* TO DO WITH HIS *SCIENCE-SIDEKICK* BACKGROUND

AS *BLUEJAY*, PARTNER OF PERRY "*KINGFISHER*" SOMERVILLE, GARLAND WAS AFFILIATED WITH BOTH THE *SEVEN SENTINELS* AND THE *YOUNG SENTINELS*.

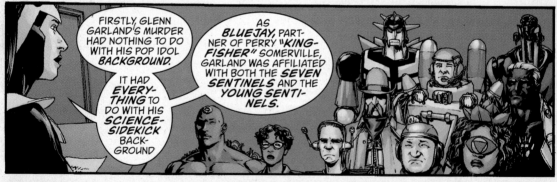

GARLAND WAS PLANNING TO SELL HIS STORY TO THE *PRESS* WHEN SOMEONE *KILLED* HIM.

WE THINK THE *SENTINELS* ORGANIZATION WAS INVOLVED.

CATHY, ARE YOU *SURE*? THEY'RE AWFULLY BIG *PLAYERS*. DIDN'T THEY DEFEAT THE *KRELL ARMADA*?

YEAH, WE WERE JUST *GETTING* TO THAT...

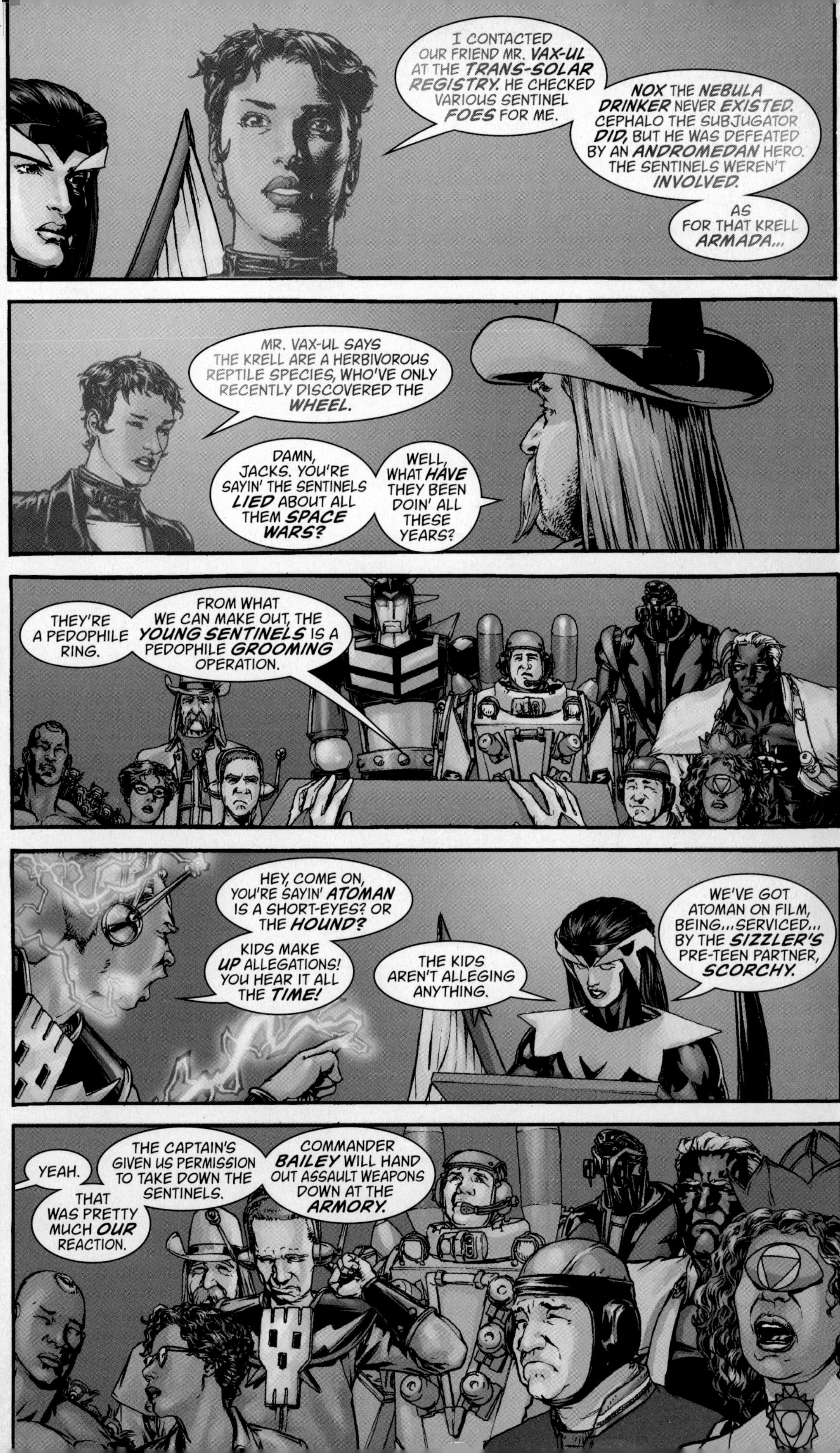

I CONTACTED OUR FRIEND MR. VAX-UL AT THE TRANS-SOLAR REGISTRY. HE CHECKED VARIOUS SENTINEL FOES FOR ME.
NOX THE NEBULA DRINKER NEVER EXISTED. CEPHALO THE SUBJUGATOR DID, BUT HE WAS DEFEATED BY AN ANDROMEDAN HERO. THE SENTINELS WEREN'T INVOLVED.
AS FOR THAT KRELL ARMADA...
MR. VAX-UL SAYS THE KRELL ARE A HERBIVOROUS REPTILE SPECIES, WHO'VE ONLY RECENTLY DISCOVERED THE WHEEL.
DAMN, JACKS. YOU'RE SAYIN' THE SENTINELS LIED ABOUT ALL THEM SPACE WARS?
WELL, WHAT HAVE THEY BEEN DOIN' ALL THESE YEARS?
THEY'RE A PEDOPHILE RING.
FROM WHAT WE CAN MAKE OUT, THE YOUNG SENTINELS IS A PEDOPHILE GROOMING OPERATION.
HEY, COME ON, YOU'RE SAYIN' ATOMAN IS A SHORT-EYES? OR THE HOUND?
KIDS MAKE UP ALLEGATIONS! YOU HEAR IT ALL THE TIME!
THE KIDS AREN'T ALLEGING ANYTHING.
WE'VE GOT ATOMAN ON FILM, BEING...SERVICED... BY THE SIZZLER'S PRE-TEEN PARTNER, SCORCHY.
YEAH.
THAT WAS PRETTY MUCH OUR REACTION.
THE CAPTAIN'S GIVEN US PERMISSION TO TAKE DOWN THE SENTINELS.
COMMANDER BAILEY WILL HAND OUT ASSAULT WEAPONS DOWN AT THE ARMORY.

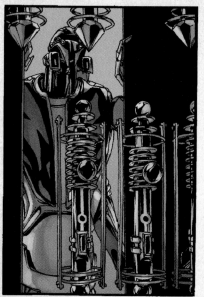

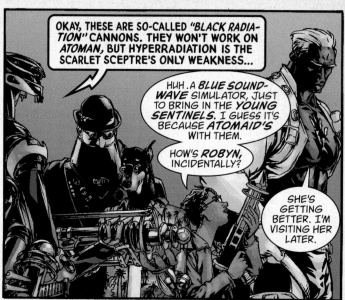

OKAY, THESE ARE SO-CALLED "BLACK RADIATION" CANNONS. THEY WON'T WORK ON ATOMAN, BUT HYPERRADIATION IS THE SCARLET SCEPTRE'S ONLY WEAKNESS...

HUH. A BLUE SOUNDWAVE SIMULATOR, JUST TO BRING IN THE YOUNG SENTINELS. I GUESS IT'S BECAUSE ATOMAID'S WITH THEM.

HOW'S ROBYN, INCIDENTALLY?

SHE'S GETTING BETTER. I'M VISITING HER LATER.

GIVE HER MY LOVE. SO, ARE YOU ON THE ATOMAN DETAIL?

YOU'D THINK. IF WALLACE DECIDES IT'S COURT ON THE STREET, WE GOT ANOTHER ULTIMA, RIGHT THERE.

NAH. TRAYNOR'S GOT ME BRINGIN' IN THE SIZZLER. GO FIGURE.

HEY, PIE-TIN! HOW COME THE LIBERAL PRESS NEVER TALK ABOUT CLICKER CHILD-ABUSE?

Beats me, Officer Cheney.

I mean, we punch the TOASTER once in a while, just like anyone ELSE.

Come on, Officer Wornow. Let's go get our VEHICLE.

PETE, YOU *&%HOLE...

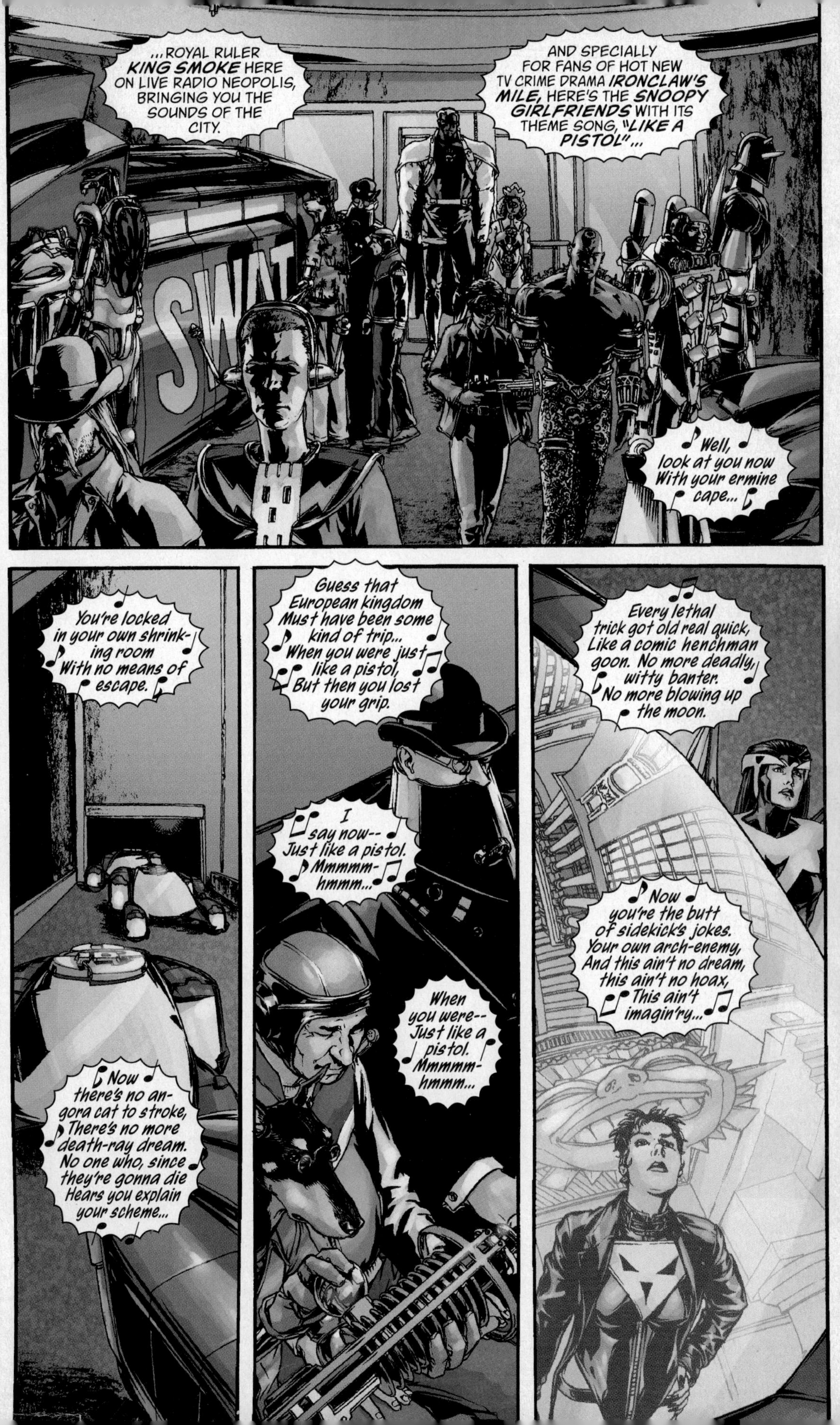

...ROYAL RULER KING SMOKE HERE ON LIVE RADIO NEOPOLIS, BRINGING YOU THE SOUNDS OF THE CITY.
AND SPECIALLY FOR FANS OF HOT NEW TV CRIME DRAMA IRONCLAW'S MILE, HERE'S THE SNOOPY GIRLFRIENDS WITH ITS THEME SONG, "LIKE A PISTOL"...
SWAT
Well, look at you now With your ermine cape...
You're locked in your own shrinking room With no means of escape.
Now there's no angora cat to stroke, There's no more death-ray dream. No one who, since they're gonna die Hears you explain your scheme...
Guess that European kingdom Must have been some kind of trip... When you were just like a pistol, But then you lost your grip.
I say now-- Just like a pistol. Mmmmm-hmmm...
When you were-- Just like a pistol. Mmmmm-hmmm...
Every lethal trick got old real quick, Like a comic henchman goon. No more deadly, witty banter. No more blowing up the moon.
Now you're the butt of sidekick's jokes. Your own arch-enemy, And this ain't no dream, this ain't no hoax, This ain't imagin'ry...

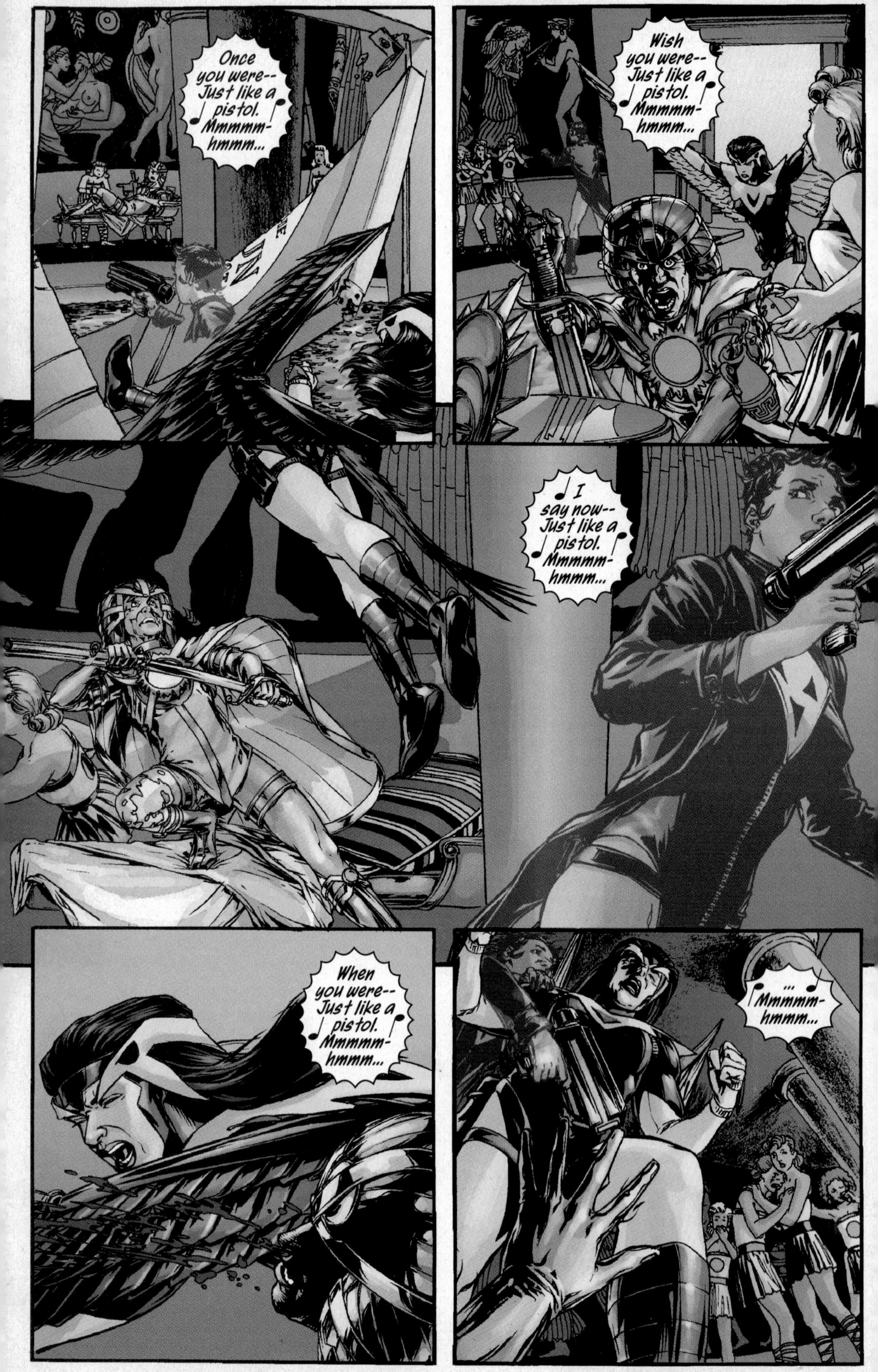
Once you were-- Just like a pistol. Mmmmm-hmmm...
Wish you were-- Just like a pistol. Mmmmm-hmmm...
I say now-- Just like a pistol. Mmmmm-hmmm...
When you were-- Just like a pistol. Mmmmm-hmmm...
... Mmmmm-hmmm...

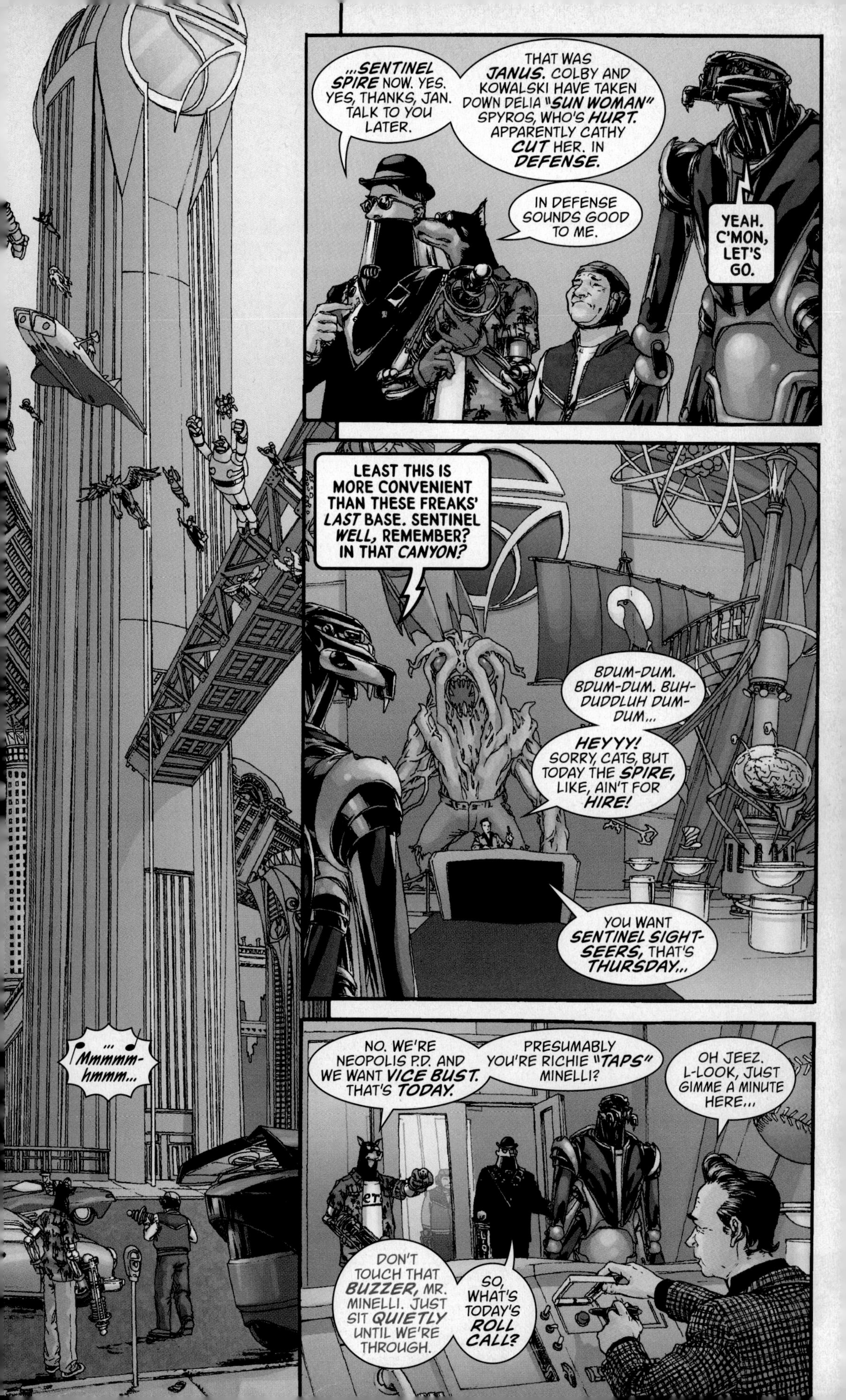

...SENTINEL SPIRE NOW. YES. YES, THANKS, JAN. TALK TO YOU LATER.
THAT WAS JANUS. COLBY AND KOWALSKI HAVE TAKEN DOWN DELIA "SUN WOMAN" SPYROS, WHO'S HURT. APPARENTLY CATHY CUT HER. IN DEFENSE.
IN DEFENSE SOUNDS GOOD TO ME.
YEAH. C'MON, LET'S GO.
LEAST THIS IS MORE CONVENIENT THAN THESE FREAKS' LAST BASE. SENTINEL WELL, REMEMBER? IN THAT CANYON?
BDUM-DUM. BDUM-DUM. BUH-DUDDLUH DUM-DUM...
HEYYY! SORRY, CATS, BUT TODAY THE SPIRE, LIKE, AIN'T FOR HIRE!
YOU WANT SENTINEL SIGHT-SEERS, THAT'S THURSDAY...
...Mmmmm-hmmm...
NO. WE'RE NEOPOLIS P.D. AND WE WANT VICE BUST. THAT'S TODAY.
PRESUMABLY YOU'RE RICHIE "TAPS" MINELLI?
OH JEEZ. L-LOOK, JUST GIMME A MINUTE HERE...
DON'T TOUCH THAT BUZZER, MR. MINELLI. JUST SIT QUIETLY UNTIL WE'RE THROUGH.
SO, WHAT'S TODAY'S ROLL CALL?

IT'S OKAY, HARRY. I GOT THAT FROM HIS *HEAD.*

THERE'S FOUR HERE TODAY: *KINGFISHER, SCEPTRE, BOOMER-ANG, DAVY JONES...*

C'MON. LET'S CHECK THE *REC* ROOMS.

NOW, JUST YOU REMEMBER: NICE AND QUIET, EH?

O-OH GOD...

...TELLYA? AFTER A COUPLE O' TIMES, IT'S OKAY.

ANYWAY, *THESE* GUYS, THEY'RE *NOTHING.* LOMAX, HE'S *NASTY.* AND *WALLACE*...WELL, THAT'S SOMETHING *ELSE.*

UHH...M-MARTA?

AWW, S***, LOOK AT THIS. "RUGRATS DOES DALLAS."

OH #%@*! I KNOW DOG-GUY THERE. THESE GUYS ARE *COPS.*

MARTA *WESSON? BOOTS?* WHAT ARE *YOU* DOING HERE?

WH-WHAT WAS I *SUPPOSED* TO DO, WITH *STEF* GONE? I JOINED THE *YOUNG SENTINELS.*

LISTEN, BLACKIE HERE'S *NEW.* LET HER *GO,* OKAY?

READ THE DIAPER DUO THEIR *RIGHTS,* HARRY.

KEM, LEX, YOU GUYS WITH *ME.*

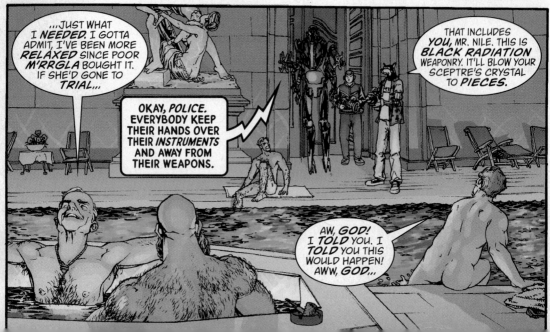

...JUST WHAT I *NEEDED.* I GOTTA ADMIT, I'VE BEEN MORE *RELAXED* SINCE POOR *M'RRGLA* BOUGHT IT. IF SHE'D GONE TO *TRIAL...*

OKAY, *POLICE.* EVERYBODY KEEP THEIR HANDS OVER THEIR *INSTRUMENTS* AND AWAY FROM THEIR WEAPONS.

THAT INCLUDES *YOU,* MR. NILE. THIS IS *BLACK RADIATION* WEAPONRY. IT'LL BLOW YOUR *SCEPTRE'S* CRYSTAL TO *PIECES.*

AW, *GOD!* I *TOLD* YOU. I *TOLD* YOU THIS WOULD HAPPEN! AWW, *GOD...*

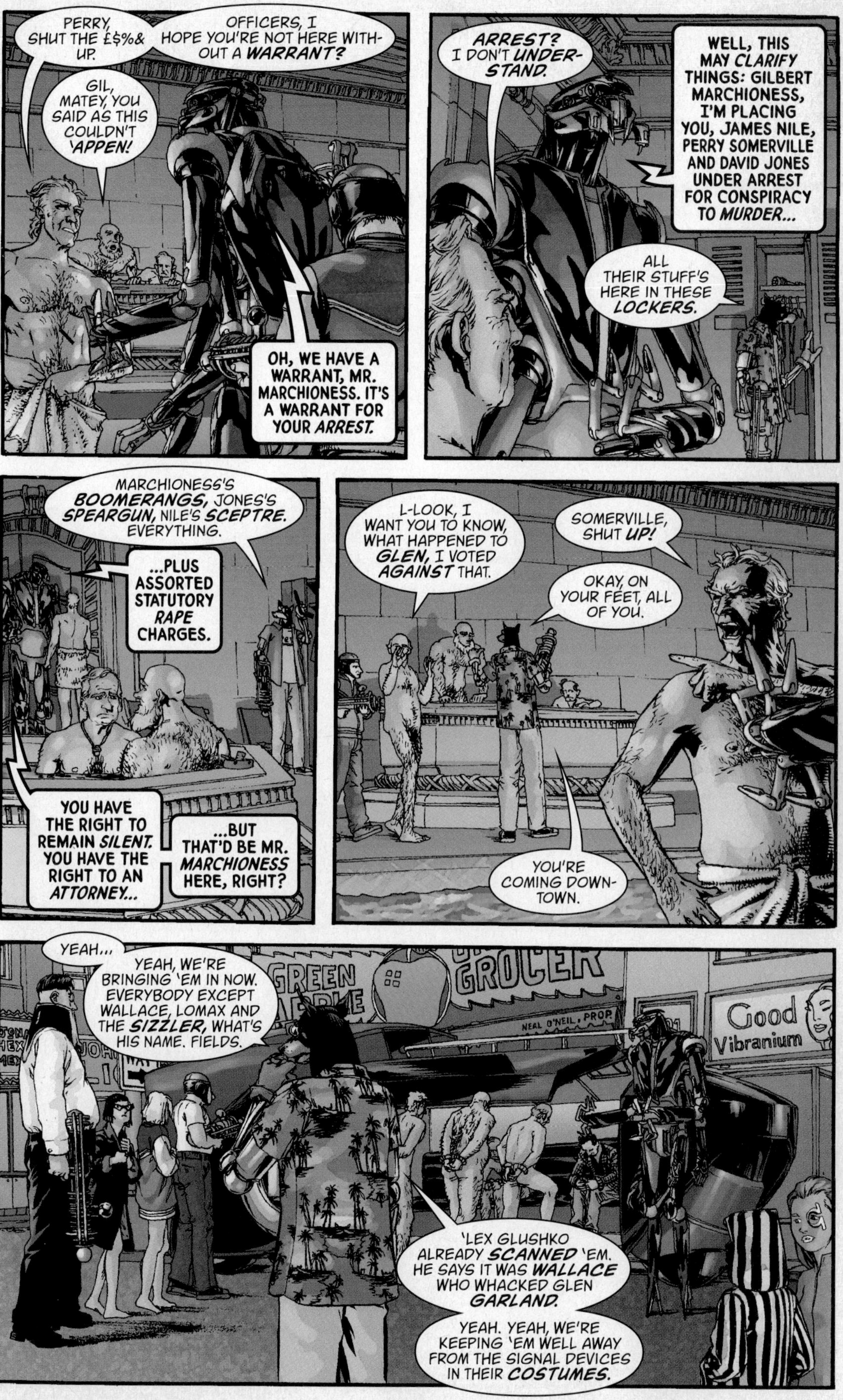
PERRY, SHUT THE £$%& UP.
OFFICERS, I HOPE YOU'RE NOT HERE WITHOUT A WARRANT?
GIL, MATEY, YOU SAID AS THIS COULDN'T 'APPEN!
OH, WE HAVE A WARRANT, MR. MARCHIONESS. IT'S A WARRANT FOR YOUR ARREST.
ARREST? I DON'T UNDERSTAND.
WELL, THIS MAY CLARIFY THINGS: GILBERT MARCHIONESS, I'M PLACING YOU, JAMES NILE, PERRY SOMERVILLE AND DAVID JONES UNDER ARREST FOR CONSPIRACY TO MURDER...
ALL THEIR STUFF'S HERE IN THESE LOCKERS.
MARCHIONESS'S BOOMERANGS, JONES'S SPEARGUN, NILE'S SCEPTRE. EVERYTHING.
...PLUS ASSORTED STATUTORY RAPE CHARGES.
YOU HAVE THE RIGHT TO REMAIN SILENT. YOU HAVE THE RIGHT TO AN ATTORNEY...
...BUT THAT'D BE MR. MARCHIONESS HERE, RIGHT?
L-LOOK, I WANT YOU TO KNOW, WHAT HAPPENED TO GLEN, I VOTED AGAINST THAT.
SOMERVILLE, SHUT UP!
OKAY, ON YOUR FEET, ALL OF YOU.
YOU'RE COMING DOWNTOWN.
YEAH...
YEAH, WE'RE BRINGING 'EM IN NOW. EVERYBODY EXCEPT WALLACE, LOMAX AND THE SIZZLER, WHAT'S HIS NAME. FIELDS.
GREEN APPLE
GROCER
NEAL O'NEIL, PROP.
Good Vibranium
'LEX GLUSHKO ALREADY SCANNED 'EM. HE SAYS IT WAS WALLACE WHO WHACKED GLEN GARLAND.
YEAH. YEAH, WE'RE KEEPING 'EM WELL AWAY FROM THE SIGNAL DEVICES IN THEIR COSTUMES.

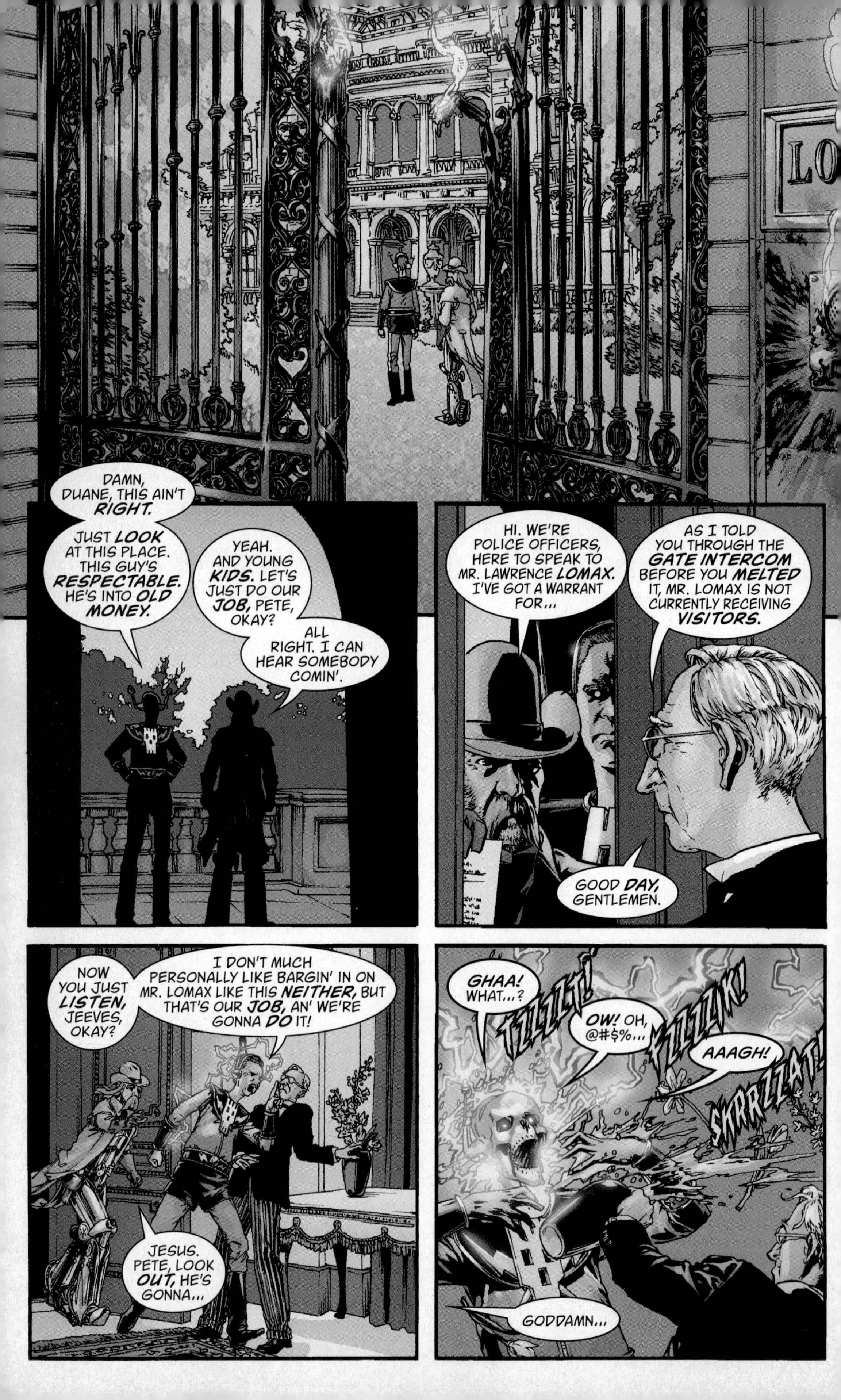

DAMN, DUANE, THIS AIN'T RIGHT.
JUST LOOK AT THIS PLACE. THIS GUY'S RESPECTABLE. HE'S INTO OLD MONEY.
YEAH. AND YOUNG KIDS. LET'S JUST DO OUR JOB, PETE, OKAY?
ALL RIGHT. I CAN HEAR SOMEBODY COMIN'.
HI. WE'RE POLICE OFFICERS, HERE TO SPEAK TO MR. LAWRENCE LOMAX. I'VE GOT A WARRANT FOR...
AS I TOLD YOU THROUGH THE GATE INTERCOM BEFORE YOU MELTED IT, MR. LOMAX IS NOT CURRENTLY RECEIVING VISITORS.
GOOD DAY, GENTLEMEN.
NOW YOU JUST LISTEN, JEEVES, OKAY?
I DON'T MUCH PERSONALLY LIKE BARGIN' IN ON MR. LOMAX LIKE THIS NEITHER, BUT THAT'S OUR JOB, AN' WE'RE GONNA DO IT!
JESUS. PETE, LOOK OUT, HE'S GONNA...
GHAA! WHAT...?
FZZZZT!
OW! OH, @#$%...
FZZZAK!
AAAGH!
SKRRZZAT!
GODDAMN...

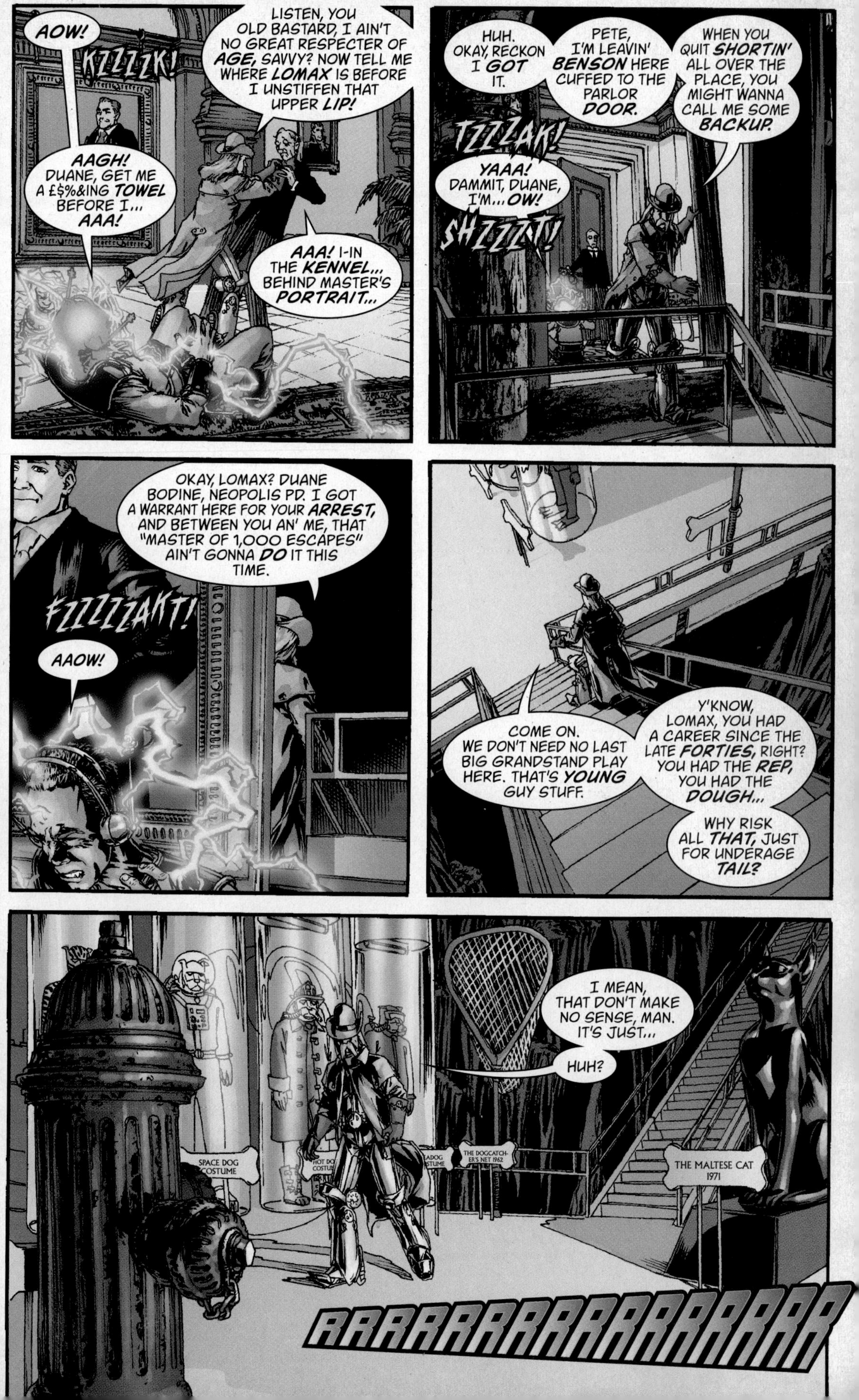
AOW!
KZZZZK!
LISTEN, YOU OLD BASTARD, I AIN'T NO GREAT RESPECTER OF AGE, SAVVY? NOW TELL ME WHERE LOMAX IS BEFORE I UNSTIFFEN THAT UPPER LIP!
AAGH! DUANE, GET ME A £$%&ING TOWEL BEFORE I... AAA!
AAA! I-IN THE KENNEL... BEHIND MASTER'S PORTRAIT...
HUH. OKAY, RECKON I GOT IT.
PETE, I'M LEAVIN' BENSON HERE CUFFED TO THE PARLOR DOOR.
WHEN YOU QUIT SHORTIN' ALL OVER THE PLACE, YOU MIGHT WANNA CALL ME SOME BACKUP.
TZZZAK!
YAAA! DAMMIT, DUANE, I'M... OW!
SHZZZT!
OKAY, LOMAX? DUANE BODINE, NEOPOLIS PD. I GOT A WARRANT HERE FOR YOUR ARREST, AND BETWEEN YOU AN' ME, THAT "MASTER OF 1,000 ESCAPES" AIN'T GONNA DO IT THIS TIME.
FZZZZZAKT!
AAOW!
COME ON. WE DON'T NEED NO LAST BIG GRANDSTAND PLAY HERE. THAT'S YOUNG GUY STUFF.
Y'KNOW, LOMAX, YOU HAD A CAREER SINCE THE LATE FORTIES, RIGHT? YOU HAD THE REP, YOU HAD THE DOUGH...
WHY RISK ALL THAT, JUST FOR UNDERAGE TAIL?
SPACE DOG COSTUME
THE DOGCATCH- ER'S NET 1962
THE MALTESE CAT 1971
I MEAN, THAT DON'T MAKE NO SENSE, MAN. IT'S JUST...
HUH?
RRRRRRRRRRRRRRRRR

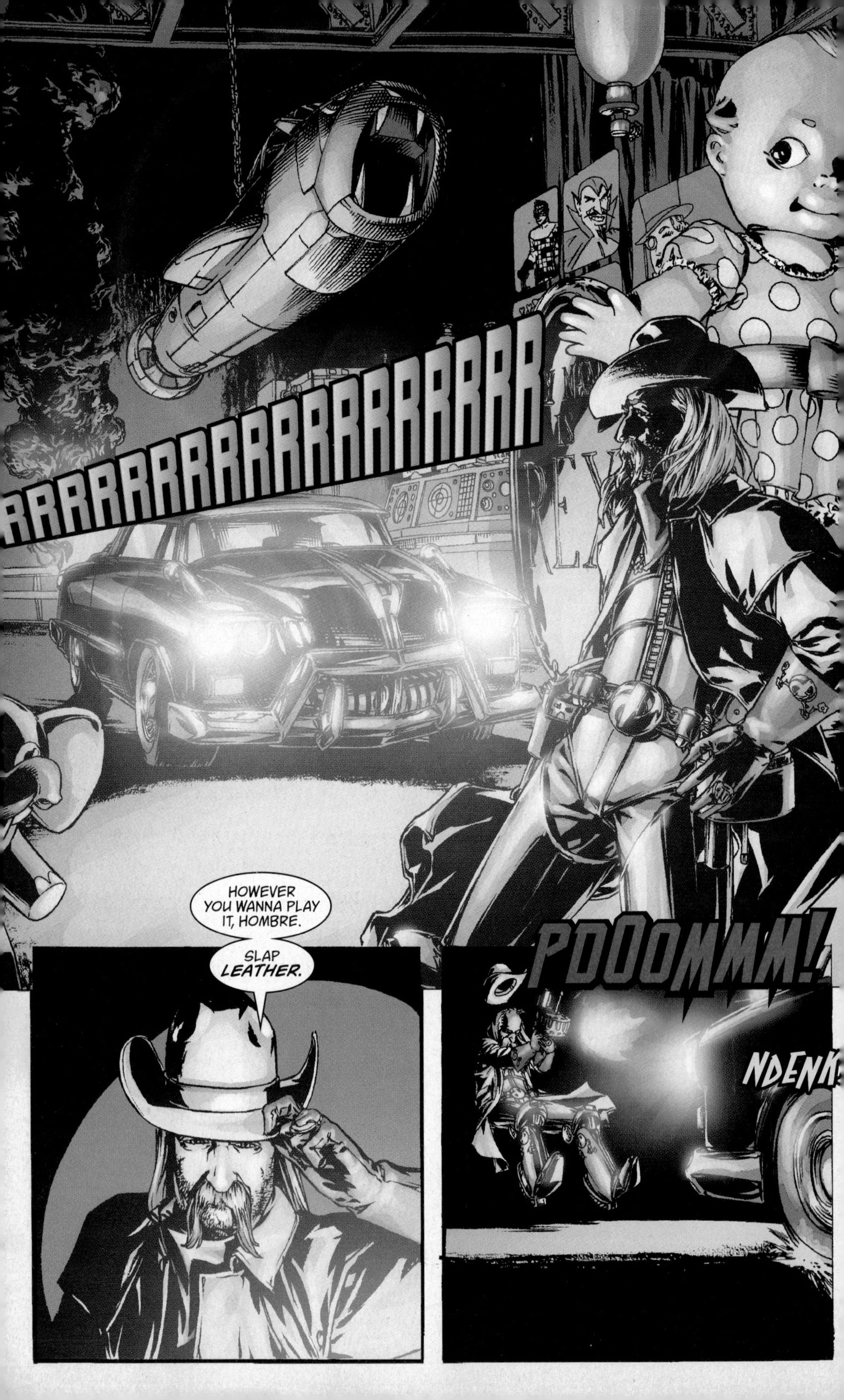
RRRRRRRRRRRRRRRRRRRRRR
HOWEVER YOU WANNA PLAY IT, HOMBRE.
SLAP LEATHER.
PDOOMMM!
NDENK

OH SH--

SHRRRANNNK

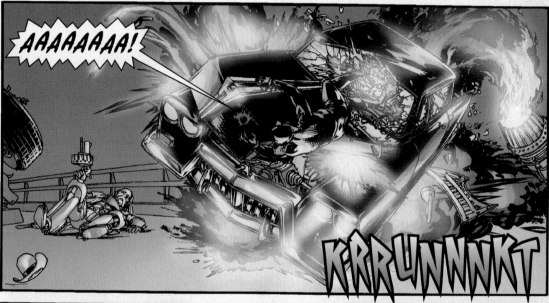

AAAAAAAA!

KRRUNNKT

AAAA...

AAAAAH...

YEAH, JANUS? DUANE.

IF THE CAPTAIN'S THERE, TELL HIM THE HOUND JUST GOT COLLARED.

AAAA...

NNHHHH...

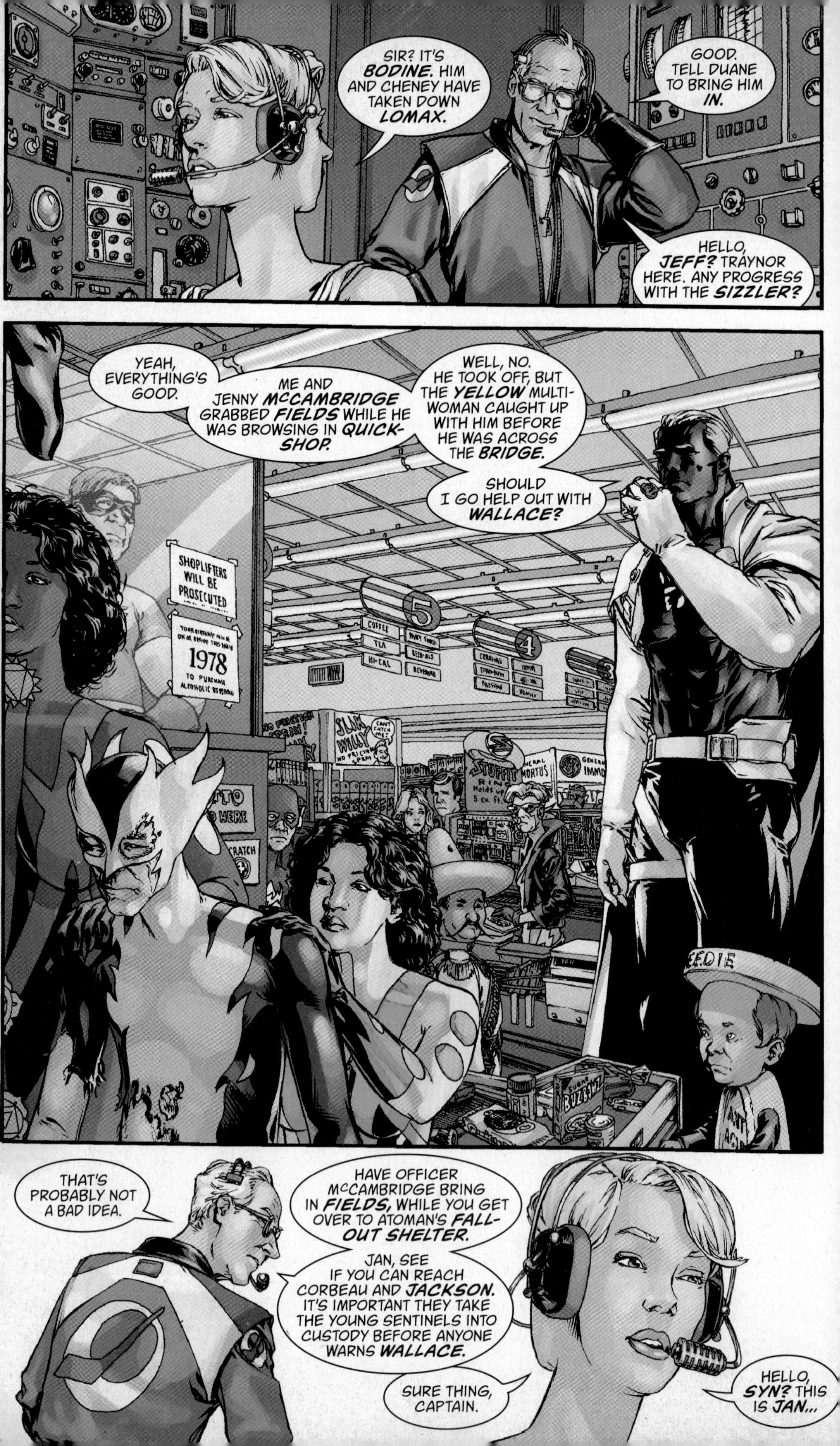
SIR? IT'S ***BODINE.*** HIM AND CHENEY HAVE TAKEN DOWN ***LOMAX.***
GOOD. TELL DUANE TO BRING HIM ***IN.***
HELLO, ***JEFF?*** TRAYNOR HERE. ANY PROGRESS WITH THE ***SIZZLER?***
YEAH, EVERYTHING'S GOOD.
ME AND JENNY ***McCAMBRIDGE*** GRABBED ***FIELDS*** WHILE HE WAS BROWSING IN ***QUICK-SHOP.***
WELL, NO. HE TOOK OFF, BUT THE ***YELLOW*** MULTI-WOMAN CAUGHT UP WITH HIM BEFORE HE WAS ACROSS THE ***BRIDGE.***
SHOULD I GO HELP OUT WITH ***WALLACE?***
SHOPLIFTERS WILL BE PROSECUTED
1978
COFFEE
TEA
HI-CAL
5
4
SLIM WILLY
CAN'T CATCH ME!
NO FRICTION SPRAY
THAT'S PROBABLY NOT A BAD IDEA.
HAVE OFFICER McCAMBRIDGE BRING IN ***FIELDS,*** WHILE YOU GET OVER TO ATOMAN'S ***FALL-OUT SHELTER.***
JAN, SEE IF YOU CAN REACH CORBEAU AND ***JACKSON.*** IT'S IMPORTANT THEY TAKE THE YOUNG SENTINELS INTO CUSTODY BEFORE ANYONE WARNS ***WALLACE.***
SURE THING, CAPTAIN.
HELLO, ***SYN?*** THIS IS ***JAN...***

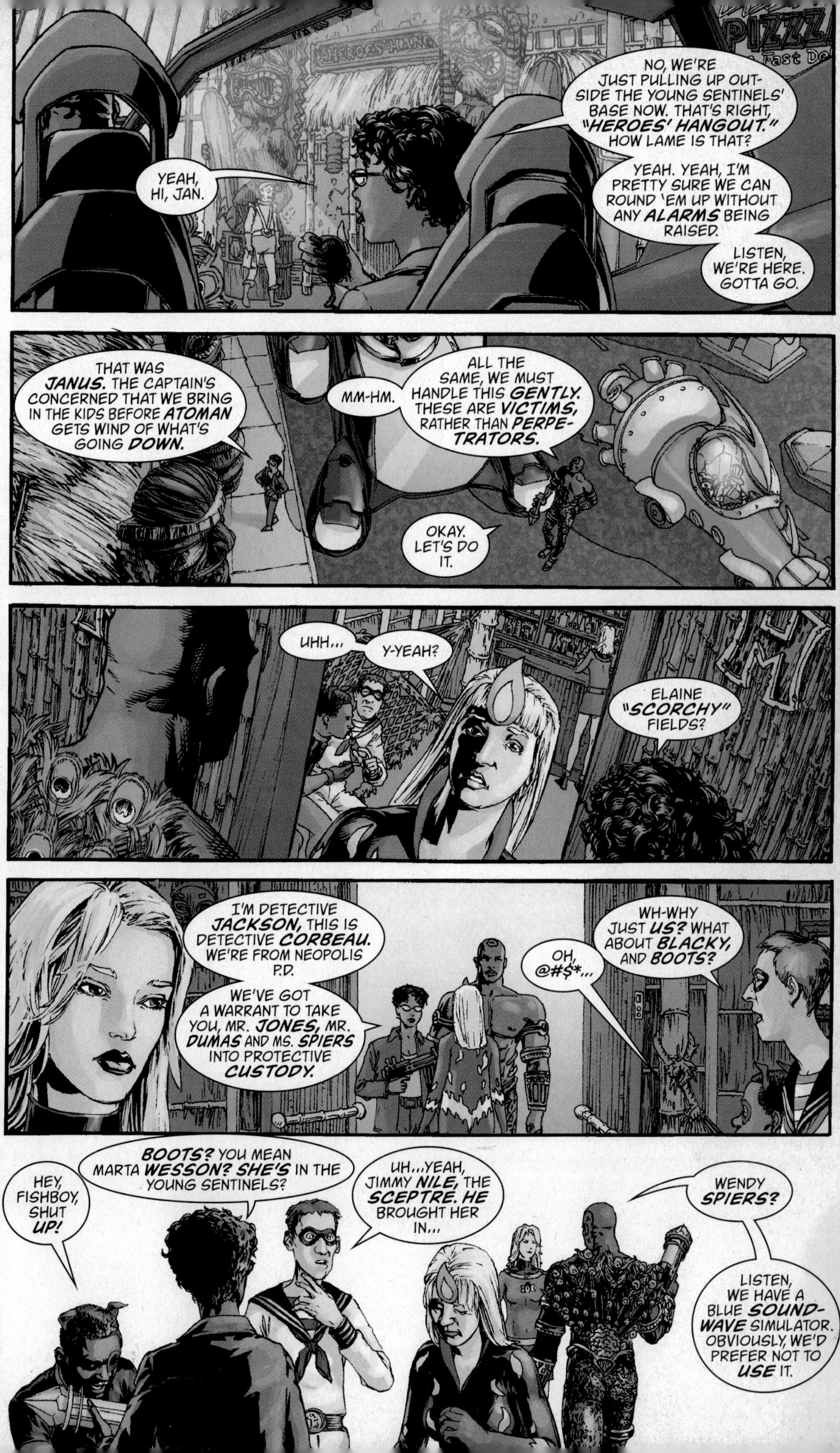

PIZZZ
NO, WE'RE JUST PULLING UP OUTSIDE THE YOUNG SENTINELS' BASE NOW. THAT'S RIGHT, "HEROES' HANGOUT." HOW LAME IS THAT?
YEAH, HI, JAN.
YEAH. YEAH, I'M PRETTY SURE WE CAN ROUND 'EM UP WITHOUT ANY ALARMS BEING RAISED.
LISTEN, WE'RE HERE. GOTTA GO.
THAT WAS JANUS. THE CAPTAIN'S CONCERNED THAT WE BRING IN THE KIDS BEFORE ATOMAN GETS WIND OF WHAT'S GOING DOWN.
MM-HM.
ALL THE SAME, WE MUST HANDLE THIS GENTLY. THESE ARE VICTIMS, RATHER THAN PERPETRATORS.
OKAY. LET'S DO IT.
UHH...
Y-YEAH?
ELAINE "SCORCHY" FIELDS?
I'M DETECTIVE JACKSON, THIS IS DETECTIVE CORBEAU. WE'RE FROM NEOPOLIS P.D.
WE'VE GOT A WARRANT TO TAKE YOU, MR. JONES, MR. DUMAS AND MS. SPIERS INTO PROTECTIVE CUSTODY.
OH, @#$*...
WH-WHY JUST US? WHAT ABOUT BLACKY, AND BOOTS?
HEY, FISHBOY, SHUT UP!
BOOTS? YOU MEAN MARTA WESSON? SHE'S IN THE YOUNG SENTINELS?
UH...YEAH, JIMMY NILE, THE SCEPTRE. HE BROUGHT HER IN...
WENDY SPIERS?
LISTEN, WE HAVE A BLUE SOUNDWAVE SIMULATOR. OBVIOUSLY, WE'D PREFER NOT TO USE IT.

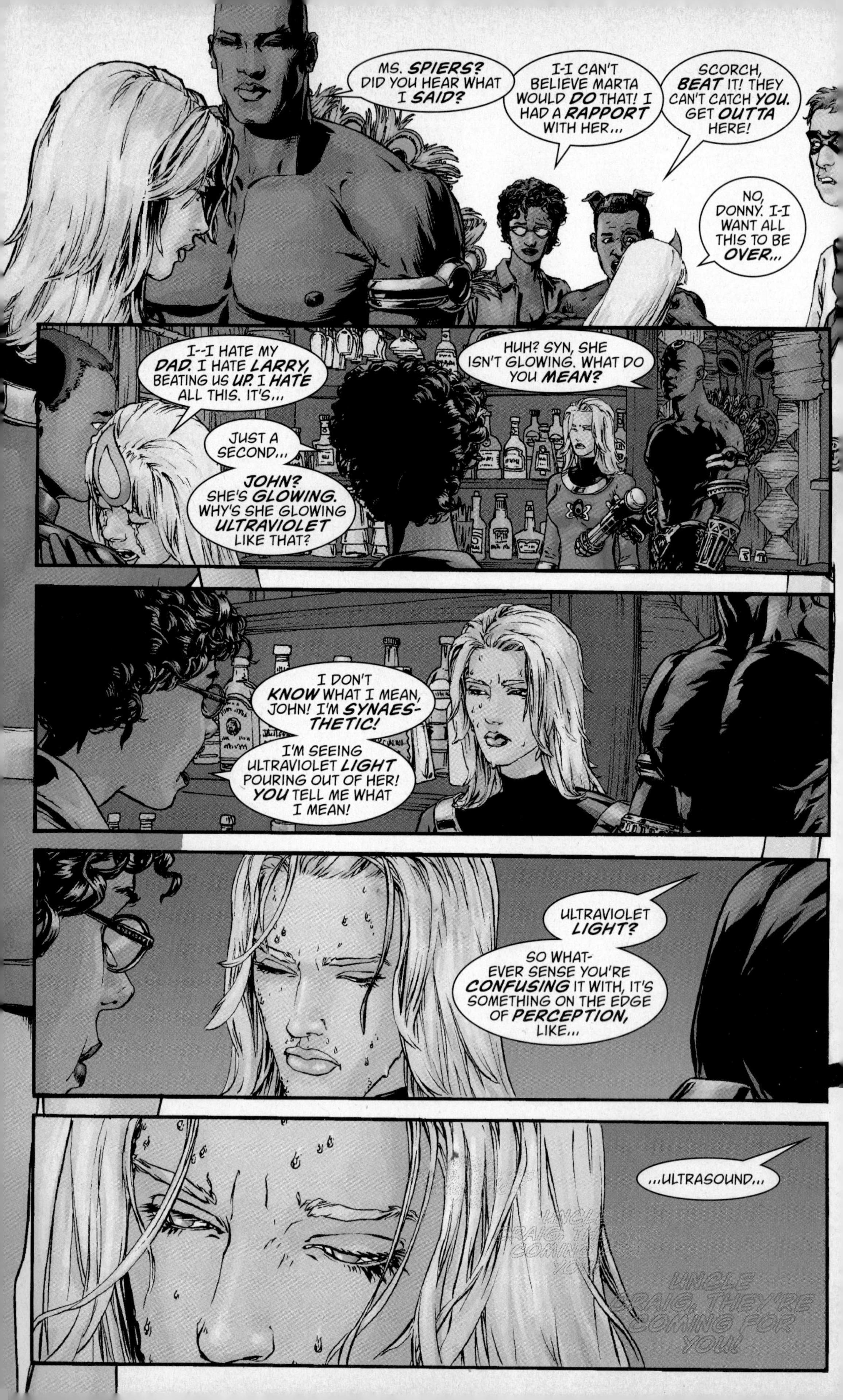
MS. SPIERS? DID YOU HEAR WHAT I SAID?
I-I CAN'T BELIEVE MARTA WOULD DO THAT! I HAD A RAPPORT WITH HER...
SCORCH, BEAT IT! THEY CAN'T CATCH YOU. GET OUTTA HERE!
NO, DONNY. I-I WANT ALL THIS TO BE OVER...
I--I HATE MY DAD. I HATE LARRY, BEATING US UP. I HATE ALL THIS. IT'S...
JUST A SECOND...
JOHN? SHE'S GLOWING. WHY'S SHE GLOWING ULTRAVIOLET LIKE THAT?
HUH? SYN, SHE ISN'T GLOWING. WHAT DO YOU MEAN?
I DON'T KNOW WHAT I MEAN, JOHN! I'M SYNAESTHETIC!
I'M SEEING ULTRAVIOLET LIGHT POURING OUT OF HER! YOU TELL ME WHAT I MEAN!
ULTRAVIOLET LIGHT?
SO WHATEVER SENSE YOU'RE CONFUSING IT WITH, IT'S SOMETHING ON THE EDGE OF PERCEPTION, LIKE...
...ULTRASOUND...
UNCLE CRAIG, THEY'RE COMING FOR YOU!

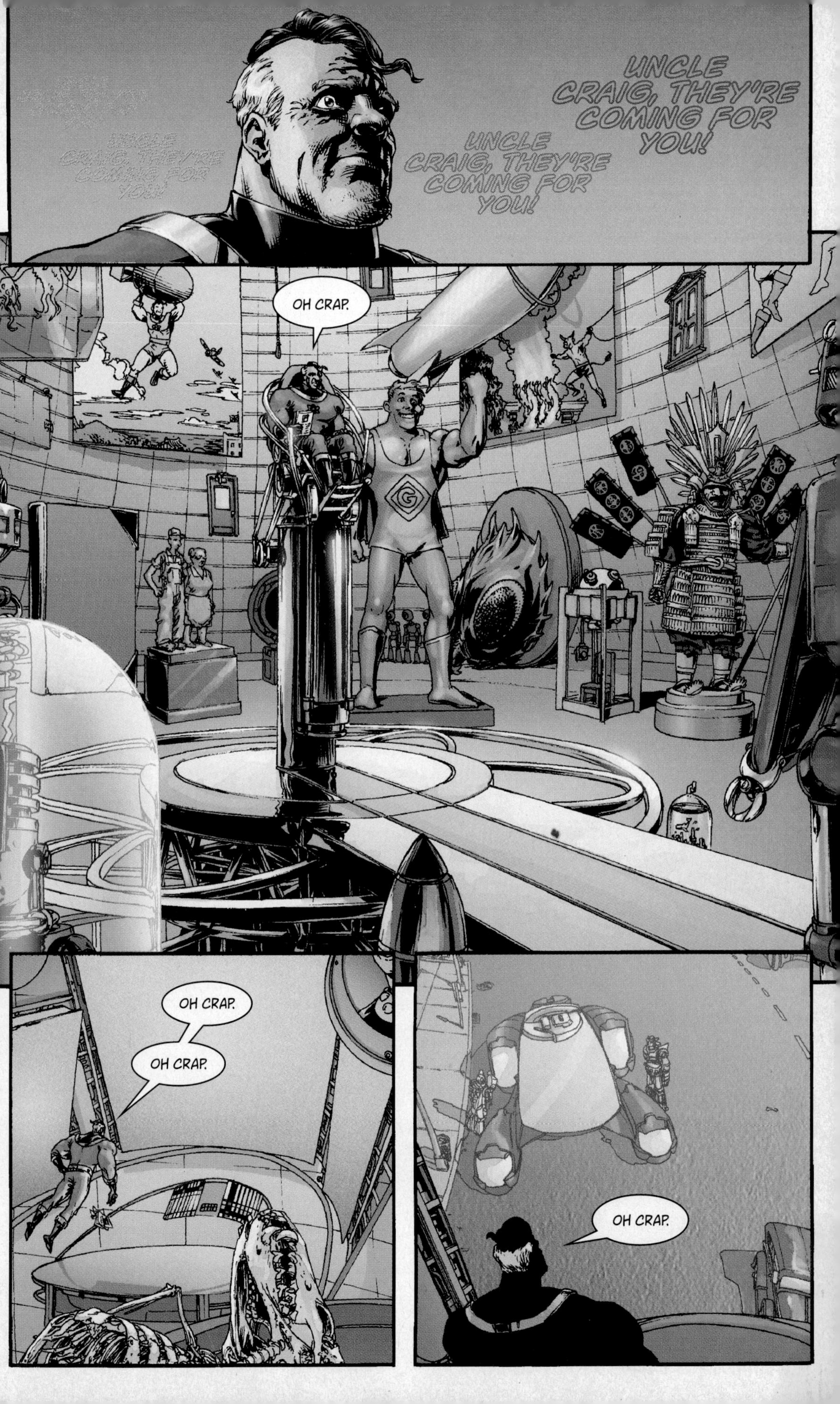
UNCLE CRAIG, THEY'RE COMING FOR YOU!
UNCLE CRAIG, THEY'RE COMING FOR YOU!
OH CRAP.
OH CRAP.
OH CRAP.
OH CRAP.

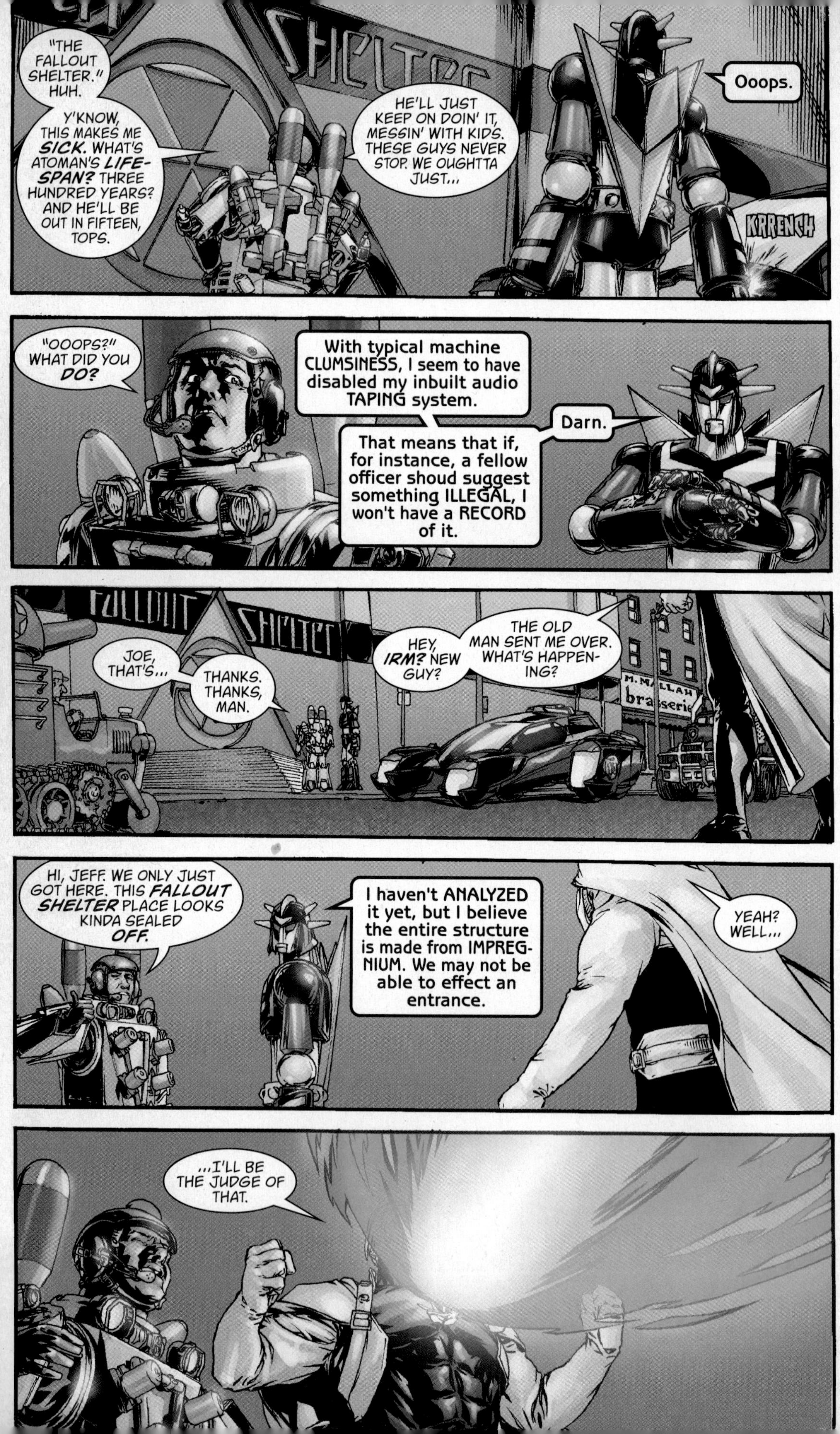
"THE FALLOUT SHELTER." HUH.
Y'KNOW, THIS MAKES ME SICK. WHAT'S ATOMAN'S LIFE-SPAN? THREE HUNDRED YEARS? AND HE'LL BE OUT IN FIFTEEN, TOPS.
HE'LL JUST KEEP ON DOIN' IT, MESSIN' WITH KIDS. THESE GUYS NEVER STOP. WE OUGHTTA JUST...
Ooops.
KRRENCH
"OOOPS?" WHAT DID YOU DO?
With typical machine CLUMSINESS, I seem to have disabled my inbuilt audio TAPING system.
That means that if, for instance, a fellow officer shoud suggest something ILLEGAL, I won't have a RECORD of it.
Darn.
FALLOUT SHELTER
JOE, THAT'S...
THANKS. THANKS, MAN.
HEY, IRM? NEW GUY?
THE OLD MAN SENT ME OVER. WHAT'S HAPPEN-ING?
M. MALLAH brasserie
HI, JEFF. WE ONLY JUST GOT HERE. THIS FALLOUT SHELTER PLACE LOOKS KINDA SEALED OFF.
I haven't ANALYZED it yet, but I believe the entire structure is made from IMPREG-NIUM. We may not be able to effect an entrance.
YEAH? WELL...
...I'LL BE THE JUDGE OF THAT.

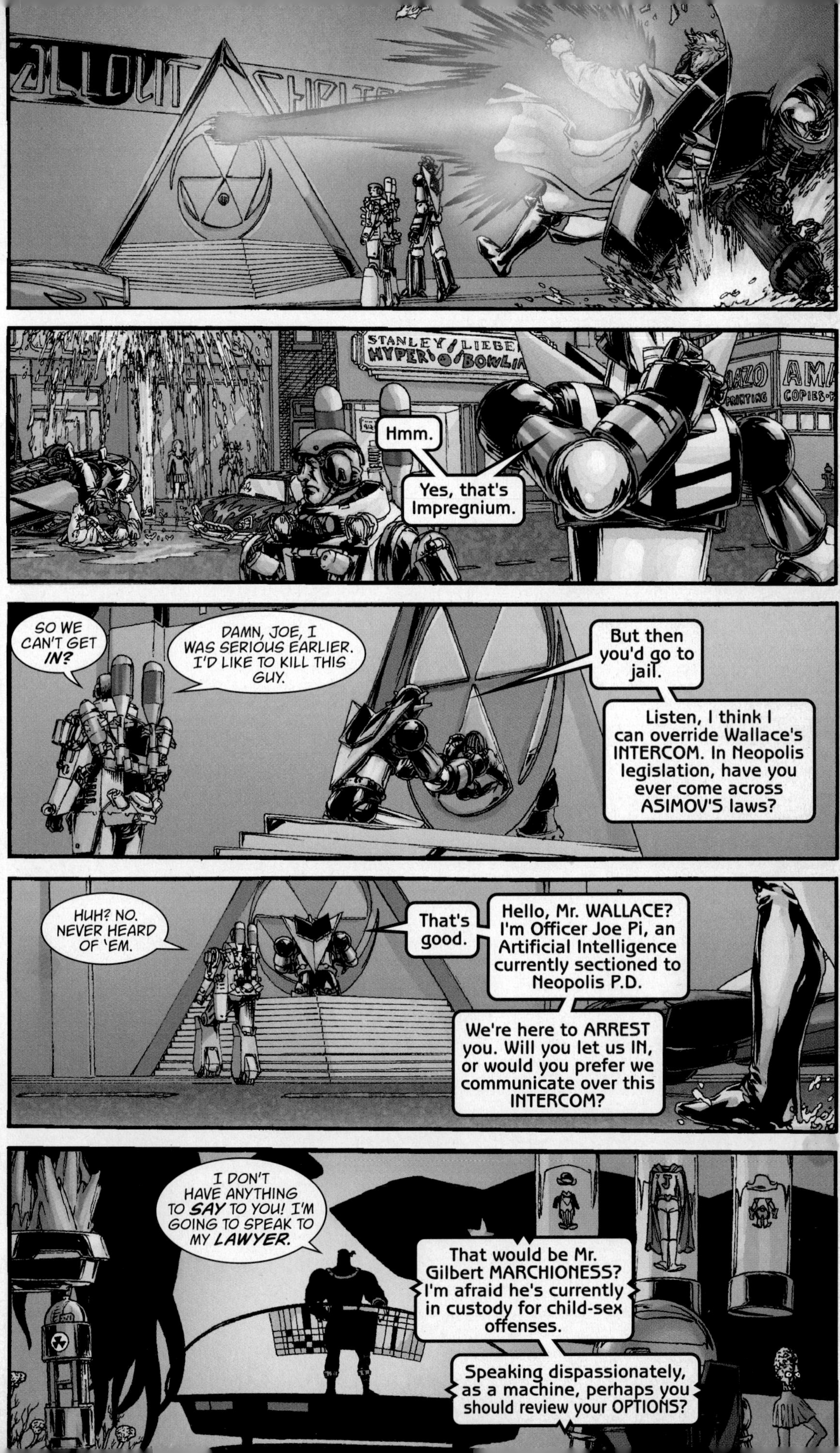
STANLEY LIEBER HYPER BOWLING
Hmm.
Yes, that's Impregnium.
SO WE CAN'T GET IN?
DAMN, JOE, I WAS SERIOUS EARLIER. I'D LIKE TO KILL THIS GUY.
But then you'd go to jail.
Listen, I think I can override Wallace's INTERCOM. In Neopolis legislation, have you ever come across ASIMOV'S laws?
HUH? NO. NEVER HEARD OF 'EM.
That's good.
Hello, Mr. WALLACE? I'm Officer Joe Pi, an Artificial Intelligence currently sectioned to Neopolis P.D.
We're here to ARREST you. Will you let us IN, or would you prefer we communicate over this INTERCOM?
I DON'T HAVE ANYTHING TO SAY TO YOU! I'M GOING TO SPEAK TO MY LAWYER.
That would be Mr. Gilbert MARCHIONESS? I'm afraid he's currently in custody for child-sex offenses.
Speaking dispassionately, as a machine, perhaps you should review your OPTIONS?

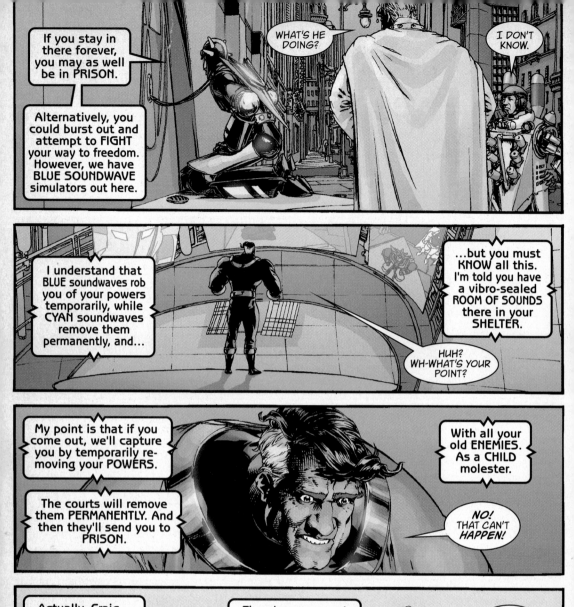

Panel 1:

If you stay in there forever, you may as well be in PRISON.

Alternatively, you could burst out and attempt to FIGHT your way to freedom. However, we have BLUE SOUNDWAVE simulators out here.

WHAT'S HE DOING?

I DON'T KNOW.

Panel 2:

I understand that BLUE soundwaves rob you of your powers temporarily, while CYAN soundwaves remove them permanently, and...

...but you must KNOW all this. I'm told you have a vibro-sealed ROOM OF SOUNDS there in your SHELTER.

HUH? WH-WHAT'S YOUR POINT?

Panel 3:

My point is that if you come out, we'll capture you by temporarily re-moving your POWERS.

The courts will remove them PERMANENTLY. And then they'll send you to PRISON.

With all your old ENEMIES. As a CHILD molester.

NO! THAT CAN'T HAPPEN!

Panel 4:

Actually, Craig... may I call you Craig? Actually, there's an 87% probability that WILL happen.

There's no way out with DIGNITY, Craig. Nothing in your shelter can HELP you. Not your WEAPONRY, not your Room of SOUNDS...

SAY, LISTEN...

LEAVE HIM BE.

Panel 5:

M-MY ROOM OF SOUNDS!

HEH. YOU THINK YOU'RE SO SMART, YOU MACHINES! NO WAY OUT WITH DIGNITY, HUH?

WELL, MR. ARTIFICIAL INTELLIGENCE, YOU JUST OPENED YOUR MOUTH AND GAVE ME A WAY OUT!

What? Craig, WAIT! What do you MEAN?

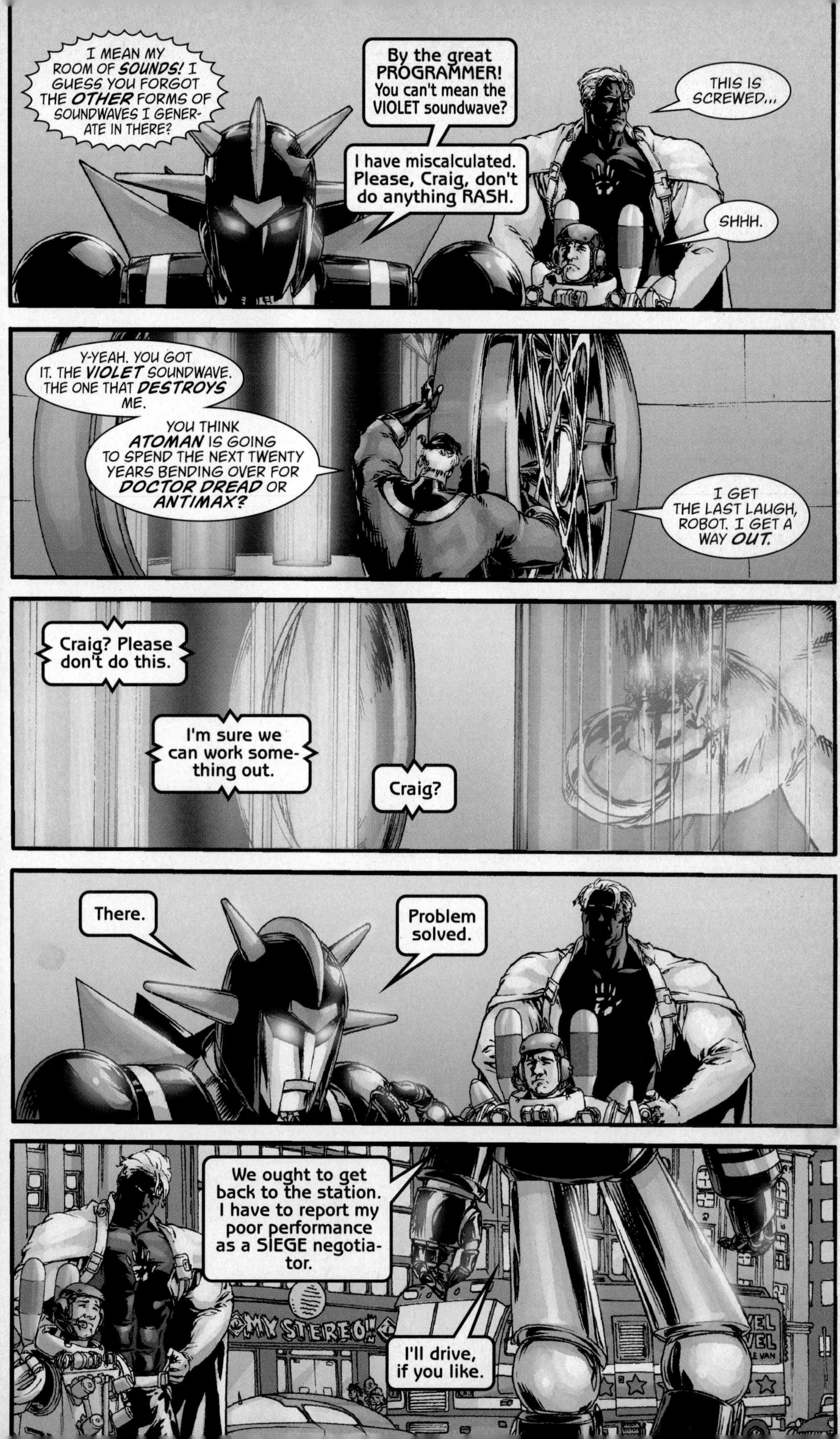
I MEAN MY ROOM OF ***SOUNDS!*** I GUESS YOU FORGOT THE ***OTHER*** FORMS OF SOUNDWAVES I GENERATE IN THERE?
By the great PROGRAMMER! You can't mean the VIOLET soundwave?
I have miscalculated. Please, Craig, don't do anything RASH.
THIS IS SCREWED...
SHHH.
Y-YEAH. YOU GOT IT. THE ***VIOLET*** SOUNDWAVE. THE ONE THAT ***DESTROYS*** ME.
YOU THINK ***ATOMAN*** IS GOING TO SPEND THE NEXT TWENTY YEARS BENDING OVER FOR ***DOCTOR DREAD*** OR ***ANTIMAX?***
I GET THE LAST LAUGH, ROBOT. I GET A WAY ***OUT.***
Craig? Please don't do this.
I'm sure we can work something out.
Craig?
There.
Problem solved.
We ought to get back to the station. I have to report my poor performance as a SIEGE negotiator.
MY STEREO!!
I'll drive, if you like.

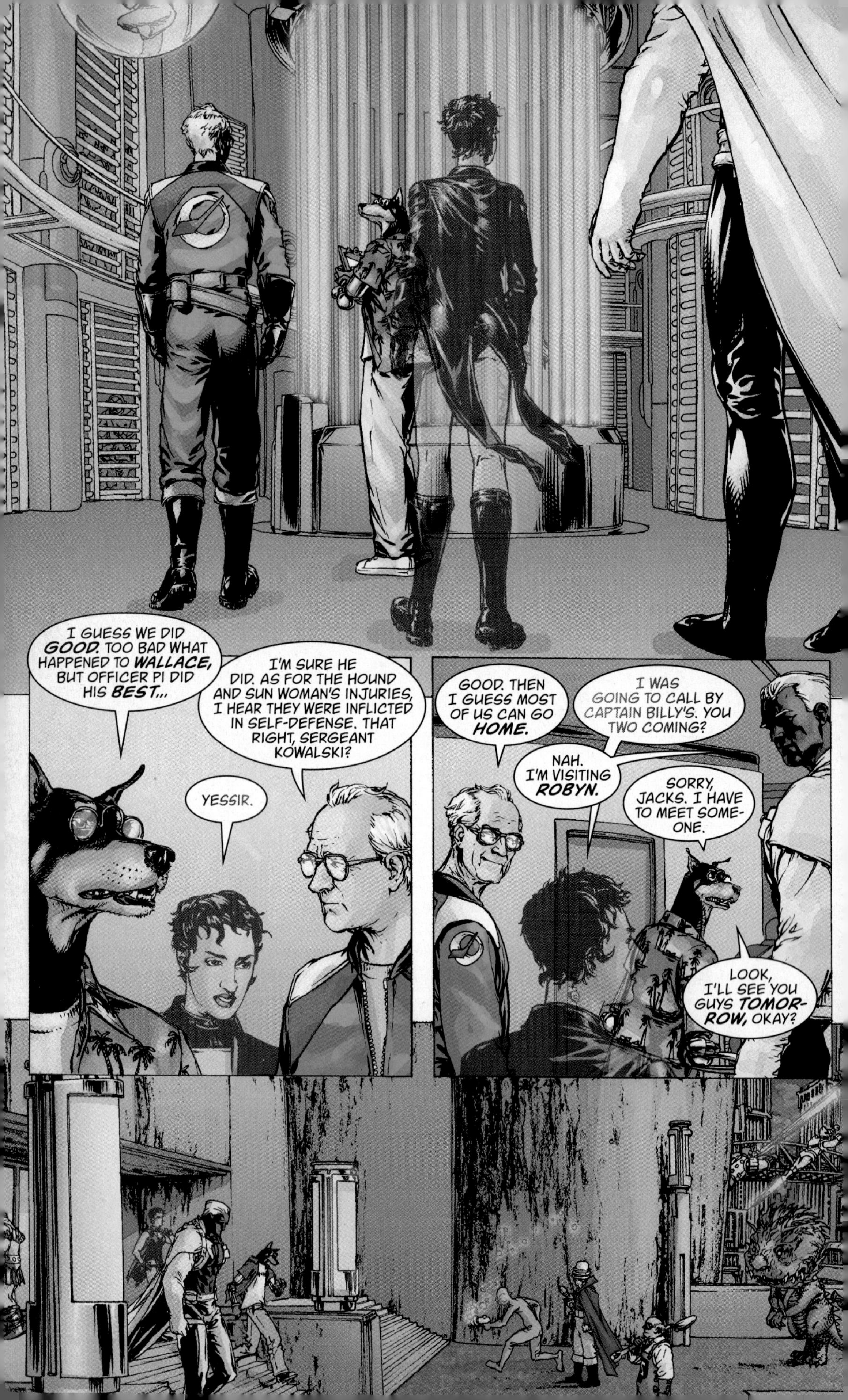
I GUESS WE DID GOOD. TOO BAD WHAT HAPPENED TO WALLACE, BUT OFFICER PI DID HIS BEST...
I'M SURE HE DID. AS FOR THE HOUND AND SUN WOMAN'S INJURIES, I HEAR THEY WERE INFLICTED IN SELF-DEFENSE. THAT RIGHT, SERGEANT KOWALSKI?
YESSIR.
GOOD. THEN I GUESS MOST OF US CAN GO HOME.
I WAS GOING TO CALL BY CAPTAIN BILLY'S. YOU TWO COMING?
NAH. I'M VISITING ROBYN.
SORRY, JACKS. I HAVE TO MEET SOME-ONE.
LOOK, I'LL SEE YOU GUYS TOMOR-ROW, OKAY?

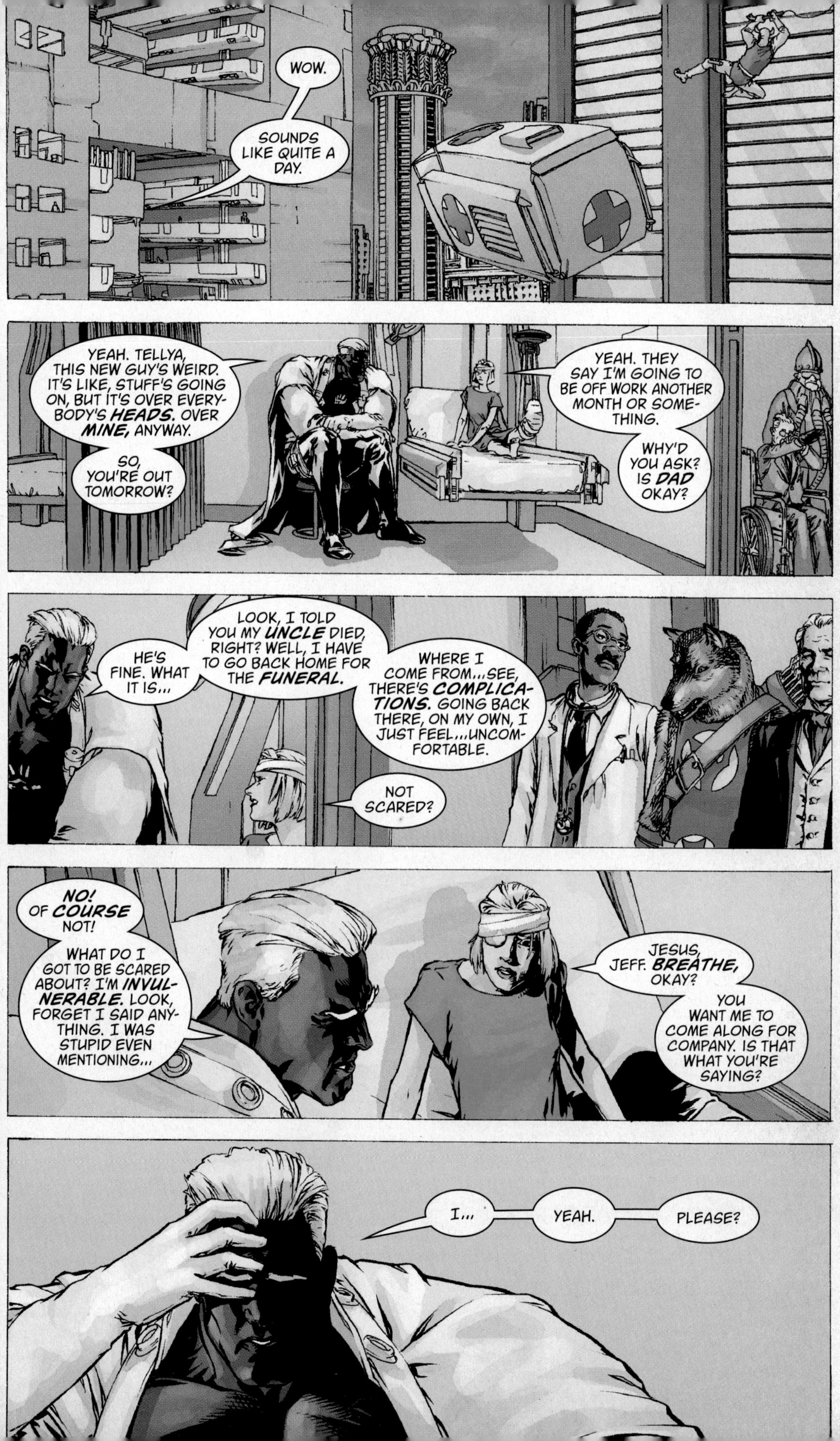
WOW.
SOUNDS LIKE QUITE A DAY.
YEAH. TELLYA, THIS NEW GUY'S WEIRD. IT'S LIKE, STUFF'S GOING ON, BUT IT'S OVER EVERY-BODY'S HEADS. OVER MINE, ANYWAY.
SO, YOU'RE OUT TOMORROW?
YEAH. THEY SAY I'M GOING TO BE OFF WORK ANOTHER MONTH OR SOME-THING.
WHY'D YOU ASK? IS DAD OKAY?
HE'S FINE. WHAT IT IS...
LOOK, I TOLD YOU MY UNCLE DIED, RIGHT? WELL, I HAVE TO GO BACK HOME FOR THE FUNERAL.
WHERE I COME FROM...SEE, THERE'S COMPLICA-TIONS. GOING BACK THERE, ON MY OWN, I JUST FEEL...UNCOM-FORTABLE.
NOT SCARED?
NO! OF COURSE NOT!
WHAT DO I GOT TO BE SCARED ABOUT? I'M INVUL-NERABLE. LOOK, FORGET I SAID ANY-THING. I WAS STUPID EVEN MENTIONING...
JESUS, JEFF. BREATHE, OKAY?
YOU WANT ME TO COME ALONG FOR COMPANY. IS THAT WHAT YOU'RE SAYING?
I...
YEAH.
PLEASE?

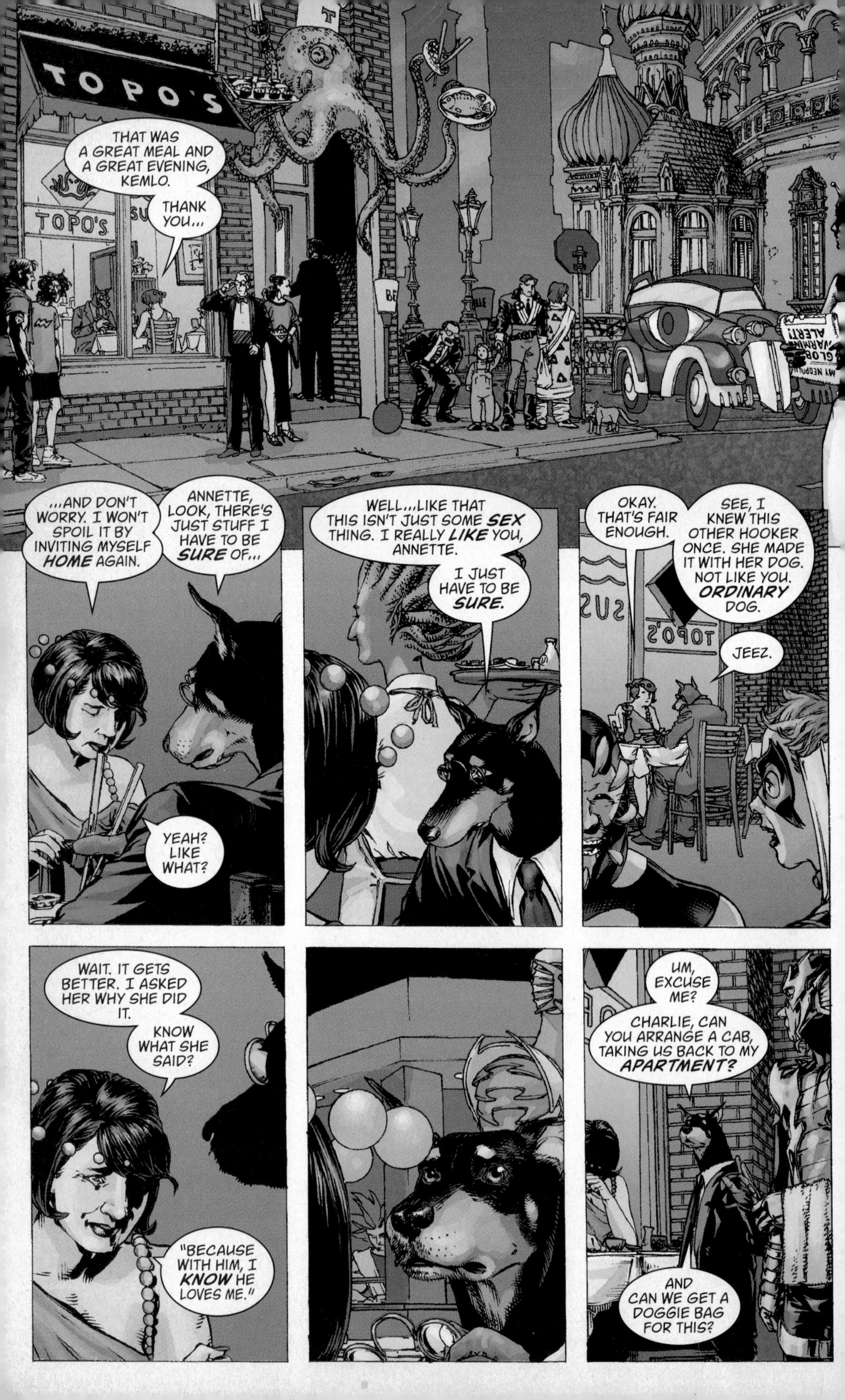
TOPO'S
THAT WAS A GREAT MEAL AND A GREAT EVENING, KEMLO.
THANK YOU...
...AND DON'T WORRY. I WON'T SPOIL IT BY INVITING MYSELF HOME AGAIN.
ANNETTE, LOOK, THERE'S JUST STUFF I HAVE TO BE SURE OF...
YEAH? LIKE WHAT?
WELL...LIKE THAT THIS ISN'T JUST SOME SEX THING. I REALLY LIKE YOU, ANNETTE.
I JUST HAVE TO BE SURE.
OKAY. THAT'S FAIR ENOUGH.
SEE, I KNEW THIS OTHER HOOKER ONCE. SHE MADE IT WITH HER DOG. NOT LIKE YOU. ORDINARY DOG.
JEEZ.
WAIT. IT GETS BETTER. I ASKED HER WHY SHE DID IT.
KNOW WHAT SHE SAID?
"BECAUSE WITH HIM, I KNOW HE LOVES ME."
UM, EXCUSE ME?
CHARLIE, CAN YOU ARRANGE A CAB, TAKING US BACK TO MY APARTMENT?
AND CAN WE GET A DOGGIE BAG FOR THIS?

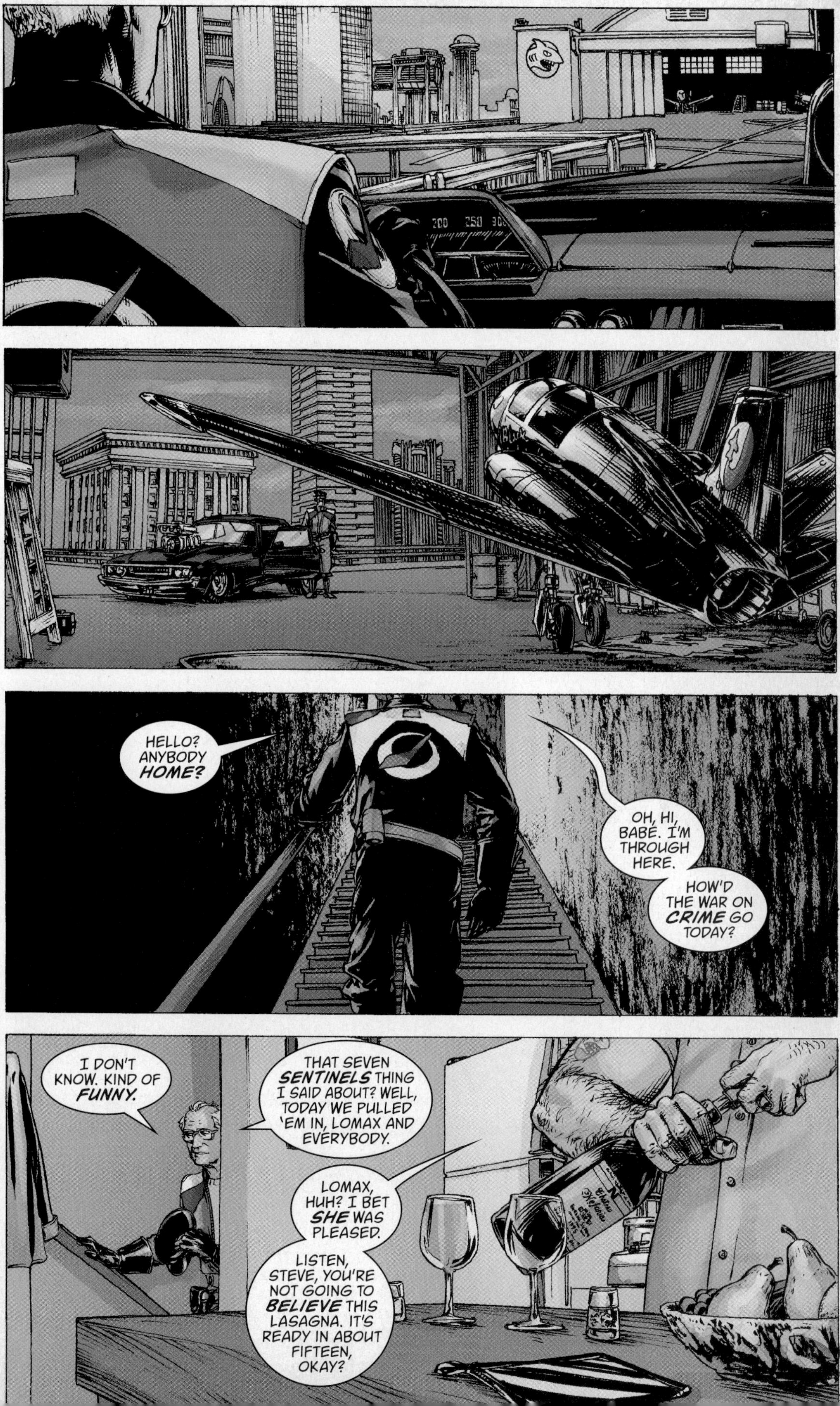
HELLO? ANYBODY HOME?
OH, HI, BABE. I'M THROUGH HERE.
HOW'D THE WAR ON CRIME GO TODAY?
I DON'T KNOW. KIND OF FUNNY.
THAT SEVEN SENTINELS THING I SAID ABOUT? WELL, TODAY WE PULLED 'EM IN, LOMAX AND EVERYBODY.
LOMAX, HUH? I BET SHE WAS PLEASED.
LISTEN, STEVE, YOU'RE NOT GOING TO BELIEVE THIS LASAGNA. IT'S READY IN ABOUT FIFTEEN, OKAY?

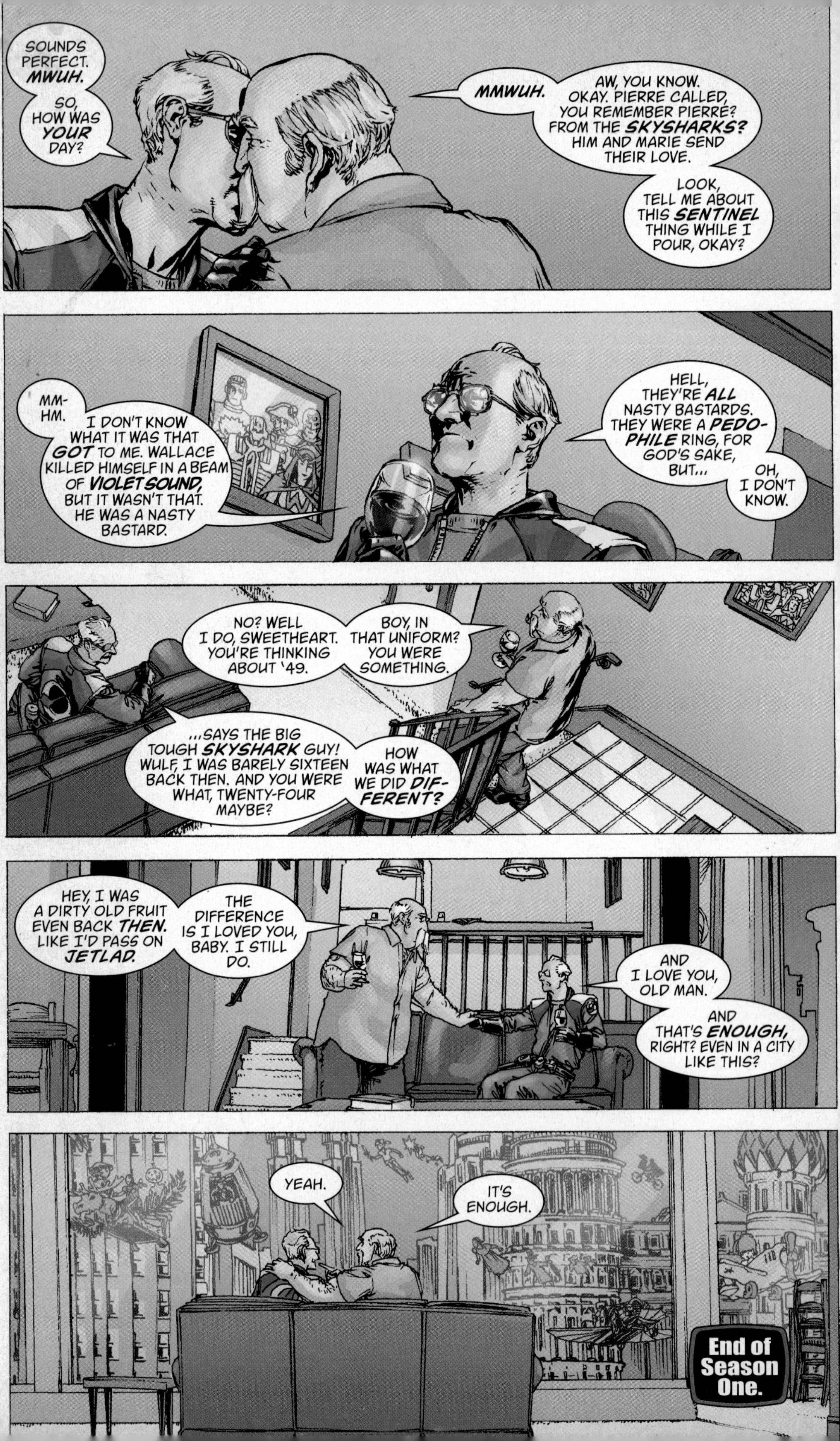
SOUNDS PERFECT. MWUH.
SO, HOW WAS YOUR DAY?
MMWUH.
AW, YOU KNOW. OKAY. PIERRE CALLED, YOU REMEMBER PIERRE? FROM THE SKYSHARKS? HIM AND MARIE SEND THEIR LOVE.
LOOK, TELL ME ABOUT THIS SENTINEL THING WHILE I POUR, OKAY?
MM-HM.
I DON'T KNOW WHAT IT WAS THAT GOT TO ME. WALLACE KILLED HIMSELF IN A BEAM OF VIOLET SOUND, BUT IT WASN'T THAT. HE WAS A NASTY BASTARD.
HELL, THEY'RE ALL NASTY BASTARDS. THEY WERE A PEDOPHILE RING, FOR GOD'S SAKE, BUT...
OH, I DON'T KNOW.
NO? WELL I DO, SWEETHEART. YOU'RE THINKING ABOUT '49.
BOY, IN THAT UNIFORM? YOU WERE SOMETHING.
...SAYS THE BIG TOUGH SKYSHARK GUY! WULF, I WAS BARELY SIXTEEN BACK THEN. AND YOU WERE WHAT, TWENTY-FOUR MAYBE?
HOW WAS WHAT WE DID DIFFERENT?
HEY, I WAS A DIRTY OLD FRUIT EVEN BACK THEN. LIKE I'D PASS ON JETLAD.
THE DIFFERENCE IS I LOVED YOU, BABY. I STILL DO.
AND I LOVE YOU, OLD MAN.
AND THAT'S ENOUGH, RIGHT? EVEN IN A CITY LIKE THIS?
YEAH.
IT'S ENOUGH.
End of Season One.

DEDICATIONS

To Leah, Amber,
and Melinda;
To all my family,
all my friends.

ALAN MOORE is perhaps the most acclaimed writer in the graphic story medium, having garnered many awards for such works as WATCHMEN, FROM HELL, MIRACLEMAN, SWAMP THING and SUPREME, among others, along with the many fine artists he has collaborated with on those works. He is currently masterminding the entire America's Best Comics line, writing PROMETHEA, TOM STRONG and TOMORROW STORIES in addition to TOP 10, with more in the planning stages. He resides in central England.

Thank you to everyone who worked on this book. Especially Zander, Alex, Alex, Todd, Eric, Jeff, Neal, Kristy, Anthony, and especially Alan. And to Scott and Jim, for bringing together my dream team for this book. And as ever, Lisa, for keeping me sane.

GENE HA is the finishing artist and co-creator of TOP 10 and resents being called a tracer. At least he isn't wanted by the Wisconsin Highway Patrol. Previously he has worked on such titles as THE ADVENTURES OF CYCLOPS AND PHOENIX, OKTANE and THE SHADE, but nothing matches the thrill of working on TOP 10. He lives in Minneapolis, Minnesota with his lovely wife and two beagle-bassets.

For Julie.

ZANDER CANNON, layout artist for TOP 10, is the creator of THE REPLACEMENT GOD, and has worked recently on projects for the Minnesota Orchestra and the NOAA Space Environment Center. He is currently pencilling and inking a SMAX miniseries written by Alan Moore. Newly married, he and his lovely wife Julie live and work in Minneapolis.

THE LEAGUE OF EXTRAORDINARY GENTLEMEN
VOLUME 1
Alan Moore, Kevin O'Neill

PROMETHEA BOOK 1, BOOK 2
Alan Moore, J. H. Williams III & Mick Gray

TOM STRONG BOOK 1, BOOK 2
Alan Moore, Chris Sprouse & Alan Gordon

TOMORROW STORIES BOOK 1
Alan Moore, Kevin Nowlan, Rick Veitch,
Jim Baikie, Melinda Gebbie, Hilary Barta

TOP 10 BOOK 1, BOOK 2
Alan Moore, Gene Ha & Zander Cannon

Look for our magazines each month
at fine comics retailers everywhere.

To locate a comics retailer near you,
call 1-888-COMIC BOOK

AMERICA'S
BEST COMICS